ENTERTAINMENT, HEROES AND VILLAINS

SUCCESS AND FAILURE AT BURNLEY FC

DAVE THOMAS

Author **Dave Thomas** retired as a Leeds headteacher in 1996 and did supply and consultancy work until writing football books gradually took over. As a lifelong Burnley supporter and season ticket holder at Turf Moor, Dave is well placed to write about his team. *Entertainment, Heroes and Villains* will be Dave's ninth book and he's currently working with cult Burnley hero Roger Eli on his autobiography.

ENTERTAINMENT, HEROES AND VILLAINS

SUCCESS AND FAILURE AT BURNLEY FC

DAVE THOMAS

VERTICAL EDITIONS

www.verticaleditions.com

First published in the United Kingdom in 2011 by Vertical Editions, Unit 4a, Snaygill Industrial Estate, Skipton, North Yorkshire BD23 2QR

www.verticaleditions.com

ISBN 978-1-904091-50-9

A CIP catalogue record for this book is available from the British Library

Cover design by HBA, York

Printed and bound by Jellyfish Print Solutions, Hampshire

ACKNOWLEDGEMENTS

Thanks to all who helped with the book in any small—or large—way.
Special thanks go to:
Chris Boden and the *Burnley Express*
Jamie Beatson at St Johnstone, Perth
Darren Bentley and BFC
Alastair Campbell
Clarke Carlise
David Conn
Kevin Clarke
Stephen Cummings
Brendan Flood
Suzanne Geldard and Andrew Greaves at the *Lancashire Telegraph*
Frank Keating
Jack Keogh
Barry Kilby
Richard Moore
Piers Morgan
Alan Nixon
Paul Sandiford
Mark Ogden
Phil Whalley
Henry Winter
Jim White
And Mrs T. who sorts out all my computer problems

CONTENTS

INTRODUCTION

He was the Anointed One, taking Burnley Football Club from impoverished obscurity to Premiership riches. At the beginning of the Premiership season the Burnley Football Supporters Club wrote Owen Coyle a profuse and glowing letter of thanks for the magic carpet ride he had given everyone so far. Reproduced in full in chapter 10, it ended: 'Mr Coyle your name will go down in the history of Burnley Football Club and we at Burnley Football Supporters Club were privileged in being able to say we were there in the 2008–09 season to watch our team play football under one of the greatest managers we have had.'

And then in January, 2010 he was gone. As management goes, it was a brief tenure. He was the Messiah one minute, and then branded as Judas when he left. It was remarkable. He came from nowhere, here today, gone tomorrow. A club and town were left reeling. On Tuesday, 22nd September, 17,600 people attended the Carling Cup tie that brought him back to Turf Moor. Under normal circumstances there might have been no more than 6,000. The majority came to vent their spleen and hurl their opinions at him as he took his place in the dugout as the manager of Bolton Wanderers; in their eyes hero to villain in a matter of months.

Why?

In total contrast to the Supporters Club letter; Jack Keogh on Friday 15th January, 2010 in the *Burnley Express* wrote about the legacy of Owen Coyle (chapter 13). It seemed then, and still does, quite astonishing that Keogh could write in such a way about a man that had brought success and financial salvation to the club in such a short space of time. They were his personal feelings but reflected the mood of the club, supporters and townsfolk. This book looks to explain why Jack Keogh wrote his letter. He wrote of the 'magical mystery tour . . . and famous victories . . . the memories . . . then the devastating news . . . the timing . . . the unexpected departure . . . the complete shock . . . the mixture of emotions . . . the hurt and disillusionment . . . the decimation of the backroom staff . . .'

'It would have been fitting if he could have left with the blessing of his beloved fans, and not with a bitter taste in their mouths,' he wrote. Jack Keogh's letter was emotional, but then so are all football supporters. Whilst the world of football outside Burnley in years to come will care little about the events of January 2010 at Burnley Football Club, the supporters of Burnley Football Club will have longer memories. But Owen Coyle put emotion to one side when he made his career decision as might many of us when faced with such a choice. Had emotion swayed the day, he would have stayed at Turf Moor.

Coyle's predecessor was Steve Cotterill, currently at Portsmouth and if a football club's history is a continuum, it is difficult to tell the Owen Coyle story without knowing something of the struggles of the preceding seasons. Cotterill's importance and contributions to Burnley were significant. But, the contrast between the two was so great, the changes so immediate, the transformation of players so successful, that to appreciate the impact Coyle had, it is essential to understand what went on before. That Cotterill will be forever compared with Coyle at Burnley is an unfortunate burden he must bear.

Not that Steve Cotterill was a poor or an unpopular manager. Far from it, for with little money he kept the club in the Championship and managed to gather the majority of the side that Coyle would take to Wembley and the Premiership. That, in fact, would be something Cotterill was quick to mention on Sky Sports. But, Cotterill's style was different and his teams at Burnley played a brand of football that would seldom be described as 'pleasing to the eye'. Even before Cotterill, the part played by Stan Ternent has to be acknowledged. In his final season he kept the club in the Championship (it was he who brought them up in the first place) and considered it, bearing in mind the constraints, his greatest achievement.

But Cotterill's part is crucial to the story. It was quite astonishing that much the same collection of players was transformed into the cavalier group that became known fondly as 'The Band of Brothers'. Cotterill's players blossomed under Coyle and certainly four of them went on to have astonishing seasons in 2008–09—Robbie Blake, Graham Alexander, Clarke Carlisle and Brian Jensen. Season 2008–09 was truly astounding for not only was there the joy of promotion, but there were wonderful games against the big Premiership sides—West Brom, Fulham, Chelsea, Arsenal and Tottenham. It was Owen Coyle's season. They were his triumphs.

Cotterill's football was losing spectators. His final season was one of boredom. Someone like me, a season ticket holder, travelling 40 miles from Leeds for every home game, seriously wondered how much longer I wanted to do this. In the previous season his team had set a club record for the number of games without a win. Entertainment was at a low level. But he did wonderfully well in his first season, was a genuine man, wracked his brain for answers, had precious little money to dabble with, the smallest of squads, spent sleepless nights, and wore his heart on his sleeve. If he was not the easiest man for journalists to deal with (Coyle quite the opposite), nevertheless, he left the club, still respected and appreciated by supporters. Stan Ternent too left with the thanks of supporters who will be forever grateful for what he did and the promotion he achieved in 1999–2000.

But with supreme irony, the man who took Burnley to Wembley and guided themto the Premiership, working a football miracle and astonishing the football world, may never be remembered with the same affection. Most supporters will thank him for the success he brought but will not forget the mid-season walkout and the decimation of the backroom staff. Where they might wish Stan Ternent and Steve Cotterill the best of luck in all they do in future, many supporters will not grant Owen Coyle that same accord.

Of course some might argue there is no sentiment in football, that for those who work in it, it is a business and an industry. But for supporters, emotion is hard to put to one side when thinking about his decision to leave the club at the particular moment he chose. The move was widely analysed and dissected in the press. Whilst some pundits wrote how they understood his motives, others were highly critical of the timing.

So: this book looks at events leading up to his appointment and then his time at Burnley. The change to the new style of football was immediate but his first few mixed months gave little indication of the sensation to come. When it did come, it was a wonderful time but heartbreaking when it ended.

The story looks at the manner of his departure, the reactions and the shattered aftermath as his successor, Brian Laws, attempted to keep the club in the Premiership. It was a dreadful time for club and fans. It is no cliché to say that the heart and positivity had been ripped out of the club. The final outcome was unsurprisingly one of failure; and the new man, Brian Laws, could do little to restore the fractured spirit. As the season neared its end his future at the club looked insecure, but he was retained to build his own team and attempt to get back the Premiership place.

Although Owen Coyle's departure to Bolton Wanderers was controversial and feelings ran high for months, it was always important that this book should not belittle his achievements. How could it? What he did for the club was too important for that and as many supporters eventually agreed, life goes on, a club moves on, and every manager plays his part in the never-ending story. Football is all about coming and going, arrivals and departures. He brought a £60million payday at a time when the club could barely pay its bills and only more directors' loans kept the ship afloat in the weeks leading up to Wembley. Another £48million was assured from parachute payments after that. In monetary terms alone his contribution to the club was simply immense.

Owen Coyle was at Turf Moor for not much more than two years. But what a two years they were. If it is possible to put a money figure to his value to the club, it is impossible to put a value on the sheer enjoyment and pride he brought to Burnley's supporters and the whole town of Burnley, for that brief period of success.

Mark Griffiths was on the second open-top bus that toured Burnley after the Wembley victory:

> I can't get over what I witnessed. There's real poverty in Burnley—there were young women with teeth missing holding their grubby babies up like it was some kind of papal blessing. There were whole Asian families waving and shouting at the roundabout by Centenary Way. It was magnificent. Our little town turned itself inside out to applaud—nay worship our team. They were on walls and rooftops and leaning perilously out of office windows and hanging banners from bridges over Yorkshire Street and Finsley gate. It was magnificent. Leaving the Town Hall, a chill descended and the crowds thinned a little, but the buses were pursued by young girls and middle-aged men waving home made flags, and tattooed adolescents who'd ripped their shirts off. When we approached the Turf again the crowds were still there, deeper and even more urgent, with some having sprinted across the town to get there. When we crossed some of the junctions you could see people running along the parallel streets. It was utterly heart-warming to see that people cared so much.

The whole team had performed on the day but it was Owen Coyle's personal triumph. The inspiration was his. The amazing processional scenes were unforgettable and the enormous cheering crowds were paying him homage. Burnley had seen nothing like it for years. It was, and still is, a town that has a host of problems and deprivations. Coyle brought success and glory to a place that desperately needed something memorable. 'Like some kind of papal blessing,' Mark Griffiths wrote.

Banners appeared declaring that 'Owen Coyle is God'. But only months after that, new banners would declare him 'Judas'.

As a die-hard Burnley supporter of over 50 years, this was a tough book to write. Feelings had to be put to one side. A balance had to be maintained; personal opinions kept in check, fairness, neutral enquiry and objectivity the target. My own diaries and notes I kept during the period are anything but objective, but where they are reasoned and appropriate, I have made use of them.

I am particularly indebted to Brendan Flood who gave me permission to use sections of his book, *Big Club, Small Town and Me*. Brendan was operations director, on the inside at Burnley, involved in everything that was going on, instrumental in ending Cotterill's time and then bringing Coyle to the club. The book and conversations with him were illuminating. Barry Kilby, Burnley FC Chairman, was unfailingly accommodating and willing to talk and Owen Coyle took time to meet and talk with me at the Euxton Training Ground. Clarke Carlisle also spoke at length about working with Owen Coyle and his impact on the players.

Mirror and *People* journalist Alan Nixon provided match reports, plus several sources of material and permission to use them. His knowledge of what went on at the time came from his working relationship with Owen Coyle. His invaluable and frequent assistance is gratefully acknowledged. Henry Winter, Mark Ogden and Jim White of the *Telegraph* gave me use of their reports and features. Chris Boden at the *Burnley Express* made his reports and features available along with Suzanne Geldard at the *Lancashire Telegraph*. Stephen Cummings and Kevin Clarke let me reproduce their blogs.

Thanks also to the following: Alastair Campbell who gave me carte blanche to dip into his Burnley articles; Piers Morgan who kindly let me use his piece about Owen Coyle published in the *Mail on Sunday;* David Conn who let me use his *Guardian* piece about Barry Kilby; Frank Keating of the *Guardian* who previewed the Blackburn game; Darren Bentley at BFC, where the matchday programme and the club website were sources of great help and material.

The magazine of the *London Clarets Something to Write Home About* was in constant use; my thanks to Phil Whalley in particular. The Claretsmad and Longside websites and messageboards were equally important. Jamie Beatson at the St Johnstone fanzine *We Are Perth* was extremely helpful as were all the contributors to the questions I put on their website.

Time has passed by since Owen Coyle left but I still wonder, had he stayed, if we would still be a Premiership Club. I think the answer would have been yes. And irony of ironies, if Steven Hunt had not equalised for Hull City against Bolton Wanderers at the Reebok at the end of December, 2009, then Owen Coyle might still be Burnley's manager. When Hunt scored his second goal, Bolton manager Gary Megson's fate was sealed, and Owen Coyle's time at Burnley was as good as over.

Dave Thomas, April 2011

1

STEVE COTTERILL

Inheriting a parlous position, with very limited financial resources, Steve Cotterill kept Burnley Football Club in the Championship, worked incessantly to improve things, and even took the club into the play-off places on a couple of occasions. It is well documented that when he took over from Stan Ternent there were not even enough first-team players to form a team, but by the time he left, the majority of the team that triumphed at Wembley and took the club into the Premiership, had been signed by him. And yet, by and large, these were the same players who went on a run of 19 League games without a win, setting an unfortunate club record two seasons earlier. Even so, when the new season started after that terrible run, in the pre-season friendly at Turf Moor he was given a great reception and welcome when he walked onto the pitch. He was a fighter and grafter; he put his heart and soul into the club, and was much respected for that.

If Burnley fans had an early problem with Steve Cotterill, it was simply that with his sky-high reputation they wondered how long he would be at the club. At the back of people's minds was always the question; how long will it be before a bigger, wealthier, more ambitious club poaches him? Supporters wondered if Burnley was just a stepping stone for him on the way to better things. Would budget restrictions, working on a shoestring, struggling to make ends meet, having to sell players, be the catalysts that would frustrate him and drive him away? Many felt it would only be a matter of time before he went to perhaps even a Premiership club. Several ex-Premier clubs littered the Championship demanding a return to the top level—West Brom, Derby, Leicester, Southampton; Coventry, Crystal Palace, Wolves, Norwich, Ipswich, Leeds and Sunderland. Which one of them would tempt him away? Cotterill's star was high and still rising, certainly at the beginning of season 2006–07.

The opening game that season was against QPR and as he jogged onto the field there was no sign of his popularity waning. Perhaps it was because people saw a passionate man who wore his heart on his sleeve. What you saw was what you got. Who would forget how visibly upset he was at a dinner in 2006 when he stood and paid tribute to a young fan who had died and whose funeral he had attended? When Ade Akinbiyi was sold in January 2006 Steve's head might just have agreed that

£1.75million was too good to turn down, but Burnley supporters were acutely aware that in his heart he was distraught to see the sale of his talisman. Months later, he still referred to it. 'I'd sooner a striker scored 30 goals than the rest of the team chipped in with goals, but people here don't score 30. We sell them after 15.' Burnley folk appreciated a man who could work on limited resources, speak his mind and just get on with the job. It is a character trait embedded in Burnley people.

Steve Cotterill, like his successor Owen Coyle, might be the first to admit he was never the world's greatest player but then how often do great players make great managers? It is no job requisite. Most of the world's great managers seem to have been average players, in fact some of them not even average. But all of them would say they were hard workers and made the most of their abilities. Perhaps it meant that they had to have other qualities to succeed in management. A will to work, single-minded ambition, the ability to give never less than 110%, a determination to use what talent they have, a willingness to learn the job, in most cases by starting at the bottom, and a fundamental belief in teamwork.

'What happens when you don't have a lot of money is you end up with team players rather than star individuals,' Cotterill said. 'If you have lots of money, you might have a lot of very good individuals, but then you don't always get a team.' At Burnley he always argued that his players were team players, and it was he who first introduced the team 'huddle' before a game, and at some games, even afterwards—away at Blackburn in the FA Cup replay even though they had lost, and away at Luton after a particularly heroic winning performance. In that way he espoused the team ethic; Burnley legends Potts and Adamson would have been proud of him. The team ethic was the basis of their philosophies.

When Cheltenham Town beat Burnley in an FA Cup game, the name of Steve Cotterill went into Chairman Barry Kilby's mental filofax. As a result of that he was one of those interviewed for the Burnley job when it became vacant in June 2004. At that time he was 'between jobs' and was spending time on a temporary basis at Leicester City assisting with coaching. Prior to that there had been a short spell at Sunderland with the professorial, sombre-faced Howard Wilkinson. Prior to that there was a short and controversial spell as manager at Stoke City. Talk to a Stoke City supporter and they will not smile at his name. They were not best pleased when he left so soon after joining, but then which supporters ever know the full facts behind any story? Was he happy at either club?

He started his playing career in the non-Leagues at Cheltenham Town, Alvechurch and Burton Albion. He then signed his first 'big' contract at Wimbledon after a £30,000 deal with Burton. This was a huge step going from non-League to first-class football in one go. Cynics might say that the Wimbledon brand back then was anything but first-class. His appearances there were infrequent and he was sent on loan to Brighton.

From there it was back to Wimbledon and then on to Bournemouth for his best years as a player. He was signed for £80,000 and in the next three seasons picked up three Player of the Year Awards, no mean feat. He was a great hit with the fans with his guts, bravery, honest play and 100% effort. A severe knee injury ended his career. There were the inevitable attempted comebacks, including a spell at Hereford but he never really recovered his form. The next step was to move into coaching and gather the necessary badges and qualifications. He was on his way.

In the mid 90s he became manager at Sligo Rovers in Ireland and took them to their highest ever placing in the League of Ireland Premier Division. He also took them to the League Cup Final where they cruelly lost to Shelbourne on penalties. They played in Europe in the following season when they earned a creditable 3–3 draw against crack side Nantes and another good result, 0–0 against Heerenveen. He returned to England in 1996.

It was at Cheltenham Town that he made his name and people began to take note of his achievements. Cheltenham was a place more famed for tourism, horse racing and an annual cricket festival. He put it on the football map. Since taking over in 1997 he has been their most successful manager. They were a non-League side when he took over in the Doc Martens League. Under his leadership they were promoted to the Conference. There was also an FA Trophy win at Wembley beating Southport 1–0. Then, from the Conference there was a promotion to the Football League Division Three, as it was then. After a season of consolidation, the next season there was a Millennium Stadium victory over Rushden and Diamonds in 2002 and this took them into the Football League Division Two. It had been five amazing years and by the fifth year his name was on various influential people's lips. The title 'promising young manager' was bestowed on him by the Press and on other occasions 'one of the most respected young coaches'. One newspaper went as far as to include him in a list of young and potential England managers. In 2001–02 the club reached the fifth round of the FA Cup, a tremendous achievement. The run included victory over his future club Burnley, and was only ended with a 1–0 away defeat at West Bromwich Albion.

He remembers his time there vividly and is fiercely proud of what he did. 'We had one good stand, the other three were irrelevant. Leaking gutters, puddles and holes and everything; awful pitch, a turnover of £100,000 and 400 supporters; five and a half years and three promotions on, one Cup Final at the Millennium Stadium, million pound turnover, three new stands, fantastic pitch, brilliant. An absolute fairy tale and my mum was still alive to see it. I remember me and my assistant, Mike Davis, painting the players' bar in a new stand we'd opened. My last game was seeing them win promotion at the Millennium Stadium. Wonderful, I wonder if you'll ever get that again.'

When Cheltenham beat Rushden in the Division Three play-off final it was the culmination of a season of records. They hit a club record points total of 78, a new high for goals scored, 66 and a best ever unbeaten run of 16 games. Added to that, striker Julian Alsop became the first Cheltenham player to score 20 goals in a Football League season. They reached the FA Cup fifth round. As a result, crowds rose by 10%.

He was appointed manager of Stoke City in 2002 after the peak at Cheltenham. He took over at a club that had just been promoted from Division Two to Division One (now the Championship), and his career seemed well and truly on the up. Supporters felt that the squad was strong enough to stay up in the new Division. Then, after just three months and a handful of games, quite out of the blue he left. It was announced he had joined Howard Wilkinson at Premiership Sunderland. It was Wilkinson who had encouraged him to take his European coaching certificate and Wilkinson thought very highly of him. 'He is one of the most promising coaches in England.'

Stoke City fans were incensed; the news that he had joined Sunderland coming just hours after he left Stoke. The club announced it was shocked and surprised and that they had received no communication with Sunderland prior to his departure. It was therefore surmised that he had been in talks with Wilkinson and Sunderland whilst still Stoke manager, breaching the laws of the game. Stoke were thus managerless and felt betrayed. He was branded 'Quiterall' and won no friends in Stoke.

If Wilkinson and Cotterill were seen as lacking in charisma by people in Sunderland, they would have preferred someone more flamboyant; no one could say they were not supremely equipped with coaching qualifications. When they joined the club they were only two of 13 Britons to hold the UEFA Pro Licence, Europe's highest coaching qualification. Alas, there was no money available for them for new players and it had been six years since Wilkinson had last been a club manager. However, he talked of his experience and Cotterill's ability being the catalyst for bright and exciting times. Both signed three year contracts; Wilkinson left the FA with their blessing and Sunderland Chairman Murray said there were no problems between Stoke and themselves.

'I have to adjust to being number 2,' said Cotterill. 'I have been a manager for six or seven years. It's my ambition to eventually become the manager of Sunderland.'

A piece in the *Northern Echo* gave an illuminating insight into Cotterill's personality. It portrayed a man determined to get to the top, with the chance to take over at the club if he impressed. 'He is a confident man with an arrogance that will not be welcomed by the waiting Press, but what he lacks in front of the media he more than makes up for in the dressing room where he is known to be a tremendous man manager.'

Derek Goddard of the *Gloucestershire Echo* who covered the

Cheltenham football team for five years and knew him well, described him as, 'A very emotional coach and a very sensitive bloke. I first knew him as an 18 year-old and he was always a little cocky then. Then he left to go to Wimbledon, where he was plagued by injury. But he was always tetchy and cocky. He is not one to get on with the Press. He is one of those that if you ask him his name, he would want to know why you were asking. I think the men at BBC Radio Stoke will be pleased that he has moved on.'

Ambition fired Cotterill as it so often does with players whose careers are ended early by injury. 'It has been a burning ambition of mine to manage in the Premiership. I gave myself a time-scale when I was about 35, because sometimes a time-scale makes you work harder, of managing in the Premiership by the time I was 42.' He almost achieved this at Sunderland where he might have slipped into the post when Wilkinson left. The understanding amongst fans was that he was being groomed to succeed Wilkinson. But his stay was brief. Sunderland were relegated with a then record low number of points. In the 20 games they managed before they were sacked they won just 10 points from 20 games. But Cotterill remained unscarred, his confidence and aspirations were undimmed. At Burnley he felt that one day he could indeed become an England manager, or at least progress to the Premiership.

If his experiences at Sunderland were not particularly pleasant, he felt he had learned from them. 'Your bad experiences in life are your best ones if you are intelligent enough to learn from them. Sunderland was a great club and to have managed them would have been fantastic but it never got to that. Maybe if the opportunity arose,' he added, 'to manage in the Premiership I will be a lot better and a lot wiser.'

He is on record as saying that he would loved to have rewarded the people of Burnley with a Premiership place having met so much good-will. At a meeting with a supporters group he said he was truly amazed that stories that northern folk really did leave their doors unlocked for their neighbours to pop in, were actually true.

> There is so much good-will in the area. A local guy, I won't name him in case it embarrasses him, came to me with a cheque, made payable to me for £6,000. He knew I wanted netting round the new training pitch so that we wouldn't keep losing balls. It ended up costing £9,000 and he came back with another cheque for an extra £3,000 to pay for it. He came back the other day with a cheque for £3,500 so that we can take the train to away games rather than sitting on a coach for seven hours. You can't beat things like that. Another guy bought all the lads £2,500 worth of training watches, terrific gestures from those people.

Much as he would have liked to have brought success to the club he was careful with his ambitions and statements, never promising top two targets, but sometimes, carefully, mentioning the possibility of a top six place when things were going well.

When he took over at Burnley his brief from Chairman Barry Kilby was simple: to keep the club in the Championship. 'I just had to keep them up but the chairman said that if I got relegated with them, I wouldn't get the sack.' He found the place to be a very hard-working area that would not accept anything less than hard work from its football team. 'It's very, very working class and the only thing against it is the constant bloody rain. If we had better pitches at the training ground and the ball rolled in the right direction, the weather might not bother me so much.'

He was interviewed by Alastair Campbell shortly after he arrived.

> If you walk down the road you don't see Manchester United or Arsenal shirts, they'll be claret and blue. Alastair Campbell seems pretty happy with what's going on at Turf Moor but he told me the weight this club carries in the town. If I was to achieve half here of what I achieved at Cheltenham, I'd get the key to the town. To be honest I never got much recognition at Cheltenham. There was talk of me getting the freedom of the borough but somebody rang up and said to qualify I would have to do something for 25 years.

In between Sunderland and Burnley there were 11 months when he looked at other jobs but considered them unsuitable.

> I'd had a hard time, professionally and personally. My mum died just before I left Sunderland. Dad died at an early age so there was just me and mum and she meant everything to me. I turned down eight job offers. I didn't want to be disrespectful to those clubs but if you want to be a manager in the Premiership you've got to be selective. This, Burnley, is the right one. There's something about this northwest corridor. Burnley have the tradition and the chairman is a man I can work with. Everyone here, including the famous old players, has been very supportive and I've been reminded there are wonderful people in our game. I got a warm reception when we went to Sunderland. The people said I hadn't been given a chance there and I appreciated that. It helped a lot. You have to aim as high as you possibly can but it would be too ambitious to talk of Burnley in the Premiership yet. And, there's no point in me saying I'll never leave here.

He joined Burnley at a critical time. Stan Ternent had just managed, against all the odds, to keep them in the Championship. With no expectations of being 'dismissed' he chose not to renew several players' contracts and had a list of new people to bring in. Thus, when he left, the club consisted of a threadbare first-team squad. Chairman Barry Kilby wanted a young and hungry manager. Cotterill was exactly that with several points to prove after his Sunderland experience. He quickly signed five players and it was noticeable that four of them were defenders; John McGreal from Ipswich, Frank Sinclair from Leicester City, goalkeeper Danny Coyne from Grimsby, and his ex-player Michael Duff from Cheltenham. The fifth was a creative midfielder Micah Hyde from Watford. Later came the inspired loan signing of centre back Gary Cahill. The defensive signings were crucial and formed an almost rock solid back four that gave a firm bedrock for survival in the Division, conceding only 39 goals in 46 games. The problem was at the other end where only 38 goals were scored. It demonstrated perfectly the Cotterill philosophy; a philosophy that was based on not conceding goals, not losing and very much holding on to what you had got. With a collection of bargain basement boys, old heads, free transfers, short term fixes and loans, this was never going to be a season, anyway, of scintillating football heading towards promotion.

Unfortunately that season Cotterill would experience the basic problem at Burnley. With no money, players had to be sold whenever any other club came with a decent offer. Courtesy of Robbie Blake, three consecutive 1–0 wins took Burnley to the heady heights of 8th place and supporters were warming to Cotterill and developing a new optimism. But then Blake was sold. Unsettled by approaches from Wigan, he eventually went to Birmingham for a reported £1.25million. When Burnley beat Wigan 1–0 at Turf Moor the game was memorable for the abuse hurled at manager Paul Jewell. Cotterill probably thought in that moment, when Blake was sold, that he would not see the Premiership with Burnley. It was a defining moment for him and supporters, an unfortunate reminder that Burnley would always struggle financially, and that managing at this club would be with one hand tied behind his back. Young star Richard Chaplow was sold to West Brom not long after.

But, there were notable high spots of the season; a 3–0 victory over Premiership Aston Villa at home in the Carling Cup; the 1–0 win over Liverpool in the FA Cup third round, and then the FA Cup tie against Blackburn Rovers. The win over Liverpool was totally unexpected and was one of those memorable Turf Moor nights reminiscent of the glory days in the early 60's.

Basically, on a raw, cold night, manager Rafa Benitez totally underestimated what it would be like to bring his 'shadow' team to Turf Moor, a small, compact place but fiercely passionate and raucous. He brought a team consisting of two regular first-teamers padded out with bit-part players. He made the mistake of thinking that the little Championship club would roll over and surrender. With Blake having departed Burnley supporters too could be forgiven for thinking that this might be a valiant defeat rather than a memorable win. To their delight, however, Liverpool were poor, dispirited, disinterested and almost easily dispelled. Burnley won 1–0 with as bizarre a goal as you could wish to see. Traiore the full back, under no pressure at all, performed a sort of slow-motion drag back as he turned, and then watched as the ball trickled in the opposite direction to that which he intended, slowly rolling over the line. It was no more than Burnley deserved although Benitez made wild claims that Liverpool had controlled the game. What else could he say to placate the 3,800 angry Liverpool fans who gave their team hell as they left the field at the final whistle? Only when Baros came on and he ran at pace at the Burnley defence did Liverpool look at all interested. For Burnley, Chaplow, Camara and Jean Louis Valois threatened constantly, making chance after chance. The game even ended with a bit of Burnley showboating. The result inspired a joke that did the rounds for weeks afterwards in the Everton side of Liverpool. 'What's the difference between Liverpool and a teabag? A teabag stays in the Cup longer.'

Next up were Rovers, the last time the clubs having met, was back in Stan Ternent's time when both were in the Championship. This time, Blackburn were the established Premiership side with money to spend and star players. The anticipation was electric and Steve Cotterill had a new experience to add to his CV—a local derby like no other. Within hours of the draw he set out from his home near the Blackburn training centre at Brockhall to find a statue draped with a Burnley shirt. All police leave was cancelled on the day, riot vans were parked outside the ground, but the game itself was dour and drab whilst overhead police helicopters waited for trouble. Neither side wanted to lose or even concede a goal. 'We didn't play for a draw but we didn't want to get beaten in front of our own fans.' Predictably it was a 0–0 stalemate. The only high spot was a fan threatening Robbie Savage on the pitch and the obligatory streaker.

Blackburn won the replay 2–1 but in between the two games, something rare had happened at Turf Moor. Manager Cotterill was allowed to spend £600,000 on striker Ade Akinbiyi from Stoke City. Prior to this he had sounded out Les Ferdinand, due to leave Bolton Wanderers, but Ferdinand wanted to move back south. Cotterill spoke to him four times but in the end Reading signed him, with Cotterill adding the comment that once Reading expressed interest there was no way Burnley could match their wages. Akinbiyi was unavailable for the replay at Blackburn. Around 7,000 Burnley fans made the short journey. Although they lost there were two memorable moments. The first was Hyde's stunning 20-yard goal that levelled the game. The Burnley end erupted. For Hyde to score at all was a rarity, but this goal was stupendous, as he controlled it on his knee, swivelled and crashed an unstoppable shot into the top corner over Brad Friedel. Extra-time was the least that Burnley deserved but a second Blackburn goal five minutes from the end won the tie. Burnley players were crestfallen but Cotterill lifted them with a team huddle in the corner of the pitch that left an image that will last for years in the minds of all fans that saw it. It was a masterstroke of man-management.

Less of a masterstroke was the debut of Ade Akinbiyi against Sunderland in March. Pumped up and raring to go after his delayed first appearance, due to injury, he was so up for it, he wasted no time in head-butting a Sunderland defender after he had been on the pitch just three minutes. No one knew whether to laugh or cry at the absurdity of it. Less spectacularly, the season faded away. Blake's loss had been critical. His goals were sorely missed. Akinbiyi was not the answer—just yet. He would score goals the next season, whilst at the end of this one, Burnley finished 13th. Of course there had been ups and downs; games that could have been won, should have been won, the usual number of last minute goals conceded, debatable referees' decisions, bad luck and so on. Every manager will point to them all. If Cotterill was disappointed overall, he need not have been. His collection of odds and sods had performed creditably in many games, he had organised them, cajoled them, and from the touchline orchestrated them. McGreal, Sinclair and Cahill had been inspired signings. The fans had warmed to him and appreciated his efforts. One in particular was Kevin Clarke who in March 2005, two thirds into Cotterill's first season, summarised some of his achievements so far for the magazine: *When Saturday Comes*.

At the end of 2003–04 Burnley Chairman Barry Kilby decided to dispense with grizzled Stan Ternent. Stan's idea of conflict management involved a smack in the face, his idea of team-building a week in Magaluf. But he had been a success, achieving promotion to the First Division and keeping the team there for four years. In the past two seasons though, Burnley had become a running joke, conceding more than 160 goals.

On his arrival at Turf Moor, the club had nine players and a pressing debt of £750,000 that needed to be paid to finance companies to stave off administration. Cotterill spouted the usual platitudes but also talked of building a team, and then a squad, of organisation and teamwork. Rather than the traditional pre-season jaunt to the Isle of Man for games against Wrexham and Stockport, Cotterill took the team to Austria to play friendlies at altitude against Bundesliga sides.

He began to earn fans' confidence by rejecting substantial bids for the jewel, England Under-21 midfielder, Richard Chaplow. Free signings included Mr Own Goal, Frank Sinclair, while fees were paid for Danny Coyne, £25,000 and Michael Duff, £15,000. Fans were heartened by the signing of a goalkeeper and three defenders. 'I watched videos of all last season's games,' said Cotterill. The small squad was further bolstered by loan signings, the prize one being defender Gary Cahill from Aston Villa. Few had heard of him but he made a dramatic impact, helping the side keep seven clean sheets in the first nine games he played. As entertaining as Stan was, nobody could imagine him chucking an 18 year old into the first-team; he preferred 36 year old mono-paced David May.

After 28 games Burnley were eight points off sixth place with two games in hand. The star player Robbie Blake had gone to Birmingham, which would have been a disaster under Stan but is now seen as an opportunity to invest. Burnley have the second best defensive record in the League, have beaten Villa and Liverpool in the Cups and won at Stoke despite their fans using every insult available towards Cotterill, despite suffering a number of injuries—Coyne and Chaplow out for three months. Cotterill advocates ice baths, masseurs and under-water pressure tanks to increase blood circulation and the First XI has remained largely the same throughout.

Sinclair is now club captain, transformed from joke into rock-solid centre half (nicknamed, The Power) and Cotterill has worked magic on others, none more so than left back Mo Camara, who used to bomb down forward and then launch crosses into Yorkshire—apparently to the constant amusement of Ternent's staff. Cotterill had him perform 1,000 crosses a day in pre-season, and now he attacks with intent and accuracy, to the extent of being renamed Moberto Carlos.

We have a gem, who in his short time here has already been linked with Leicester, Wolves and Portsmouth. But Cotterill says he is going nowhere and is building an infrastructure and planning an indoor dome with the Blake money. Burnley have more qualified coaches within the youth set-up than any club in the country and there is talk of Academy status. Cotterill will leave Burnley for a Premiership side in the next three to five years. We will not begrudge him that, as it is certain he will leave us in a better position than when he took over.

Clarke provided a good and accurate appraisal. In addition, as an aid to diet, players had club breakfasts and lunches. In the following season the individual coaching given to players certainly paid off with Ade Akinbiyi. In fact he became so prolific, he was sold to Sheffield United, this being the event that inspired Cotterill's famous observation: 'We don't have players who score 30 goals; we sell them when they get to 15.' And yes Cotterill did leave after three and a half years. But it was not to a Premiership side, and when he did return to football after a lengthy interval it was to lowly Notts County before taking over at Portsmouth. How ironic that was. They were more destitute than Burnley when he had arrived there.

The 2005–2006 season started with a defeat at Crewe Alexander. Defender Wayne Thomas and striker Noel Gifton Williams had joined the club. The capture of Thomas showed the lengths Cotterill went to in order to sign players, when he flew out to Florida to catch Thomas during a family holiday. James O'Connor joined Burnley permanently having already earlier been on loan. And Cotterill raided Bournemouth for three players, Wade Elliott, later to score the fabulous winning goal at Wembley in 2009, Garreth O'Connor and John Spicer. The defeat at Crewe was further marred by racist comments that Cotterill heard aimed at Burnley's black players. 'I don't take too kindly to that,' he said. 'I'd rather not say who it was directed at but we've got a few Stoke players here, which spiced things up a bit.'

In truth, other than an occasional convincing win, the season got little better. Only 14 games were won out of 46. Akinbiyi's goals brightened things up and the win at Luton was one of the few memorable games. This was the game where with Burnley down to ten men when Jensen was sent off, they still managed to win 3–2 thanks to a heroic goalkeeping display from midfielder John Spicer who volunteered to take over after a two-minute team meeting (there was no sub goalkeeper on the bench), and a marvellous Akinbiyi hat-trick. It was undoubtedly his game and entered the list of 'great' Burnley displays when people proudly say, 'I was there.' He scored with two rasping wonder-goals from distance and a penalty. Even the Luton fans applauded Burnley off the pitch and the picture of the after-game huddle is an iconic reminder of a marvellous performance against the odds. Teams can often win when down to ten men, but when the man missing is the goalkeeper and one of the ten then has to go in goal for the second half, and on top of that when the main striker was once a figure of fun yet scores a terrific hat-trick, then the victory is all the more special.

Steve Cotterill hailed the win as the greatest of his career.

> I've been lucky enough to have some big wins in my career but this is the best. Ade is a gem. There were a few eyebrows raised when I signed him but I told him at half-time to make sure he went out there and got the match ball. I love him and so do the players.

There was a swift exit from the FA Cup and Aston Villa gained revenge and knocked Burnley out of the League Cup. Akinbiyi who had been knocking in the goals and certainly benefited from Cotterill's coaching was then sold for a fee totalling £1.75million. There was no way impoverished Burnley could turn down this offer. With his departure, the goals dried up. Gifton-Williams was no prolific scorer, there was no Blake of course, and there was only one more occasion during the season's remaining 21 games when Burnley scored more than one goal in a League game. Just 10 goals were scored in those 21 games. It made for depressing reading, and even more depressing viewing. Added to this was a run of six consecutive defeats spanning February and March. At the end of this run the club had sunk as low as 18th place. The season finished with them in 17th position but at least with two new added players— striker Andy Gray, ironically bought from Sheffield United, and midfielder Alan Mahon. Both were quality players and Gray would come good in the first half of the next season. But Mahon was an enigma, never fulfilling at any club his undoubted silky smooth potential.

Nobody knew that the forthcoming season would test Cotterill, the Chairman, supporters and the Board to the limit. But the signs were there. Just 16 points were won from the last 19 games.

2

TREADING WATER

A Chris Boden, *Burnley Express*, pre-season interview in August 2006 gave a fascinating insight into Cotterill's philosophies, football thinking, and views on the forthcoming season; a defining season that would set a new club record—of the wrong sort.

Ambitious Clarets boss Steve Cotterill is realistic enough to admit the Championship is getting tougher. But he feels his squad, as they showed in patches last season, will make life difficult for the big guns in the Division. Incredibly Burnley and Preston, promoted together in 2000 are the longest serving clubs in the Championship, with every other club in the Division for the 2006–07 season having either gone up or down in that time. The likes of Leeds, Southampton, Leicester, West Brom, Birmingham, Sunderland, Wolves, Crystal Palace, Derby, Ipswich, Norwich and Coventry have all plied their trade in the Premiership in the intervening years.

'Punching above our weight,' is a phrase that has often been heard around Turf Moor, but Cotterill feels Burnley will not be out of place among esteemed rivals. 'It probably is going to be harder. I went on record last year and said it was going to be like Premiership 2, and it probably is now. It's tough, obviously we know that, but we've just got to make sure that we get ourselves sorted out and in the best shape we can, because we know on our day we can give teams a game, without a shadow of doubt. We've just got to hope for no injuries, for good performances, good confidence levels and a bit of luck along the way.'

Injuries massively affected the Clarets last term, with Wayne Thomas and Danny Coyne both missing the vast majority of the season but with more numbers and depth this time round, Cotterill is looking for an improvement on the 17th place finish. There has been no need for major surgery this summer, after two close seasons spent building up squads almost from scratch, but he said: 'You always get through rebuilding in the close season, you can never stand still because as we saw last season we thought we had our defence absolutely nailed down. That isn't necessarily the case, because if you look at us last season we were nothing like as miserly as we were the season before. It always has to start with you trying your best to keep clean sheets and you can be as good as anybody, but if you leak them, you're not going to score every game. Scoring goals is normally the most difficult part of the game because it's normally a player's individual brilliance, or a couple of players, with passing and good movement, that go together to make that one goal. But, collectively you can try and get that team together to stop conceding goals. So, for me, last season, a disappointing side for me was conceding too many goals. If you get beat 1–0, that doesn't dent your confidence as much as if you get beat 3–0, because the following week the defenders are on edge.'

Cotterill was hugely encouraged by the form displayed in the run-in last term: 'Towards the end of last season, things changed a bit, a few bodies were missing, and the last eight games we won two, drew five and lost one. The game we lost at Millwall, we were awful, and that was our worst game. Of the five games we drew, we certainly should have won two of those. The two games we won we felt we deserved to win. If you took that points tally, goals for, clean sheets and put them into a season, broken down, that eight game block, if you work it out, and I did down to decimals, would have taken us to eighth in the League with 63 points. If you had looked at that, you would have thought "hang on we're doing something right here". And if you could match the spell we had from September to December you would win the League probably. I remember being bottom of the League and out with the chairman one Friday night presenting a shirt to one of his relatives and felt we didn't deserve to be there. We had dominated a few of the games still getting beat; and it was a major disappointment. But hopefully the players have learned from that, will be closer knit than they were last year. But we have to carry on and keep working for the future; there's no point in looking back and seeing who was the best player last season and the season before that, it's all about who will be best player this season. And that best player whoever he is; has to be one of 11. We haven't got, I'm afraid, room for a talent if he's not going to be one of 11 players.'

The return of Thomas to full fitness is a massive boost, and Cotterill again underlined why he went to such lengths to land the former Stoke man: 'If Wayne is fit and he listens, that's important for Thommo because he has always got an opinion, not to say he's always wrong, but not to say he's always right. But he's got an opinion which is fine. I'm happy for players to have opinions before you start the discussion, it saves a row. But I think he could be, and we spoke about this, I hope for Wayne Thomas' sake he fulfils what he could fulfil because if you look at some of the players in the Premiership, if Wayne gets things right and is tough and determined, mentally strong, I think Wayne could be playing higher than here. He's quick, he's strong, he's aggressive, sometimes he takes a risk because he feels comfortable, but that's sometimes the confidence we don't want to take out of players. You just hope he doesn't dance on too many balls in our box. I'd rather he headed it and put his foot through it.'

Cotterill is eager for a return to the 'Thou Shalt Not Pass' nature of the defence in his first season, and the central defensive area is the most competitive in the squad. He hopes the pressure to keep hold of a shirt will make Burnley meaner: 'We are strong there. But it was an area, to be fair, whether it was lack of competition, whether it was age, whether it was getting over injuries quick enough, that caused me a massive headache. I don't want that headache. If we've got four who can play there, we've probably got more than four—we might have five—but we've probably got four that can play there because the other one will end up playing right back. But if we've got four who can play there, and two are playing there for 46 games, like Sonko and Ingermarsson did for Reading, then good.'

Cotterill feels there are more goals in this side, from the back four and midfield as well as the front men, and has been disappointed in the return from the defenders: 'We've got potentially people who can score. We are disappointed with the amount of goals we've got from defence. We have been disappointed with that, make no bones about that. We seem as though we are harping on about defenders here, and I don't mean it to be that way, but for the aerial ability we've got in the team and for the times they have gone into the box, we are disappointed with the amount of goals. For me a major disappointment is Michael Duff because I know he can score and yet here it's as though he can't. He used to get his head on most things when he went up for corners. So that disappoints me. I think that when balls come in your box, invariably you will see defenders get their head on it. We don't have a problem in our box. It seems to be in the opposition's box we haven't opened teams up enough. To be honest that's down to the individual because I think we've given them so many different runs, so many different set plays, I think it's now down to the individual and his own desire to attack the ball. I am sure this season, even in this short space of time, Steve Foster and Thommo will score. How long it will take, I don't know. Hopefully it's very, very early, preferably the first ten minutes against QPR. But they will, score, that I am convinced of. Steve attacks the ball, he takes a run up to the ball. To be fair, it takes bravery.'

While the defenders battle it out for starting berths, there are a couple of other areas where shirts are up for grabs and Cotterill said: 'We really want a couple of people to nail down positions. Obviously I have the nucleus of the side in my head but I think there are a couple more positions that need to be fought for in my opinion. The right side is proving somewhat difficult to nail down because I am not convinced that everyone who has played there to date has taken their chance. I wouldn't say it's our problem side but someone needs to grasp that for me.'

Alan Mahon has filled the right-sided role as well as playing centrally on the left and just off the front, and Cotterill said: 'Because of what we're doing with Alan Mahon, we have to be a bit more midfieldish than right-wingerish, but I think that might depend on who you're playing against, what type of full back you've got in there, and who plays full back for you—one will potentially attack more than the other. We give Alan Mahon licence to come in off the line, to go wide and to come in behind the front two at specific times. When the move breaks down, he has to get back with the rest of the team and that will probably be the thing I have to talk to Alan about this season more than about the final third, where we know he can unlock doors for us. He has to be part of that unit because there is no point in him being able to do all those special things in the final third if he is not going to help out Jon Harley or Frank Sinclair, depending where he plays.'

While Mahon's impish quality has already made him a firm favourite among supporters, his deadly accuracy from set pieces in pre-season have caught the eye, and Cotterill admitted: 'We had a few free kicks we worked on last year to good effect, but when your team changes, and one of those people standing over the ball changes, sometimes it has a bit of a knock-on effect. But you can either try things, work on things, or just let anyone have a shot, and we might have to give Mahony his head a little bit when he's in and around the box because we don't quite know his shooting range yet, although we've got a pretty good idea. Hopefully that will be a source of goals, but there was a lack of goals from our two central midfielders last year with Micah and Ginge—we didn't get enough goals from them. Chris McCann didn't do too bad and then all of a sudden he seemed to dry up.'

If 'we have to get more goals' was the underlying theme of the pre-season talk with reporter Chris Boden, it was a problem that would remain and would have serious consequences from the end of December until early April. If Cotterill had possessed a crystal ball and been able to foresee what was coming he would no doubt have had sleepless nights long before they actually began to haunt him.

But all that was to come, and until October Burnley played well and got results, none better than the televised game away at Norwich City where there was a terrific 4–1 win and classy football to admire. Another stunning result was a 4–2 win against Barnsley when they came back from a 0–2 deficit. A run of six unbeaten games came up and for the first time in his Burnley career Cotterill won a manager of the month award. With a 1–0 win over Ipswich Burnley were just two points behind leaders Cardiff. In mid November they were the last team in the League to be unbeaten away from home. Sadly Cardiff put an end to that. A win at home against Leeds United got them back on track but it was a crucial game in that an injury to striker Andy Gray put him out of the team for much of the remainder of the season. It was a hammer blow.

By the end of that game Burnley were in fourth place. An approach from Leicester City for Cotterill's services was rebuffed by the chairman. There were reports that West Brom wanted him. His reputation was high and rising. With the run of the ball and freedom from injuries there was no reason to suppose that Burnley could not maintain the progress they had made under him. But it was not to be and the Sunderland game on 16 December 2006, provided defining moments. At 2–0 up and only ten minutes to go Steve Cotterill made changes and went on the defensive to shut up shop and see out the game. Ignoring the old maxim, if it ain't broke don't fix it, the substitutions did not work. Sunderland scored twice in those final minutes and it is fair to assume that Cotterill was as stunned and angry as the supporters. The game was number three of a total of 19 games without a win spread over four months.

Significantly, also in December, a new director joined the Board. This was Brendan Flood, Managing Director of Modus, then a thriving property development company. He was ambitious, go-ahead and had money to invest in the club. With Flood's money Cotterill was able to replace Andy Gray with Ade Akinbiyi, bringing him back from Sheffield United where he had eventually languished. Alas, Ade was not a success in this second spell and there were at least two directors angry at the wasted money and the way that his return had been sealed without their consultation.

The dreadful run of results continued, the football was poor.

Supporters eventually began to question Steve Cotterill's ability to stop the slide. After a defeat away at QPR the manager referred to the loss of Andy Gray:

> Everybody is hurting and at the moment it is tough but I will support the players all the way, even when they do things that upset and disappoint you. We have shown we can do it and we know we can do it but at the moment we are down and need a lucky break. We need something to go for us because at the moment they are the same players they were earlier in the season. We will get back there but one thing you can't do is give them a confidence pill. We were undone by corners, today we had a nightmare with corners, we faded, and we looked devoid of confidence.
>
> It's funny but we haven't won since we lost Andy Gray. If you lose your best players it doesn't help. People say that one man doesn't make a team. Well I'd like to change that statement—I think one man does make a team. You look back at all the great sides; would Argentina have won the World Cup if Maradona hadn't played for them? I think one man does make a team. Look at Chelsea without John Terry.
>
> We've brought in Ade but Ade is nowhere near as fit as he was last time he was here. He's yards off the pace, we know that and there's more we can do about that. At the moment we've just got to keep going.

There were touches of desperation in those words and the references to the missing Andy Gray were almost plaintive. Ade had come back muscle bound, having spent too much time pumping iron at Sheffield. He scored just two goals.

The agony was far from over. Not even the acquisition of international centre half Steve Caldwell in the transfer window made a difference. But the 0–1 defeat at home to Leicester was indicative of the poor luck that befell Burnley. It was a McGreal own goal of the comedy variety, the sort of goal you could show on a Christmas video. The ball ping ponged around in the Burnley box. Thomas cleared it but the ball rebounded off McGreal's knee into the net. The manager was as forthright as ever.

> It certainly looks as though our luck is out after that 90 minutes. On another day we'd have got the points, we had enough chances to win two games. We're desperate for something to happen, never known a spell like it; it's maybe the worst of my career. What you get from me is an honest opinion, and when you're not winning people sometimes want to turn that round and have a little bit of a dig. That's alright because I've had lots of good things said in two and a half years here, and I can take the rough times with the good ones. It can change as it did in the last eight games last season when we lost one in eight and kept five clean sheets. We'd had a bad run then. You do your best and at the moment our best isn't good enough, so we've got to keep going, keep working, do all the things that we were doing earlier in the season that took us to great victories away from home. The run is unbelievable really; certainly when we look at how we started the season.
>
> The other night we deserved to win the game, and one goes in off Johnny Mac's knee, tell me what you can do about that one. We've had

penalty shouts over the last few weeks, and not got them. You'll get people who have a moan and groan about confidence, do they know the lads personally to comment? It's all well and good mimicking my remarks, taking the mickey out of what I say, but do they know the lads and what they go through? They're playing their way out of it, they are determined. At the moment we're inches away from scoring a goal. When Ade and Andy get better, we'll get better. The quicker we get back to scoring goals and keeping clean sheets, the better.

At half-time during one game the DJ must have had a sense of humour when he played 'Message in a Bottle' by the Police featuring the lyrics, 'I'm sending out an SOS'. At half-time in the Leicester game he played Ian Dury and the Blockhead's classic, 'Reasons to be Cheerful'. Less funny was the local radio station interview with Cotterill when it was clear that this was a man under pressure ready to fly off the handle if provoked. The interview went smoothly until the interviewer suggested that fans were seeing the next game as a 'must win' game. Cotterill turned on the interviewer and grilled him. 'Who's told you that then . . . how many have told you that . . . how many people was that . . . how many . . . I'm waiting for you to tell me . . . How long was the radio show . . .? So how many calls . . . twenty, thirty, forty, fifty?' Somehow equilibrium was restored and the next question was asked: 'What would you say to fans worried by the League position and results?' Cotterill terminated the interview.

Listeners were divided in their response. Some thought the manager was embarrassing and handled it all badly. Others sympathised seeing him as a man under pressure fielding some stupid questions. It was, however, reasonable to think that he was frustrated and baffled at the sequence of results, a sequence that had included a number of draws where he might have felt a win was deserved. Never comfortable with the media, always looking and sounding on edge, this was one interview too far under the circumstances. This was a man seeing his team having no luck, the tiniest mistakes punished, penalty claims being ignored and not really having any answers. The best striker was still unfit. Akinbiyi was a shadow. There had been directors' meetings where there had been strong differences of opinion. He was not every director's cup of tea. There was no one to blame but himself. This was his team. He had bought or acquired them. They were not inherited so he could not blame any previous manager. This was probably not the best time to go on 'live' radio and presenter Gary Hickson later revealed that it had certainly been Cotterill who had ended it.

And still there was worse to come and endure. A 0–1 defeat at lowly Southend United was the last straw for many supporters who wanted Cotterill replacing. Southend, to make it even more depressing, had scored in the last minute from a gifted opportunity. There have been many grim displays in Burnley's long history and this was one of them.

Andrew Firmin in the *London Supporters*' magazine expressed his opinions. There was a problem however, a recently renewed contract made it costly for the impoverished club to dismiss the manager.

The day after the Southend defeat, I found myself periodically checking my mobile phone for text messages. What I was half expecting—hoping—was to see that Steve Cotterill had been dismissed as Burnley manager. It seemed to me after Southend to be absolutely the right thing to do, and the best course of action to maximise our chances of remaining in this Division. If I had been Barry Kilby, the first thing I would have done on that Wednesday morning would be to offer the manager my best wishes and then set about identifying a temporary replacement who could motivate the team and get them playing to the best of their abilities for the final ten games.

I am aware that this is all rather easier said than done. It isn't so long ago that Steve Cotterill was the beneficiary of an extended contract, something that made me uneasy at the time.

There would presumably be a substantial pay-off to negotiate, and one can only hope that if dismissal were to be considered, the likely cost of action wouldn't be a decisive factor. Then we'd have to find a replacement at short notice, at an awkward time of the season, and with a backroom lacking in plausible candidates to succeed, even on a caretaker basis. I remain convinced that the short term boost given by a new manager, particularly one who could revert to the basics, start picking the players in their best positions, and get the team playing honestly and working hard again, would have made the difference in keeping us up. A couple of wins and the odd draw should still be enough to do it, but it's hard to see where those might come from when we haven't won a match since November and scored only one goal this month. We're now level on points with sides which have been fighting relegation all season; time to end denial, surely. Calling for a change at the top always looks extreme, although I can tell you I wasn't the only one hoping for that message on Wednesday. You are entitled after such a barren run to ask questions of the manager.

I can't think of a Burnley manager in recent decades who would have got such an easy ride over such a sustained period of poor results. Our manager has always been an impressive talker about the game, and clearly that has helped him. Of course Barry Kilby doesn't make hasty decisions about managers, a policy which has been borne out in the past, so in reality there has probably always been little prospect of getting that message. For me, if it was going to be done, then after Southend was the time to do it. So now, for better or worse, we have to assume Steve Cotterill is our manager for the rest of the season and the next game at home to Luton looks utterly crucial.

The next game against Luton, a team down at the bottom, was one of the worst ever seen at Turf Moor and ended in a 0–0 draw. A win was seen as essential, a win was expected. No one thought that the barren run could continue against a team as poor as Luton. But it did, and by now supporters were voting with their feet as attendances fell and even season ticket holders found better things to do on a Saturday afternoon, as Burnley sat just two points above the bottom three. And yet the team received a long and loud reception as they came out willing them to a victory. But it was not to be and the pre-game cheers were replaced by boos and abuse at the end. It was reasonable to think that any other manager would have been dismissed by now. The game set a new club record for a run of games without a win—19 in all. The manager bared his soul before the next game at home to Plymouth on 3 April.

> After two and a half years here, working on the budget I have had and potentially leaving to go to three other clubs, which I haven't done to sign a new contract here, then somewhere along the line I think that is earning time and credit. I do more than the average football manager does at the club and there is enough fight in me to keep our players going. One thing I don't do is give in and I will fight on until it is right. We need that little bit of something different to spark us. We are in this run where we haven't won for 18 League games but we have drawn eight of them. If you isolate them, there is an injury time penalty at Ipswich, a penalty given against us at Coventry that wasn't, an own goal against Leicester when we dominated the game. You could go on and on and even in the games we have lost we have only lost two by more than one goal. The goal difference tells you there is not a lot wrong with us. But our 'goals for' column tells you where the problem is this season. Perhaps not scoring an early goal makes them edgy. That belief factor can last us so long and we have to maintain that strength of character and belief factor for longer. Nobody was more disappointed or angry than I was about not winning against Luton. I have never been on anything like this in my life. The longest it's gone on for before would be something like five games, before winning the next few on the spin. It's amazing the pressure that is put on clubs to win football matches. We are competing in a League that is very difficult to compete in against teams who have between 20,000 and 30,000 people watching them, and it's tough. But you have to show the fighting spirit to make sure we get enough points on the board between now and the end of the season.
>
> It's tough down at the bottom and we've got to try and make sure we fight our way out of this. It's a fine balance between trying to whip them up too much and getting them to go out and pass a ball. There's a happy medium but when the players are a bit short on confidence, or there are a few moans and groans, my view is to get them angry. I would be angry and more aggressive, and that is the only way you can come through times like this, to fight your way through them. I don't think there's any other remedy. The tough times in life are probably the best times because you don't learn anything in the good times. You take them for granted. In the tough times you have to come out fighting tooth and nail and that is how Steve Cotterill is. But I cannot give every player the same mindset and determination. 95% of supporters have been very good to me and nothing changes my view of them, just because you haven't won in 18 games. You are bound to get a few shouts when the ground is quiet and the team's not up and running. But you have to do your best to ignore those isolated shouts. I tell you what could be worse—not looking to change anything to try and make us better.

One thing he did try was an addition to the squad. Ade was dropped and in came nippy striker Paul McVeigh from Norwich. What a difference he made and the inevitable happened on 3 April with a home win over Plymouth Argyle. This wasn't just any old win, this was a convincing win. The football flowed and as soon as the first goal went in you could see heads lift and confidence roar back. The half-time score was an astonishing 3–0 with McVeigh getting the second and then Elliott capping the night with a fourth in the second half. This was proper football totally the opposite of the dire stuff against Luton. Pace appeared from somewhere, with accurate passing and intricate one-touch stuff fit for a football connoisseur. Another loan acquisition, Djemba-Djemba, pulled all the strings. Gray was sublime even though he failed to score. Every player was up for it.

At 9.45 Steve Cotterill walked around the touchline very slowly and deliberately, punching the air and applauding the fans. The players had gone. As he approached the tunnel he turned again to face the fans and pointed to his heart. It was a show of emotion and a fantastic touch with which to end the night. His post-match comments were brimful of genuine pleasure and relief.

> I am delighted for the players, for the chairman and the directors who have stood beside me because it has been tough. Early mornings, late nights, waking in the middle of the night to write things down and trying them the next day. I think it is probably the toughest time I have had to face in my managerial career. There will be a percentage of supporters I need to convince, but those who have stood by me have been first class. Our chances went in tonight and there were lots of people who could vie for man of the match, but for me, Andy Gray was absolutely immaculate and I am sorry he didn't get his goal. Football is my life and over the past few months there hasn't been much of it, so I am going to enjoy tonight and tomorrow.

Skipper Steve Caldwell made a telling comment: 'He wears his heart on his sleeve and he cares.' The Plymouth win amazingly was the first of five in the final eight games of the season. There was an astonishing 1–0 win away at soon to be promoted Birmingham. West Brom who finished fourth were beaten 3–2. But the final two games brought defeats to end things tamely. For over four months during the winless run, Steve Cotterill had lived on the good will, patience and appreciation of the supporters and chairman. That appreciation was based on their understanding that money was tight, there was never going to be a big squad where players would compete for places, and that this was a place where managers were always hamstrung by the sale of their best players. Kyle Lafferty would be the next, although it would be a new manager who would see to that one.

Manager Cotterill summed up season 2007–08.

> I think what can be described as a good season for me would have been in the top six, because that's an aim that would have been difficult. But,

certainly, what I've done personally is tread water for another year. I think this year is one I won't ever forget, how we started—we always knew it would be tough anyway to stay up there, irrespective of injuries or suspensions. But when they kick in with us we struggle. We do that every year, not having the strength in depth of replacing your key players that make others play. I don't know if that will change. I don't know the answer to that yet. We do need to have a stronger squad, because that's why we end up in the scenario we end up in, and we will need to bring players in. Players will have to go and other players will have to be addressed to make room for new arrivals. I would have thought there would be a few discussions at the end of the season as regards that.

Cotterill's comment about treading water for another year suggested that he thought this had been a wasted year for him personally. His plan to manage in the Premiership by the age of 42 was becoming less likely barring a miracle. It would certainly not happen at Burnley with a player budget of just £5million to eke out; whilst other clubs had budgets three times that. The book that director Brendan Flood brought out in 2009 would illustrate the frustrations Cotterill was feeling.

3

STEVE COTTERILL AND
THE LAST SUPPER

Sadly for Steve Cotterill it was becoming clear that the new season, 2007–08, was developing into just more of the same when a run of ten games with just one victory, and some very poor football, provoked supporter discontent and resulted in declining attendances.

It was such a shame, but things were not working out even though new players had been brought in. The return of Robbie Blake was a masterstroke. A real crowd favourite, he had not had a happy time at either Birmingham or Leeds where he subsequently went. Cotterill brought him back and fans were delighted. 'I have unfinished business here,' said Blake.

Another masterstroke was the sale of the lumbering Wayne Thomas who had never really sparkled, to Southampton for £1million. In came his immediate replacement, the eloquent and elegant Clarke Carlisle, for a steal at £250,000. If this wasn't a terrific deal, then nothing was. Thomas had been plagued by injuries and red cards, the number of which had become a club joke. Another incomer was full back Stephen Jordan from Manchester City.

What nobody realised at the time was that here then was the nucleus of the side that two years later would triumph at Wembley: Jensen, Duff, Caldwell, Carlisle, Elliott, Gudjonsson, Alexander, McCann and Blake. Cotterill had signed seven of them including the re-purchase of Blake. McCann had already been at the club before Cotterill arrived but Cotterill nurtured and developed him further. The most fascinating perhaps was Graham Alexander. Already in his middle thirties when he was signed from local rivals Preston, it was a signing that lifted fans' eyebrows in surprise. What was the use of someone already near the end of his career? Three years later he was still an integral part of the side; fit, wiry, influential, so much so that he was later appointed as a coach, and was possibly the world's best penalty taker. He came as a full back but eventually switched to midfield.

But by now, perhaps the person with increasing significance and influence at the club was the ambitious director, Brendan Flood. He had arrived the season before, able to dip into his own money and that of his company, Modus, in order to bolster the club's finances. As joint Operational Director he was in a position to make far-reaching decisions. He assumed a growing profile both in the club and the media. He wanted more than mediocrity and did not want to settle for the mid-table comfort zone. His book, published in 2009, would reveal more than a little of what went on behind the scenes, Cotterill's increasing frustrations, which some might have seen as growing paranoia, and his reasons for the poor displays.

Yet, his final season started so well with a win over promotion favourites West Brom, 2–1, in front of a good crowd of over 15,000. But, by Tuesday 5 November, there would only be three more wins. Four wins, six draws, four defeats and 18 points had been garnered by then. Not unreasonable, if mid-table survival was the only aim. But what the bare statistics did not show was the poverty of the football, by now known as Cotterball, the direness of the displays, and that by the time of the fateful Hull City game, the attendance had slumped to a depressing sub 10,000, an alarming 50% drop on the opening game.

If the 0–0 game against Luton Town in the previous season had sunk to new lows, or the 0–1 defeat away at Southend, then the Hull City game was even worse when it ended with a last minute winner for Hull, and a 0–1 defeat for Burnley. By now Cotterill had come up with the most bizarre reason ever heard for the continual poor performances, when he told the Press that the players were now under too much pressure placed on them by the new plans for ground development and the resultant raised expectations. He described the weight of expectation undermining their confidence at home. Supporters simply raised their eyebrows in amazement. His gloomy demeanour, plus the tortured excuses and reasons did not go unnoticed by his employers. To be fair to him, injuries to Duff and Caldwell had been disruptive, and it was the old Akinbiyi that re-surfaced, the player who scored few goals.

The Hull game was the nadir. This was an inept, ineffective and utterly abysmal display. There had been something like nine wins in the last 45 games. It was clear to all that Cotterill had lost his way, and possibly even lost the dressing room and the confidence of some, if not all, the players. The football had become dreadful and spectators, frankly, were bored.

The game was the last straw for Brendan Flood in particular, although one may assume other directors and the chairman held the same views. It was 8th November when the news broke and the club announced that Cotterill had left the club by mutual consent after a stay of three and half years, making him at that time the longest serving manager in the Division. This time, however, instead of enduring another four-month winless run, the club acted.

Cotterill's last interview for the local Press, illustrated the problems he felt about the ground development announcements:

The crowd are more anxious this year than they have been before because of the hullabaloo that's gone on off the pitch. That's a definite fact. There's less patience with the boys at home now and I don't think that's fair. We shouldn't get edgy about playing at home.

'Perhaps it was no surprise,' wrote Phil Whalley, 'that a manager so desperately looking for scapegoats, anywhere but in his own coaching and tactical preparation of the team, had been jettisoned. Looking back through the season', he continued, 'perhaps the real undoing of Steve Cotterill was the arrival in the Boardroom of Brendan Flood, a powerful man who remained to be convinced by the merits of the manager. Perhaps Cotterill's self-generated PR about his ambition and his own potential had stopped fooling people. As long as he kept telling fans that he was 'getting there' and as long as he sounded sure of himself, fans might have continued to give him the benefit of the doubt, even in the face of dour, percentage football and extremely poor results. But, then when he was eventually and clearly crumbling under the pressure, with the shield of self-confidence evaporating, people were then seeing the manager as the problem and not the team.

Flood's words earlier in June had hinted at his ambitions and what he wanted from a manager.

The immediate plan is to get a good entertaining team and we are doing our best to do that now. Steve Cotterill has been out there shopping and is very careful who he goes for. This is his big, big chance. His heart is definitely in the club and he's massively ambitious. I think he's got the brains and the willpower and with the right people around him we'll get the best out of him and he'll get the best out of his players. I'm confident that he's as good as you get and he just needs the breaks and he'll grow into it.

Reading between the lines there, if entertainment was what Flood was after, he was perhaps aware neither he nor the supporters were getting it. 'This is his big chance' were more words that hinted that it could well be his last at Burnley Football Club, and that he was now under close scrutiny.

There were more than just a few fans who wondered why it had taken so long to look for a new man asking; has any other manager ever got away for so long with producing one of the lowest-scoring Burnley sides ever, and a four-month run of 19 games without a win? 'Cotterill was, and is, a remarkable character, and a canny operator in a football world full of confidence tricksters and chancers', wrote Phil Whalley. 'His aura and charisma was used to good effect for a long time but eventually in a results oriented business, persona could only take him so far.'

In an unusual twist to the usual 'dismissal' Press conference arrangements, Cotterill actually sat in on the conference, next to Chairman Kilby and Flood. Kilby told the gathering that Cotterill still had the capabilities to manage in the Premiership.

> However what has happened in the last ten games and the slide down the table, maybe the directors thought it was time for a change. We played poorly against Hull and bad home defeats never help. That was a defining moment. I think we are fourth lowest in the Division in terms of attendances. People want winning teams more than anything else. If you can win and entertain, then that's all the better. We still have ambitions to get into the top six and I was very conscious we were sliding down the table.

Flood also congratulated the departing manager, who, sitting alongside, slumped in his baggy grey tracksuit, looked as though he was bewildered and shell-shocked by the whole thing. His heart was at Burnley there is no doubt of that, and he had come to identify strongly with both club and town. But it was a massive blow to his personal ambition, denting any future CV. Flood admitted that the manager had done a lot for the club but he considered him unable to take the club further. Again reading between the lines, there were hints that he had spoken to the playing staff about their attitude towards Cotterill's tactical approach.

> Maybe Steve has done everything he can here and his opportunity lies elsewhere. He has already done a lot and I think those extra yards might feel too much for him, whereas someone else might see them as small steps. We have to entertain, and we have been entertaining in some games, but we have been fragile in others. From my point of view, knowing what I do about the players, they have probably got into a mentality that is maybe not their natural way of playing. Perhaps with a greater freedom and different tactics, we might see a team that is consistent every week and does attack teams from the off. They are good footballers and we just have to see if a better team can be got by having a different person leading them. There is a big ambition beating away in the club and hopefully we can do better and entertain ourselves doing it.

One wonders how Cotterill felt hearing these words. They were tactful and diplomatic rather than brutal and hard-hitting. Yet behind them there was a clear and unmistakeable message. These were good players. Cotterill was not getting the best out of them. His tactics were negative and stifling. The players didn't want to play his way. Doing any more with them was seemingly beyond Cotterill's capabilities. Someone with a different philosophy might take them to the next level.

Steve Cotterill, though he may well have been inwardly fuming at the subtle criticisms, was himself the diplomat. If any rank and file supporter had said these things to him, he would have received short shrift. One wonders what Cotterill's reaction to one supporter would have been who wrote: 'The Cotterill book of excuses was rivalling *War and Peace*.' Phil Whalley himself had been on the receiving end of a Cotterill blast for something he wrote in the *London Clarets* magazine. But in public Cotterill was restrained.

If ever there was mutual consent this was it. There are no problems at all, no bitterness with the Board of directors. It is a big shame that it has happened. I have had a great time here. It has been a tough couple of days for me, but that is something I will have to come to terms with. It's a great club; I have loved every minute of it.

Brendan Flood said more in later articles that revealed the state that Steve Cotterill was in. He had gone as far as he could and was pretty much down and out, the suggestion being that he just didn't know what to do next.

'We need someone who's going to light the touch paper . . . You've got to have people who are clever at getting things done; Steve's energy levels were getting low and that's a problem when you're a manager.'

In *Big Club, Small Town and Me*, Brendan Flood gave his account of the decision to replace Steve Cotterill. My thanks go to him for permission to reproduce the pages in their entirety.

As the season got going we beat Oldham 3–0 in the Carling Cup on a Tuesday night. It was a good result but Oldham could have had a hatful and the only difference between the two sides was the finishing. The following week we had a disappointing home draw with Blackpool and then we had a bit of a sticky spell. We won our next match at Sheffield Wednesday, but they were dreadful, having lost their last six games and they visibly had no confidence. I'd have backed North End to get a result that night. Then we went on a run of nine games with only one win, a home result against Norwich who are often as kind to us as Plymouth. As the poor run gathered pace Steve was getting more and more agitated. Slightly bizarrely in my opinion, he was expressing regret that we'd sold Wayne Thomas.

Steve and I had built up a friendship over the previous ten months or so and he was quite open with me. When Sammy Lee was fired at Bolton and Chris Hutchins at Wigan, he hinted to me that maybe he should try his luck and go for jobs there. I knew that he had made a couple of strategic phone calls to Wigan and Bolton. And he had actually asked Sir Alex to give him a reference for the Wigan job. He was feeling under more pressure at Burnley and was acutely conscious of what happened during the nineteen game winless run in the previous season, when we hadn't dismissed him. But this spell certainly wasn't good. We'd spent a lot of money by Burnley's standards and brought nine or ten players since I'd been at the club but I could see he was becoming more and more aggravated and impatient with the players. You could see it during matches on the touchline.

Steve had started commenting that Burnley was a small club. I don't think he felt he was getting the rewards for all the effort he had put in, even though he was fairly well paid. And to make matters worse there was a growing tension between Steve and one or two members of the Board. In his conversations with me he referred to his growing frustration with the 'energy sappers on the Board'. After a 3–2 home defeat by Southampton he came into the chairman's lounge after the game, clearly angry and swearing. He was venting his spleen quite spectacularly about the players, the club, and everyone who was at fault apart from himself.

Going back to my general philosophy that I always give people 12 months to prove themselves, I started to review our progress and what we had achieved in that time. I had to admit I was concerned that we might have wasted some of the financial investment. Steve was still asking me if we could go in for more players like Darren Huckerby at Norwich and Lee Bromby at Sheffield United. I felt they were older players who wouldn't add anything to the club; and we'd be laying out more cash for little benefit. The difference in our views about the sort of players we should be signing was widening at this point. Steve was becoming concerned that by October I no longer supported him, and he wanted more players.

Then on a miserable night on 6th November we played Hull City at home. They were near the bottom of the Division and a team that we should beat if we were well organised. Ellen and the whole family came along and we invited some friends who were Hull fans. It was a cold night and a desperately poor crowd of about 9,900. The atmosphere was terrible and it was obvious that a lot of people were beginning to feel the recurring pain of the nineteen games without a win from the previous season, and fans were starting to question what we were doing. But most of the fans didn't know that Steve had already expressed that he didn't believe that he had long left at Burnley and, naturally for an ambitious man, he had one eye on a Premiership job.

The game was absolutely dire from start to finish and Steve was getting some criticism from sections of the fans in the Bob Lord Stand. The supporters were becoming as impatient as he was and they had every right to be. At the start of the season I thought we had a reasonable chance of making it to the top six. But three months into the season it was obvious that we still weren't good enough overall.

We lost the game 1–0 and I was completely horrified. It was such a bad performance that we had been outplayed by Hull. At the time we had no idea that they'd end up being promoted and they just looked like a workmanlike Hull team. This was a real milestone. Bloody hell, we'd just been outclassed by Hull.

The next morning I woke up at five o' clock. I usually sleep very well and I only struggle if I have something big on my mind. As I got up I said to Ellen:

'I think we need a need a new manager.'

I went down into the kitchen, made a coffee and started putting together a list of people we'd consider if Steve wasn't our manager. And as soon as it was a decent hour I rang Barry and told him that I was convinced that we needed a change:

'Barry I think we should take the bull by the horns. If we change now we'll probably have more choice, but if we wait until January there might be fewer decent managers available. If we open up the running now we might get some good candidates and it allows a new manager the chance to recruit a few players in January.'

We shared our concerns over the club's current difficulties and agreed that I should meet with Steve. Steve and I always exchanged phone calls the day after a game, and he had rung me twice on the Wednesday afternoon but I hadn't taken the calls because I was still annoyed. At about 4 p.m. and at the third time of ringing I answered the call:

'Hi Steve.'

'Okay.' He paused sensing a problem. 'How are you mate?'

'Well, not good, it was shit last night.'

Over the past year we'd got to know each other pretty well and Steve could read me, certainly on this occasion:

'Yep it was. Have you got something to say Bren?'

'Yeah, it's time for a change Steve.'

Even though I think in his heart he knew it may have been coming he was a bit taken aback and I could tell that he was understandably upset. So I said to him:

'Look, why don't you come round tonight for dinner and we'll talk it through. I'm sorry Steve.'

Then I rang Ellen and said:

'Can you rustle something up? I've got Steve Cotterill coming round and it's not going to be the best evening.'

This clearly presented Ellen with a bit of a dilemma:

'What do you want for an evening like that?' And she started talking about the type of food you do when you're changing the manager. 'Do you want beers or do you not want beers?'

When Steve arrived he was dropped off by a driver so I think he was expecting a few drinks. He later described the meal as 'The Last Supper' and I don't think he was referring to the fish. As we sat talking he was quite upset and I was genuinely moved. He'd put a lot of effort in over the last few years and he'd done a good job for the club, but I explained to him that I didn't think he could take us up and we needed a different style to make things happen. And maybe it would be better if he tried to focus on going for jobs in the Premiership, because I knew he wanted to.

So we agreed that he'd leave by mutual consent. At that moment it was the best thing for Steve and for the club. It was one of the most difficult days I have ever experienced and it genuinely scared me that I was then responsible for changing Burnley's manager. I actually expected Steve to walk into the manager's job at Wigan or possibly Preston shortly thereafter but it didn't happen for him.

The following morning I was on the 7 o' clock train from Manchester to Euston when I rang Barry. I had my hand over my phone as I explained to Barry what had happened and that Steve had taken it well, all things considered. Barry was in Germany that day so we agreed we'd do the Press Conference on the Friday.

As I sat in my meeting later that morning my phone started ringing non stop. And when I went outside to look at my messages they were from newspapers and Sky Sports. Steve had gone into training the next morning and told the players, who true to form texted their agents and off it went into the ether. And, in a further bizarre twist it turned out that my hushed conversation with Barry had been picked up by a Burnley fan opposite me on the train and then downloaded onto the Claretsmad website. I couldn't believe it.

So, we had a hurriedly arranged Press conference back at the club on the Thursday afternoon. I met Steve before the Press arrived and he went over a couple of points on his contract. He's always been a strong negotiator and that had served the club well, and he left with a healthy compensation package.

Looking back, that Friday, I was convinced that we'd done the right thing. After all, we had been sliding down the League. We couldn't afford to have another winless run of matches and we had to do better. But the next two weeks were daunting. Without doubt they are on the shortlist for the worst weeks of my life. I had people ringing me all the time and you can't help watching Sky Sports and listening to comments when the topic is discussed on the radio. There were phone-ins on Radio Lancashire with guys ringing up and saying, 'I don't think we should have got rid of Steve Cotterill so quickly.' And: 'It's obviously Flood who's sacked him.'

The consensus was pretty much 50:50 and for the half who supported Steve it was clear that whoever was brought in would be 'Flood's man'.

Cotterill duly left, and Owen Coyle duly arrived and it could be argued that the appointment of Owen Coyle was simply the result of good fortune and coincidence rather than a good selection process. Chairman Kilby just happened to have a Gleneagles weekend booked at the time of the search for a manager and he was able to meet Coyle at breakfast in Scotland. His arrival would spark two of the most dramatic chapters in the club's history. There was the season that ended in Wembley and promotion; and the second was the following season that saw Coyle's sudden departure and Burnley's subsequent relegation.

Cotterill remained without a job until early in 2010 and then, refreshed and re-invigorated he took over at Notts County with immediate success. Under his guidance they finished Division Two Champions. He was next appointed manager of cash-strapped Portsmouth in time for the 2010–11 season and at the time of writing was enjoying a spectacular renaissance.

His time at Burnley can be viewed in a number of ways. He was the man who got the impoverished club back on track in his first season. He was the man who was in charge during the winless run of 19 games. And he was the man who gathered the players who went on to achieve the astonishing promotion feat. And yet, despite the fact that there were occasional games that supporters slept through, his legacy will be remembered overall with gratitude and respect.

4

THE MESSIAH ARRIVES

How will Owen Coyle be remembered at Burnley Football Club? As the man who led the club to an improbable and unexpected place in the Premiership? Or as the man who left them in the Premiership in mid-season and in so doing contributed hugely to immediate relegation?

His achievement was immense. But, his untimely departure was widely condemned. The promotion season of 2008–09 was one of the most stunning and exciting seasons in the club's history. The Carling Cup run during that period was unforgettable. But, if there was elation and joy at Wembley in May and the accolades poured down on Owen Coyle, there was a huge contrast at Bolton Wanderers only months later and at Turf Moor in a much later Carling Cup tie, when vitriol and bitter abuse was hurled at him by thousands of Burnley supporters.

Just how did this change happen?

* * * * *

The search was on for a new manager. It was time to find the replacement for Steve Cotterill. Operational Director Brendan Flood believed the time was right for a new man to take the steps needed to achieve the club's 'burning ambition'. Since Brendan Flood had arrived at the club and invested money it is true to say that ambitions and aspirations had definitely been lifted. Here was a man who had brought a new burst of energy into the Boardroom and a welcome injection of money. As in his Modus business, he was not satisfied with just treading water and mid-table mediocrity. Eventually his business would fold, but until that happened he was, as one journalist, Alan Nixon, described him, 'Burnley's go-to man'.

'We haven't got anybody lined up,' he said on 10th November, continuing:

> We spoke (with Steve) about what the ambitions of the club were and what Steve had on his plate in terms of trying to achieve those ambitions. He has already done a lot and I think those extra yards might feel too much for him at the moment whereas someone else might see them as small steps. So someone different and new faces might do us all good. Tuesday's defeat (the demoralising 0–1 home loss to Hull City) hit us hard. On the way to the

game what has happened since was not on my mind. It was only when I was reflecting on where we were and Steve and I were chatting that we both asked what the other thought. Maybe Steve has done everything he can here and his opportunity lies elsewhere. We have to entertain and we have been entertaining in some games but we have been fragile in others. There is a big ambition beating away in the club and hopefully we can do better and entertain ourselves doing it. At the moment, a couple of wins and we are straight back into the top three.

'Knowing what I do about the players they probably got into a set mentality that is maybe not their natural way of playing. Perhaps with a greater freedom and different tactics we might see a team that is consistent every week and does attack teams from the off. They are good footballers and we just have to see if a better team can be got by having a different person leading them. We will take our time though. The club has been here for 125 years and we can afford a few days to pick a new manager, so with the international break we have time to make a sensible decision and get the best man who can add value to the club.

'We have great foundations for anyone coming in to work with the players and off the pitch we have exceptionally good finances because we have not incurred any debt as a result of Barry's excellent handling of the books.'

In fact the club was about to announce at the AGM a year end loss of £4.3million, an increase of approximately £1million on the previous financial year; a loss that would have been higher had Brendan Flood not bought over £3million of shares making him the second biggest shareholder. Other directors too had invested loans in the club.

Brendan Flood said in the *Burnley Express* on 12th November 2007, just a couple of days later:

We're looking for someone to light the touch paper and help achieve ambitions of Premier League football. I'm doing all these chairman's lunches, trying to get to know everyone, so they're all ringing me up now, telling me who they think. Phil Gartside told me who had applied for the job at Bolton, and Dave Whelan told me who Wigan are looking at, so I get decent feedback from other people, which helps to educate our process, and you've got to go on references. It's like appointing an employee in your own business. You've got to find out what habits they've got and you've got to make sure they fit the culture you're trying to set. We're trying to set high standards, and we don't want anybody who may be a big name, but have bad standards.

Flood spoke of the profile of the man being sought:

Younger definitely. Steve Cotterill had big strengths, honesty, he's passionate, he's committed, thinks deeply and analyses everything . . . But I think we want maybe someone who's got that bigger picture who can say, 'Right, I'm aiming for this position, what do I have to do? Somebody who can add value to the club, do something the club hasn't got just now. We can ring up certain clubs on the back of our reputation and get certain players through our Boardroom, relationships and reputations, but we need a manager who can deliver something so that we say 'that's interesting', and just a bit different. We're looking for someone who stands out. I think they've got to have the potential to manage in the Premiership. In that case you've got to be a good ambassador, a good communicator, can inspire the troops and capture the fans' imagination. All those things are what we're after, and at the end of the day they've got to care about Burnley. We don't want negative things about Burnley rammed down our throats at Board meetings, we want positive things.

One candidate was Steve Davis already at the club but Flood had reservations. 'I think it'd be a lot of pressure for Steve to take on the post of manager. I think Steve Cotterill has said it might be too early for him. In time I think he would be capable. Who knows? We don't want someone using this as their learning zone.'

The club had a broad view of who to select from, not just out of work managers but one or two who were already in employment which would have meant making official approaches through the correct channels. One such was Brian Laws at Sheffield Wednesday, reported to be the preferred candidate, but his club would not entertain any approach. (Ironically he would arrive much further down the line in January 2010, having been sacked by Sheffield Wednesday.)

I'd say there were definitely three or four, and there might be one or two who are in employment, so I think we can't give any details. A couple we've been told would be interested in coming to Burnley. I think it will be something that will happen reasonably quickly, within a week or two, because I think there is the interest for managers to come here. We're a sound club, we're one of the best managed clubs financially in our League, so from that perspective it's a good start for the manager, and we've got some reasonable players on the pitch. If you look at the line-up, it's not too bad. We've got options and we can take advantage of the January transfer window. I don't think we need to massively change the team. I think we just need two or three players who can just really finish this squad off. There's a cracking team spirit and some good leaders there and a nice blend of youth and experience. I think it's 90% a winning squad. I think a couple of players will make all the difference. We just need somebody who's going to light the touch paper.

It would be the unknown Owen Coyle who lit that touch paper and I am indebted to Brendan Flood for permission to use pages of his book: *Big Club, Small Town and Me*, TH Media, 2009. In this he describes how Owen Coyle arrived at Turf Moor.

The ending of Steve Cotterill's era at Turf Moor was without doubt the hardest thing I'd had to do since I arrived at the club barely twelve months earlier. But it was done, and having made that decision, we now had to figure out how we could get someone to make a difference. We were determined to find someone who was capable of taking us up to the Premiership.

I was acutely aware that I didn't have the unequivocal support of the town at this time. I had picked up very early in the process that the consensus in Burnley was, quite rightly, that I was being judged for this decision. As you can imagine I now felt immense pressure to make sure that we got the next appointment absolutely right.

When I first joined the Board at Burnley I had decided to get some guidance from figureheads who were successful and experienced in the game, so I went to see Dave Whelan at Wigan to pick his brains. Dave is quite sensible with his money, which I guess is partly why he is so successful. So much so that when we went for lunch he even went to the extent of ordering tap water to drink. I thought he was winding me up, but he wasn't. I took the chance to ask Dave for his advice on buying players, which agents we should use and which we should steer clear of. After he'd sat back and thought about it for a moment he said:

'You know Brendan; it's all down to the manager. If you make the right decision on the manager you'll do well. If you make the wrong decision you'll do badly. It's as simple as that.'

The clarity of Dave's words had struck me and we were now in that very position. They had become more relevant than ever. Throughout the next couple of weeks there was a hotline to my mobile from the Press. Radio Lancashire, Suzanne Geldard and Chris Boden were on the phone almost every day.

As the furore seemed to gather pace, I knew that the best thing to do was to get on with the job in hand quickly. So Barry and I got to work agreeing the criteria that we were looking for in our next manager and this is what we came up with.

We need someone who is familiar with Burnley or a very similar club. They need to have a good knowledge of the Championship. They must have a good track record. Someone with modern coaching skills. Someone who is passionate about the academy. And has the ability to bring in promising young players who could join the first-team squad immediately.

We also agreed that we would prefer a young manager if possible, but this wasn't an immovable prerequisite. These criteria were essential for us to be able to find the right man and gave us a fairly vivid profile, so it didn't look like finding our man would be an easy job. But there was no way we were willing to settle for second best. We simply had to get the right man. But the criteria we had set didn't seem to narrow down the field much.

We were bombarded from all sorts of avenues and I began to make a detailed list to add to the one I'd started on after the 'Last Supper'. The sort of names that were cropping up were Gary Speed, Mike Newall, Peter Reid, Billy Davies, Nigel Worthington and Paul Jewell. I made a note of every contact we received. I did have a plan to ring every applicant personally, which I immediately scrapped. And so we set to work in narrowing the list down a bit. We were nearer the mark with the likes of Sammy McIlroy who was doing a solid job at Morecambe, and Simon Grayson who had worked wonders at Blackpool with very little resources. Mick Phelan was an obvious name that came to mind. He's a Burnley lad and still lives in the area. He still comes to matches when he can and he's got a fantastic pedigree having worked for Sir Alex for so long. I rang Mick but he didn't return my call.

My personal favourite was Brian Laws. He'd been an outstanding player for Burnley and like a lot of our ex-players was still very fond of the club and its supporters. And, he had done his shift at Scunthorpe and moving up to Sheffield Wednesday, in his first full year in charge, he had a very good win ratio of 44%. But, one of our directors warned me off him because of a little fracas he was involved in when he was manager at Grimsby Town. Brian spent just under two years as manager there but his relationship apparently took a turn for the worse when during an argument on a night out, he allegedly threw a chicken wing at his Italian player Ivano Bonetti, which hit the player in the face, and then a full scrap ensued. The alleged incident took place in a Kentucky Fried Chicken restaurant and consequently Brian was given the nickname, 'The Colonel' which followed him to Hillsborough.

So, ignoring my co-director's advice I made a direct approach to Sheffield Wednesday and asked for their permission to speak to Brian. Wednesday still weren't playing particularly well but they turned down our approach. Obviously we wouldn't speak to the manager directly in a case like this, but I did find out that Brian would have loved to come to Burnley and he wasn't best pleased with the Board at Hillsborough to say the least. The owners he didn't like there at the time have gone now, but I'm sure he would have relished the job at Burnley at that time.

So, we turned our attention to the other candidates. We thought about Mike Newell who had caught our eye because of the good style of football that they had played at Luton. But his Blackburn connection might have worked against us. You can't afford to be too parochial, but on the other hand you can't be exactly sure that an ex-Blackburn player will end up having a love affair with the Longsiders at Burnley.

When we had parted company with Steve Cotterill, he had recommended Joe Royle to me as he thought we'd struggle to do better. I thanked Steve because I knew how much he admired Joe, but he didn't really get near to fitting our brief. By the end of the week I had spoken to all of the serious candidates on the phone and we were getting close to a shortlist made up of Paul Jewell, Peter Reid and our own Steve Davis, who was an assistant coach under Steve Cotterill and a legend with our fans.

Then out of the blue the club received an email from a journalist in Scotland, Alan Nixon, who said that Owen Coyle might be interested in the job. Alan was a friend of his but I didn't know who Owen Coyle was. He wasn't on my first or second list and when I found out he was at St Johnstone I decided it wasn't really worth following up. I thought that it would be difficult to justify the decision if things went wrong after we appointed a candidate from outside the mainstream. So I decided to give it no more thought. Barry and I agreed that we needed someone with a good standing in the game, someone who had either played for Burnley or who had a safe reputation.

That evening as I sat in my kitchen I was running through all the names again—Steve Davis, Peter Reid, Paul Jewell—and then I looked at some of the others—Simon Grayson, John Gregory and Steve Staunton. I began to wonder if we had enough good candidates on the list or whether we'd need to go back to the drawing board. I was starting to feel the pressure of the decision and it was making me unusually nervous. It wasn't quite like making a decision for Modus. When I did that I did it for the good of the business, it might make us money and it might lose us money. But whatever the decision was, it wasn't publicly aired, ready to be slated by forty thousand people who have every right to do so because it affects their lives in some way or another.

The more I looked at the list, the more I felt obliged to research each candidate thoroughly. So I thought I had better ring Owen Coyle, the St Johnstone manager. His name was vaguely familiar to me but I couldn't remember who he'd played for. He'd been at Bolton probably around the time I was watching QPR and Arsenal in London, so obviously my football knowledge of the time had been dulled somewhat.

I rang Owen at about 10.30 in the evening. I just felt that I needed to leave no stone unturned and through the week I had spoken to everyone with half a chance just to be clear in my mind. I got Owen's answer-phone so left him a message and he rang back at about eleven. We were on the phone for about an hour as I went through the interview form that I'd prepared to ensure the questions I was asking each candidate were consistent. He had a fairly broad Glasgow accent and I found myself saying pardon a few times. I began by asking how he went about getting the best out of his players and I was quite impressed by how his reply developed:

'I think I've got good people skills. I'm very happy to make decisions at the football club and communicate them to the players. I always tell them if they're going to be left out of the team.'

He told me he was at peak fitness and that he occasionally turned out for the team.

'I want the players to be the same as me. I want them to be the best that they can possibly be.'

That really struck a chord for me. Owen went on:

'I want to get every ounce of effort from my players and I want them to be up front and honest. I make sure that they have respect for me and I have a huge amount of belief in them. They have a real "day at work" attitude and a strong sense of community.'

He told me that he felt it was vital to be there on the training ground every day but that, during the week, Sandy Stewart his number two, often spoke to the players to avoid them hearing the same voice all the time. So far so good. So I asked Owen what he knew about the English game and he told me that he came down every week to watch a reserve game. He continued:

'If I worked in England I'd have to be very selective in sourcing players from Scotland. But there's a player at Dundee United and one at Hearts that I'd want to bring down. They're good enough to play at Championship level. And I know that Ireland is a real hotbed of young talent.'

It appealed to me that it looked like Owen would be able to source players from lower cost areas such as Scotland and Ireland, and within twenty minutes of speaking to him I was glad that I had. I was starting to think that this was a man who was not a million miles away from what we were looking for. He hadn't said anything that worried me so far, so I asked him what his views were on the Youth Academy and he answered:

'It's so important Brendan. Eight out of my first-team at St Johnstone are 22 or under, you've got to have young legs in your side. I'd want to get younger players into your football club, getting younger players in always revitalises the rest of the squad.'

Owen had worked with strong role models like Bruce Rioch and Alex McLeish and had also spent some time with Jack Charlton in Ireland. He had great admiration for Jack and spoke passionately about the simplicity of the big man's philosophy:

'I learned a lot from Jack. Players need to have a sense of spirit and a sense of community and from a leadership point of view that's absolutely vital at the football club. And home games are so important. We have an obligation to entertain our fans.'

And that hit me right between the eyes. That obligation has been loud and clear at Burnley for most years of our history but I hadn't felt entertained for a few years. Owen was getting on a roll now:

'I love to attack when we're at home. We've only lost two home games in the last two and a half years at Saints.'

Owen had certainly struck a chord. We'd lost two home games at Turf Moor in the last two and a half weeks and I'm certain I'd have been more entertained at Burnley bus station. So I asked: 'How keen are you to come and work here in England Owen?'

'Brendan I'd do absolutely anything to work in England at that level. I'd come and do it for nothing.'

As we said goodbye I felt Owen had definitely got his name on the list. He'd made a big impression on me. But I was still concerned about the nature of the gamble. He still wasn't quite proven enough and he didn't have a connection with Burnley, so all of that remained an issue. Everything he had said to me made me think he would do everything in his power to be successful if he was given the chance. And when I looked at his record on Wikipedia; it strengthened his case as well. Anything over 40% is a good win ratio for a manager. Both Paul Jewell and Peter Reid were in the early 40's. And although he'd only been a manager for three years, Owen was up at 50%. In my own mind we now had a shortlist of four.

* * * * *

The following morning I spoke with Barry and I told him that I'd had a conversation with Owen and I thought it had gone really well. But Barry wasn't easily convinced, mainly because Owen was from St Johnstone. He asked me what I thought of him:

'Well he sounded a bit like Bill Shankly. Do you remember how Bill Shankly was? He's a strong family guy, three kids and a good catholic and he's teetotal.'

That'd make a change for Burnley. And I could certainly relate to Owen's family background. As it turned out Owen came from the same part of Glasgow as the great Shankly. I only hoped he might be touched with the same kind of genius. I told Barry how his philosophy and work ethic had really made an impression on me, but he still wasn't sure:

'But he's from St Johnstone Brendan. He's an unknown entity.'

That looked like it was going to be a sticking point for everyone. Not that St Johnstone is a poor club, quite the contrary and Owen had obviously had some success building up there. The year before they'd hit the Scottish national Press by beating Rangers at Ibrox in the quarter-final of the League Cup. And their recent record was excellent. But with the best will in the world, the Scottish League One isn't the Championship, and St Johnstone isn't Wolverhampton Wanderers.

But later that morning a slightly odd thing happened. I received a text from Phil Gartside, the chairman at Bolton Wanderers. It read:

'Hi Brendan don't know if you're fixed up but have you had a look at Owen Coyle?'

I wondered what was going on so I rang Phil and asked:

'What do you know about Owen Coyle?'

Phil knew Owen only from his playing days and it turned out that Bolton actually considered him to replace Sammy Lee before they appointed Gary Megson earlier in the season. Now Phil's quite a measured thinker so it gave me more encouragement that he thought so highly of Owen. So, as soon as I'd spoken to Phil I rang Barry and asked him if he would be happy to meet Owen. And as luck would have it Barry was on his way to Gleneagles for a romantic weekend with his partner Sonya, so he agreed to meet him for breakfast on the Saturday morning.

I wanted further evidence of his desire to get the job, so Owen had offered a reference from Alex McLeish, the Scotland manager, who was preparing the national team for a massive game against Italy on that Friday. I really didn't expect Alex to ring but, sure enough, within half an hour Alex was on the phone and he said:

'Brendan, Owen's a great fella; full of passion for the game and I have no doubt he will be a great success in the Championship. And I'm sure he'll be a Premiership manager one day.'

I thanked Alex and I felt stronger again to push Owen on to the shortlist. That Saturday, while Barry was meeting Owen, I was having breakfast with Paul Jewell. Paul had flagged up his interest in the job after someone in his family had heard me talking about it on the radio. I'd agreed with Barry that following our respective meetings we'd compare notes at lunchtime. I was interested to know why Paul hadn't gone back to Wigan when Chris Hutchins had left a few weeks earlier.

'The players up there are on thirty, forty thousand a week and they're not interested. If I went in I would have to come down hard on the players. And—I got into a bit of social when I was there last time.'

Initially I wasn't sure what Paul meant by that but the tabloids later printed allegations of an affair. We got to discussing money at which point Paul was at pains to say that he wanted complete control of team affairs and he would need three to four million to spend in the first transfer window. So that was a 'no' then. I agreed that we'd ring Paul again on the Monday. Paul had a few other opportunities and we agreed that Burnley wasn't at the top of his list. Before I rang Barry I decided to take the dog for a walk and while I was out Owen was on the phone and he sounded chirpy.

'Hi Brendan I think I've had a good meeting with Barry and I liked what he said about the football club.'

Owen had enjoyed the breakfast and he was now even keener to move things on. He asked what the next step was. I said:

'Barry and I need to discuss it further and we'll get back to you in the next twenty four hours and we'll take it from there.'

When I rang off I noticed that the last two digits on Owen's phone number are 18. This may sound a little strange but I am mildly superstitious and, believe it or not, my lucky number is 18. Not that this totally affected my judgement but it did help again. I do believe in fate. Now I realise that this revelation may send a lot of sensible, down to earth Clarets fans looking at all the donkeys in the Football League who happen to be wearing the number 18. But please rest assured; I do try to keep my superstitious nature in check when I'm making decisions.

And in any case when I spoke to Barry at lunchtime he had been very impressed by Owen too. He felt that he was a genuine guy with a lot of integrity, but Barry was still clearly nervous of the St Johnstone status and his relatively short track record. But we were both becoming convinced that Owen was now a strong candidate in a field of four, and in all honesty I didn't think Paul Jewell was the man for us. We decided we'd ask him to do a short interview on Monday and we'd also speak to Peter Reid and Steve Davis so that we could make a decision that day, as time was moving on. Steve hadn't done himself any harm at all because he'd looked after the team the week before at Leicester where we won 1–0. This Saturday we didn't have a game because it was an international weekend, but we needed our manager in place in time for the visit of Stoke, who were on a good run and were towards the top of the League, on the next Saturday.

Peter Reid was first on our interview list and he arrived at my offices in Manchester at nine on the Monday morning. As I approached him I noticed that he hadn't shaved and it did look like he'd had a bit of a late night. We sat down with a coffee and then Peter put this piece of paper that he'd been holding on the table. Then he nervously started his pitch in his hackneyed gruff Liverpool accent:

'I think I'll . . . er . . . you know . . . if I get this job . . . I've been learning a bit about this sports science stuff with big Sam at Bolton. It's good like... it's the way forward . . . I've got some notes on it . . . and I went on a course with that Sir Clive Woodward and I've learnt some things on that as well and I could do some of that . . . '

I looked at Barry and I was thinking, 'Has he just put this together this morning?' Barry was looking somewhat bemused too. So we asked him a few more questions. There's no doubt Peter's a likeable guy. He's got a great sense of humour but Barry and I were concerned that he'd had a couple of years out of the game and he might not be hungry enough for us. But his record speaks for itself and we thought that maybe he would come back to the game refreshed. And one thing that was in his favour was that he would bring Adrian Heath as his right arm man. Adrian had been popular here in his time as a player and manager and the Burnley factor is always a consideration. Then Peter started to chat about who he'd source his players from:

'I'm pals with Sir Alex, and I could get that kid Jonny Evans, and there's this great centre forward at Vauxhall Motors.'

I didn't try too hard to hide my surprise: 'Vauxhall Motors?'

'Yeah, yeah, yeah . . . he's been playing there because he's been a bit of a bad lad like. He's been in prison for three years . . .'

After he'd gone we moved on to Paul Jewell who we'd agreed to ring on the telephone. In reality, both Barry and I didn't see Paul as a legitimate option, mainly because of the budget he needed. And on personal terms he'd recently been offered twice what we would pay him. In all honesty we were hoping for him to let us down. When we rang he'd obviously had a phone call from Adam Pearson, the new chairman at Derby County. They were just about to let Billy Davies go and were considering bringing Paul in. He had also spoken to Birmingham City and the Republic of Ireland, so he was obviously in the market. We guessed that he was likely to go to Derby and left it at that. So in our search for a manager we were now down to just two—Steve Davis and Owen Coyle.

Barry met with Steve Davis in the afternoon. We both knew Steve well so I left it to Barry to go through the details of the job with him, before we went to interview Owen again in the evening. We had agreed to meet with Owen at Barry's house in Ribchester at eight. He'd been playing in a legends tournament at the weekend (Owen not Barry) and then driven up to St Johnstone for training with St Johnstone before driving back down to meet us. I noted that he wasn't scared of putting a shift in.

I met Owen at the Tickled Trout pub in Preston and then drove him to Barry's home. When we arrived, Barry was as convivial as ever and we just sat in his lounge drinking coffee and chatting about the club. We talked about our expectations for Burnley and whether it would be the right move for Owen. I have to say he looked very serious, certainly compared to how he came across before, and how assured he is in front of the television cameras now. But he was just as clear in what he was saying. Owen is immediately likeable, but what came over in that hour was his immense desire to get the job. We all went through our thoughts again and within an hour he was back on the road up to Scotland. As he left we told him that we'd ring later on when we'd made a decision.

Barry got us a drink and we sat down to chew things over. We both liked Owen, but Barry had his chairman's hat firmly on and initially wanted to play the safer card and go for Steve Davis. That would be a popular appointment with the fans and local Press. I can't think of any player we've had over the last twenty years who has earned the same level of unqualified respect from our supporters. There's no doubting Steve's leadership qualities and my view was that he would indeed be a Burnley manager one day. But I thought that he needed to serve his time working closely with a really good manager and gain his confidence that way. I thought that it might be too much too soon for Steve, so I was trying to push Barry towards Owen. I argued that we needed some 'non Burnley' thinking, and from a football and financial point of view, the opportunity to source players from Scotland and Northern Ireland seemed attractive to us both. We both liked Owen and we felt that we could work with him. So, half an hour later, we decided that was it.

When we rang Owen to tell him that he'd got the job he was still in his car heading towards Carlisle. We were on a speaker phone so that we could both give the message and I started:

'Owen we're just giving you a ring because we've come to a decision . . . we'd like you to take the job.' Thankfully we hadn't misjudged his desire and he didn't say he'd come back to us.

'Fantastic, I won't let you down.'

And something made me feel he wouldn't. I'd seen and heard enough in the few hours that I'd spoken to Owen to make me think we might just have struck gold. The things that differentiated him from the others were his insatiable hunger and his personal standards. Owen already had that steely determination that you don't often come across. I always believe that the guys who have come close to achieving a lot as players, but who haven't won many trophies, turn out to be the hungriest of managers.

Owen plainly showed a desire for success that all winners have. Sir Alex Ferguson has an unbelievable hunger and he constantly needs to satisfy an inner drive. But for players who have had a glittering career and won lots of medals, it's difficult to keep that impetus when they move into management. The best managers in England over the past two decades have had an irrepressible desire to achieve heights that they didn't as players, and that has driven them to the top of the game—Ferguson, Mourhino and Wenger. And now we had Owen Coyle.

The following day we had a Press conference booked for two o' clock. Barry spoke to Steve Davis in the morning and I rang Peter Reid. It was quite early when I rang him, about eight I think, but I wanted to get him early. After our interview the day before Peter must have left somehow feeling confident that he'd impressed us. So much so that he'd put it about the market that he was on his way to Burnley and the Press had taken the rumour. It was all over the *Lancashire Telegraph*, 'REID IS FAVOURITE'. When Peter picked up the phone it sounded like I'd woken him up:

'Peter it's Brendan Flood at Burnley.'

'Oh hiya son.'

'Obviously we'd like to thank you for coming to the interview and we've got a lot of respect for you. We're sure you'll have a successful spell back in football wherever you go, but we've decided to go for another candidate . . . so apologies if we've had to disappoint you Peter.'

'It's not that Owen Coyle is it?' he asked.

'Well I can't really say. Anyway I'll see you around Peter.'

'Okay cheers son,' he cheerily proffered and then hung up. I immediately thought to myself, 'imagine being in charge of him and being called son all the time. That would have been a strange one'.

I must admit that after we had made our decision I was quietly panicking. And when we rolled up for the Press conference there was a sense of, 'Well we're all glad that you've made a decision but who is Owen Coyle?' And I have to say my heart didn't exactly leap when I heard someone asking if St Johnstone was a full-time professional club. But the more I focussed on the decision, the more I became convinced that Owen was head and shoulders above the rest. As the Press conference got going my conviction grew and became stronger even more than it had been the day before. So much so, that I went as far as to call him a 'young Bill Shankly'. That was one of those moments when you hope you haven't said something that will come back and bite you in the backside. And I remembered what Dave Whelan had told me. This decision could send the club the right way or the wrong way. But we already felt that we could trust Owen, and if things didn't always go right it wouldn't be for the want of trying. We just needed to give him the right resources in terms of finance and support. (Courtesy of Brendan Flood; *Big Club, Small Town and Me*, TH Media 2009)

5

UNCERTAIN BEGINNINGS

Owen Columba Coyle was born on 14th July 1966. Paisley born he had a happy and satisfying childhood. The family were based in an area of Glasgow known as Little Donegal and they were closely involved in the Irish community:

> My parents brought us up to be well-mannered and to respect people, but equally they brought us up to be hard-working. We grew up in what was supposed to be a rough area—the Gorbals in Glasgow. I just remember being really happy. I think we just bounced off each other.

With five brothers and three sisters, space was tight in a three bedroomed maisonette.

> Mum and dad had one room, my three sisters had the other, and six boys shared two double beds in the third. I suppose it's not surprising that we were very close-knit. You knew that if anything happened they were on your shoulder. He once explained why he was so thin. 'Three boys in each bed, that's why I'm so thin. I was the last one to fight my way out and get to the dinner table.
>
> Great memories: I remember on a Sunday, from midday to about five, you could guarantee there'd be about 20 five-a-sides on the school field involving kids as young as 10 to grown men. It's a thing you don't see now but in that era everyone just loved football. It didn't matter how old you were. Everyone got a game.

He began his playing career as a slender, nimble striker in 1985 at Dumbarton, almost underweight at not much more than nine stones, and was the proverbial wanderer throughout his career, never staying anywhere for more than three years. He had signed for Dumbarton as a schoolboy whilst still only 13. His fitness might have seen its foundations laid when a paper round as a boy took him up and down tenement blocks with 23 flights of stairs. He started as a part timer working in an office the rest of the week, played most games for Airdrieonians, spent most of his time in Scotland, moved clubs thirteen times, sometimes returning to a previous club, and of a total of 669 appearances played just 54 games in England for Bolton Wanderers. His playing career lasted until 2007 at St Johnstone where he was also manager. His parents were from Donegal and he played once for the Republic of Ireland, despite being born in Scotland.

Unusually for the world of football, he was and remains teetotal; his preferred drink irn-bru. When he was a young player he was invited by Celtic to an Under-20 tournament in Switzerland. The football drinking culture was well established amongst some of his team-mates even at that early age. When the squad were allowed out one night, Derek Whyte bought a round of drinks only to be refused by Coyle. It caused some consternation and banter, even shock, but the young lad stuck to his guns. 'Many a young player would have been easily influenced, but even at that age, I was quite single-minded, quite secure in my opinions.'

His philosophy as a manager was formed whilst he was a player. 'I used to hate it as a striker when teams were negative, doubling up the full backs, contributing nothing to the game.' As a manager many years later he was firm in his principles. 'We won't do that. If we've an opportunity to go forward, we'll take it—try to make real game of it.' For him football was about a style that 'was pleasing to the eye'. In this there was an echo of the long gone Danny Blanchflower philosophy; that football was meant to entertain, not bore people to death. Home or away, attacking tactics remained the same, the aim, to win the game.

As a player he says he was prepared to run until he dropped. 'My work-rate was second to none. People knew I would have run till I dropped, that I couldn't have given any more. To be fair anything you got back then, you had to earn.' It was a view he transmitted to players. His enthusiasm and passion rubbed off on them. He thought about what they could do, not what they couldn't do.

> As a player I was delighted to do what I did. My source of frustration is that if there was a truly naturally talented player and they were not utilising that . . . that was a bugbear to me. Because being what you might call an ordinary player, you look at these guys and you think, go and show everyone how good you are. But talent is not enough. You need hard work, you need to be a team player.

At Dumbarton he played alongside his brothers Joe and Tommy. In 1988 he joined Clydebank, and then in March 1990 a £175,000 move took him to Airdrieonians. It was an inspired debut there when he scored a hat-trick. That season he was the Scottish League's top scorer. Over the next two seasons his goals helped Airdrie to promotion, a Scottish Cup Final appearance and an appearance in the 1992–93 European Cup Winners Cup.

In the summer of 1993, Bolton Wanderers paid £250,000 to sign Coyle and his two year spell in England included promotion and a brief chance to play in the FA Premier League. It was at Bolton that he experienced a side of management that he would refer to years later at Burnley before the unforgettable Carling Cup game against Tottenham. He was axed from the Bolton squad for the 1995 Coca Cola Cup Final defeat against Liverpool. Bruce Rioch, the manager who selected Coyle in every round ahead of the Final, did not name the Glaswegian on the bench at

Wembley. Rioch's decision was the moment that defined his own approach to management.

Coyle said:

> It was fantastic to get to the Final with Bolton. But despite playing in every round up to the Final, Bruce Rioch in his wisdom left me out. It was bizarre. A week before we were losing 1–0 at Portsmouth but I had done well, yet Bruce came in at the break and wiped the floor with me in the dressing room. Gudni Bergsson was sat next to me and told me he couldn't understand it. But I knew Bruce was hammering me so that he could justify dropping me for John McGinlay and Mixu Paatelainen at Wembley. Sure enough when he named the team on the Monday I wasn't in it. Then Bruce left it to his assistant Colin Todd to tell me on the Friday that I wasn't even on the bench. A couple of weeks after the Final, Bruce came up to me and said, 'You played in every round up to Wembley, so here's your medal'. He just left the medal and walked off. But he never came up with the £3,000 appearance money that I would have got had I been involved in the Final. The whole episode impacted on me enormously.

In October 1995, a £400,000 transfer took him to Dundee United. He was once again part of a promotion winning side, scoring the winning goal in extra-time in the second leg of the play-off against Partick Thistle.

His next moves were to Motherwell in January 1997 after a move to Hibernian fell through. Then in March 1999 he moved to Dunfermline Athletic. He lost his place there and went on loan to Ross County prior to rejoining Airdrie in 2001. When they went into liquidation in 2002 he joined Falkirk being promoted to player-manager in a joint managership with John Hughes in 2003. Wanting to play for as long as possible (including later in the reserve team at Burnley) he registered as a player although he was appointed as coach at Dundee United.

Airdrie were resurrected as Airdrie United and a loan there was made permanent. The manager was Sandy Stewart. Eventually the roles would be reversed with Stewart becoming Coyle's assistant at St Johnstone and Burnley. Still playing competitively, the deft goal he scored for Burnley reserves against Accrington Stanley was shown repeatedly on Sky Sports News.

In April 2005 he was named as the new manager of St Johnstone. 'I'm a great believer that everyone has to come to work with a smile on their face and that's what I'll be trying to achieve here.' A year later he achieved his first manager of the month award. He led St Johnstone to a 2–0 victory over Rangers at Ibrox to reach the semi-finals of the Scottish League Cup. Coyle's team was by far the most impressive and Rangers were jeered from the pitch. Coyle was thrilled and the style of his team embodied his philosophy of giving everything, and going for the win. 'This is one of the stadiums where we aspire to be and I told the players to go out with self belief and give it their best shot. I don't think anyone could argue with the result.'

The semi-final was lost to Hibernian after extra-time. However, Saints also reached the semi-finals of the Scottish Cup thanks to away wins against SPL clubs Falkirk and Motherwell, but lost 2–1 to Celtic in the semi-final after taking the game to Celtic and attacking at every opportunity. In the same season, St Johnstone also competed for the First Division Championship and promotion to the SPL. On 30th March Coyle was awarded his second manager of the month award of the 2006–07 season. He took the title fight with Gretna to the last day of the season, and only a last minute goal gave Gretna victory and promotion at the expense of St Johnstone. It was a result that was inwardly devastating but another part of his philosophy says that you come back stronger if you learn from setbacks.

He signed a one year extension to his contract in July 2007 and then in the early part of the 2007–08 season he led Saints to the Final of the Scottish Challenge Cup. But in the week before the Final, he left for Burnley leaving assistant Sandy Stewart in charge. On the 21st November Burnley were granted permission to discuss their managerial vacancy with Coyle and after a compensation fee was agreed he was appointed as Burnley manager the next day. The improbable dream and a whirlwind 18 months was about to begin.

The Perth club had been resigned to losing their manager and a compensation fee of a reported £150,000 was agreed. An ambitious Owen Coyle mantra had always been to seize the moment and 'cash in when your stock is high'. St Johnstone initially rejected the first compensation offer but a new offer made sure that negotiations could commence. 'Burnley have increased their offer of compensation which is acceptable to us and as such we have given them permission to talk to Owen,' said the Chairman. St Johnstone had feared for some time that he would be poached by another club and Inverness Caledonian Thistle had already been refused permission to speak to him.

The St Johnstone supporters were a forgiving group and there was no backlash or reaction to his departure immediately before a Cup Final. Their comments sometime later, when asked, were supportive and respectful. They were generally grateful for the improvements he had brought. An occasional one was critical of events on the field and the timing of the move. Others were fulsome in their praise. Just a couple of fans commented that had he moved to a Scottish club they might not have been so generous:

> I enjoyed having him as manager, performances improved on the park . . .
> When he left it was inevitable but I was disappointed . . . We improved a
> vast amount as a team and got great Cup runs out of him . . . Coyle was one
> for the fans—always seemed to have time to talk . . . The move came at the
> right time for both Owen Coyle and St Johnstone . . . He took St Johnstone
> from relegation candidates to title contenders . . . Will always be grateful to
> him for what he did . . . His man-management was superb . . . Owen Coyle laid

the foundations which allowed Derek McInnes to take us to the next level . . . I was disappointed but also thought it was good for all parties. Owen Coyle was a talented manager . . . I think he will always be an underdog manager as his motivational skills are second to none . . .

When we won that Cup our fans with few exceptions were chanting Owen's name and Derek McInnes tried to get Owen out onto the pitch to accept his recognition. He didn't come onto the pitch because his morals and manners are near impeccable . . .

Very strong minded and confident in his own ability . . . Utterly infectious and his team talks in the coaching sessions I watched were truly inspiring yet so simple . . . The best manager I have seen at Saints . . . There was a sense of inevitability about Coyle's departure . . . He'd probably done all he could and the move was at a good time for all concerned, we needed a kick start and new ideas and he needed a change . . . He was brilliant at the siege mentality stuff . . . He left at exactly the right time for all concerned, things had gone stale, we'd have preferred if he'd stayed for the Final but 99% of people now would tell you it was the right time for him to move on . . . Most of us realised it was a step up and if he turned down the opportunity it may not come again . . . I don't remember any adverse reaction about the timing . . . Good manager and turned the club around . . . Owen did a good job at Saints, he always came across as a good clever guy and an exceptional motivator . . . I think it was the right time for him to leave, had he rejected Burnley he wouldn't have got the chance again . . . We're not bitter because we could see he left to progress his career . . . Owen Coyle was but a fleeting moment in Saints' history and no-one had the rationale to react with any great venom as he hadn't achieved much of note . . .

Coyle had pretty much run out of ideas and left Perth at a good time, things had gone a little stale . . . We were heading for mid-table obscurity the year he left . . . I thought it was terrible timing given it was the week leading up to the Cup Final, obviously he was going to look after himself but while others here have been on the receiving end of treatment, Coyle escaped for some reason, the root of my annoyance lies with Burnley though . . . He's a shrewd guy with impeccable timing to ensure he does the best for himself . . .

Paul Sheerin, the St Johnstone midfielder, admitted that the players were resigned to losing him but added,

If a Championship club like Burnley want him, the manager would be crazy not to think seriously about a move. I know we have a Cup Final coming up against Dunfermline but no one here would accuse him of jumping ship. It would be a huge opportunity for him. If he goes we will wish him all the best and thank him for what he has done for us and the club. Any player would jump at the chance of playing in England. He was linked with various jobs in Scotland last season, so it doesn't surprise me that he's in demand again.

Sheerin's comments were generous. No Burnley player publicly said anything remotely similar when he left Burnley, other than acknowledging that this kind of thing happens in football and that life goes on.

'It kind of came out of the blue,' Coyle said to Alastair Campbell at the end of a pre-season training session months later in the summer of 2009. But Brendan Flood related in his book that the club were made aware of Coyle whilst he was still manager of St Johnstone, via an unexpected email from journalist Alan Nixon. The latter sent a CV and strong recommendation to Burnley. Brendan Flood eventually got back to Alan Nixon but the reply went to Nixon's spam folder. But for Nixon checking his spam folder Flood's reply would have been unopened, and in all probability, the Owen Coyle story at Burnley would never have happened.

> But it felt right. I was immediately seized of the opportunity and confident that we could do things here. Obviously I knew about Burnley's history, how they were once one of the top clubs in the country, fallen a bit on hard times, I suppose, but established in the Championship and with ambitions to get to the Premier League. It was never going to be easy, but it did feel right.
>
> 'I will leave no stone unturned,' he said at the conference where he was unveiled as the new Burnley boss having accepted a three and a half year deal. 'The fact that I'm glad to be here is an understatement to say the least. I've just got to make sure I go on and deliver what everybody is looking for. I'm very much an open book, what you see is what you get, there are no hidden agendas and I'm a very up front person. This football club is a big, big club. I've experienced that in my time at Bolton as a player and I'll look to go and achieve the goals that everyone is after. We've all got one aim—we want success for Burnley Football Club. The fans are going to be important and it is important they see the players, as a group, are giving all they've got. We want to encourage more fans to come down because we realise they are an integral part of the club. We can only do that if we are playing good football and winning games. We want to win every game but I also think we have an obligation to entertain. 'I'm not going to sit here and make any claims about 'we'll do this and we'll do that'. But what I will assure everybody is that we will leave no stone unturned and try to deliver success for Burnley Football Club.'

If some people thought the appointment was a gamble, Coyle was determined to show that it was the right decision. (Former star player Andy Payton in his newspaper column was highly sceptical.)

> I am aware that some people might say 'he's only been in the job three years' or certain things similar. But the bottom line is you are judged on what you do, not what you have done in the past. Jose Mourhino could have come to Burnley, but he wouldn't have been judged on what he has done in the past, he would have been judged on what he did at Burnley. That's the way it should be, and that's the way I'll approach it.
>
> With the utmost respect to St Johnstone this opportunity was fantastic for me. When they appointed me it was they who came after me—I hadn't applied for the job either so it was they who came and head-hunted me. I'm glad I delivered for them. I took a side that had finished eighth and narrowly avoided relegation, and turned it round to finish second two seasons running. We got to two national semi-finals and also cruelly lost out

on promotion last season, having had to sit and wait for the last six minutes of Gretna's game to finish—a time in which they scored to go up instead of us. So I know the highs and lows of football, and mental strength won't be a problem because I've had a few kicks in the teeth during my career. I've left St Johnstone a very good place to be, and turned over a profit of half a million last year, after the club had been losing money year after year. I think that shows you again that, with the utmost respect to St Johnstone, how big an attraction this job was. They are in a Cup Final on Sunday, and while I hope they win that, this was just too big an opportunity to turn down.

Brendan Flood remembers in the initial talks that Coyle was so keen to come that he joked he would have worked for nothing. So, when contract talks were started, he was reminded of that. A salary was then offered and agreed.

The Press conference and unveiling was the first opportunity for Burnley folk to see Owen Coyle's skill in front of the media, his articulacy, clarity, confidence and enthusiasm. He was media friendly, a clean cut professional; sure of his words and extremely eloquent even if the words did, and still do, come out at 100mph. His delivery was crisp and clear, his communication skills were excellent. After the austerity of Steve Cotterill's final months, Coyle's talk of entertainment, football that was pleasing to the eye, style, and wingers getting the ball across, made people sit up and listen and endeared him immediately. Here was a manager who even used the word 'panache'.

Within 18 months every supporter, director, resident of Burnley had bought into his message and embraced his philosophy. They would have crossed mountains for him. They believed everything about him. Was this man not a godsend, passionate, caring, genuine, honest, tell it like it is, a man who identified with them and the town? He was the Pied Piper, not with a flute but with football boots, and belief in him was total even before he had delivered them a place in the Premiership.

A later interview with Owen Coyle described him as: 'The eternal optimist, a bubbly fast-talking enthusiast with a positive spin for everything.' He described himself as a people-person, a sociable soul who could not bear to be in a room alone. He had never been one to tolerate miserable players who took their career for granted and he wasn't about to do that at Burnley.

Brendan Flood was confident about the appointment:

From the moment he set foot inside Turf Moor Owen Coyle looked the part. He had steely determination, clear direction and an unbelievable level of personal fitness. The players very quickly understood what he expected from them, and he engaged a striking willingness from them to follow his remarkable work ethic. He could not understand the mentality of players who were happy to pick up their wages even if they didn't make the team, probably because he'd spent his own playing career sweating blood for the cause and wishing to play football. On the whole he inherited a good bunch of players and some great leaders, like Steve Caldwell and Graham Alexander who bought into Owen's way of thinking from the outset. He had an infectious enthusiasm and a smart sense of humour, but also the crucial ability to keep himself and his players grounded. And, Owen's teams played without fear. By all accounts he had created a fantastic spirit up at St Johnstone and his win ratio of 50% was up there with the best managers of all time. (Courtesy of Brendan Flood)

Coyle said at the time:

> I bring a passion to the job and I hope it rubs off on my players. I want them to care about the team and the club. As a manager you are trying to give everyone a lift, not just the team. This isn't a wealthy town but people here are Burnley through and through. There are some who cannot afford to come to matches, some who are ill or out of a job, but it's still their team. They still care. We should be achieving things, giving them something to talk about. It's what I call a proper football club. It just feels right. There is a real sense of history and tradition about the place.

His former player at St Johnstone, Derek McInnes was effusive in his praise making use of two words (like Brendan Flood) that would be used over and again in any analysis of Owen Coyle—infectious and enthusiasm.

> Nothing will faze him at Burnley. Any manager going to a new club wants to get off to a good start and to start well with the supporters. I'm sure in his first week or so there, he will know what areas need looking at and strengthening. He's no mug. He knows the game. This is a fantastic opportunity for him. I know what Burnley is like—I played at Turf Moor four or five times during my career at West Brom. They can get big crowds and a big atmosphere. They love their football at Burnley. I think it's a fantastic opportunity for him as manager, but for Burnley, they have got a very good deal. I played with Owen at Dundee United and he's a very infectious type. He's a bubbly, enthusiastic guy. He still thinks along the same lines as the players. He keeps a happy dressing room and that's a very important part of a successful football club. He's very ambitious.

The word 'ambitious' however was telling. No-one would have predicted that not much more than just two years later, he would leave Burnley for the 'bigger' club of Bolton Wanderers. But, if supporters grumbled when he left, none of them however, could have grumbled at the events and drama that were in store for them, and that they would especially enjoy during season 2008–09.

* * * * *

The start that Owen Coyle made at Turf Moor was dramatic. If the first game against Stoke City on 24th November 2007, brought no goals for either side, it might have been thought that a 0–0 draw was no improvement on anything that had been seen before. But it was far different. The football was different, the players' attitudes were different, Joey Gudjonsson out of favour with Cotterill returned, the game should have been won. Burnley deserved to win and but for a glaring miss by Lafferty would have done so. This was a different football style, this was an attacking display and it was as if the players had been liberated and freed from the shackles and growing negativity of previous months.

This was an excellent game. Stoke were abysmal. Burnley were fluent with wide men who stayed wide. This was a basic change from cloying, dull tactics. We peppered them with shots throughout the game but over the top they went, or were saved by the keeper. One save was miraculous. This was a game at last that we enjoyed. (Personal Diary November 24th)

It was the next two games that made people sit up and take notice. Both were away games against the top two teams. And both were won. Brendan Flood felt good. Watford were outplayed by the new 'pass and move' style of which manager Coyle had spoken in his interviews.

There was a good buzz about the place again when we turned up for Owen's first game in charge, at home to Stoke. They were riding high near the top of the League and were serious contenders for promotion. The fans really got behind the team and the players deserved it. We drew 0–0 but played a lot of free-flowing football, something that we hadn't seen for months, if not years. It looked like the players were relaxed. It was very encouraging but although we deserved to win the match, we hadn't, and after the game I resolved to follow the next few matches closely to see whether I needed to plan a trip abroad!

As the weeks went when I watched Owen in action, I noticed a big difference. Steve Cotterill worked very hard on knowing the opposition, but then frequently became very concerned about them, how they played and how good they were compared to us. And often, that fear of the opposition seemed to dictate the way we played. Owen's philosophy was to let the opposition fear us. Let's just go and play and do the best that we can. That helped our players relax and to concentrate fully on what they were doing.

Which was a good thing really; because the next two away games were away to Watford, who were top, on Tuesday night, and then away to second-placed Charlton on the Saturday. At Watford the players carried on where they left off playing some good attacking football. We didn't look like we'd settle for a draw when we were holding them at 1–1, and then a good start for Owen turned into a dream start when Joey Gudjonsson hit a cracking winner.

Owen had quickly gained a foothold and effortlessly struck up a rapport with the fans who could see that our style of play was changing and that the manager talked a lot of sense. His early interviews on Radio Lancashire were upbeat but not unrealistic. He knew where we needed to improve, but from the very start he was at pains to tell of his absolute faith in the ability of our players. We knew that in time we would have to get some better players in but each member of the current squad had the manager's belief and support.

That week was as exciting as anything I'd experienced as a Burnley fan because it meant so much to me. It was as good as the two previous ones had been awful, and I felt a welcome fusion of relief and delight. And it had a perfect ending when we went to Charlton and won 3–1, bloody brilliant—what a start. (Courtesy of Brendan Flood)

Having assessed the squad it became clear to the new manager what a key player Wade Elliott was. The problem for Owen Coyle was that Elliott had not signed any new contract extension. In fact he hadn't even been offered any kind of extension in the summer by the previous manager. If nothing was done, if Elliott signed no new contract he could in fact have walked away in the following summer of 2008. In talks between Flood and Elliott's agent it emerged that the sensitive Elliott was in fact rather disgruntled that he had been offered nothing new. To have lost Elliott, possibly the team's most creative player, and on his day a devastating wingman, would in fact have been disastrous. It would be Elliott who scored the magical £60million winner in the 2009 Wembley play-off final. Getting him to sign an extension was therefore critical but Coyle was getting nowhere. According to Flood, with Coyle's agreement it was he who stepped in and sorted things, saying the things that Elliott wanted to hear, and backdating any new contract to the start of the season.

The next player problem involved striker Andy Gray a real fans' favourite. Gray was another key player on his way to a possible 20 goals for the season. In an apparent football 'tapping-up' he was approached by Charlton Athletic. He had scored twice in the 3–1 win at Charlton. Clearly they had been impressed. As a result Gray confronted Coyle with a transfer request. Having done this before the offer from Charlton was received the club put two and two together and knew that he had been approached. Gray clearly wanted to leave. It put Coyle in a quandary. Sell him, and the wrath of supporters, fed up seeing the best players sold, would descend. The offer from Charlton duly arrived, £1million, not enough and eventually it was upped to £1.5million with add-ons. Behind the scenes Gray's father was telephoning the club and imploring them to release him. This was going to be his last significant move and the wage increase was considerable. With the player's head turned Coyle had no choice but to sell and when Gray turned up for training one day and announced he was in no fit mental state to play in the next game, Coyle was hard and decisive, sending him immediately from the training ground.

> I have to say that I never wanted to lose Andy at any point and that is why we turned down the first bid. However at that point Andy came to me and said he wanted to go to Charlton. I think he had been made aware that he could double his salary, but at that time there wasn't a deal that suited this football club. Subsequent to that, Charlton made an improved offer and after receiving that I received a second visit from Andy . . . this morning Andy was again waiting to see me when I arrived at the club and when he asked I told him there had been an improved offer that the club were looking at. At that point he asked me if I was considering playing him at Coventry, which I was, Andy told me he was not in the right frame of mind and could not do himself, or the team justice.
>
> I feel that players have an obligation that whoever wears the shirt, they

do so with pride because our supporters work hard all week and pay good money to watch their team, home and away. All that I ask is that they give everything they have got to represent those supporters. But, after talking to my staff and thinking about it, we felt that we had been backed into a corner and had no option. I told Andy to go home and that he wouldn't be training with the lads as I only wanted players totally committed and focused as we prepared for a big match.

The replacement Coyle found had the football world buzzing and supporters beaming. None other than the legendary Andy Cole would play for the rest of the season on loan from Sunderland. In the away game at QPR he scored a scintillating hat-trick. Coyle had pulled a rabbit out of the hat and this particular rabbit confessed to feeling young and rejuvenated again, waxing lyrical about the effect Coyle had on rekindling his interest in the game again after languishing in the reserves at Sunderland.

Away at Wolves, Burnley won 3–2. It was the fifth game of Coyle's honeymoon period, a period that saw three wins and two draws, some scintillating football, a totally new style, and almost disbelieving supporters. To add to the glee it was televised on Sky so that thousands of fans back in Burnley could see a win at a venue at which Burnley never usually won.

'Burnley Belief Starts To Tell' wrote Ron Gubba in the *Telegraph*. He recalled Brendan Flood's comparison of Coyle with Bill Shankly.

Shankly always insisted that football was a simple game and that success was achieved by doing the simple things well. Hard work allied to good passing and movement were the key to success and so it is proving at Burnley. Working with the same group of players who managed only one win in their last ten matches under Steve Cotterill, Coyle has now overseen a run of five matches unbeaten, including away wins at Watford, Charlton and now Wolves.

The comparison with Shankly when it was made was felt to be way over the top. But inasmuch as Shankly viewed the game in simple, common-sense terms, his man-management was first class, and his down-to-earth philosophies were homespun and basic; then so too were Coyle's.

The run of five unbeaten games included a 1–1 draw against Leicester City. It was a game of wasted chances but afterwards Coyle made more revealing comments. 'I was a striker myself and will never give anybody a rollicking for trying something different in the final third.' He was referring to Kyle Lafferty's gruesome miscue late in the game after he had brilliantly broken clear along the by-line and advanced on goal. He had attempted a shot from an impossible angle. Score and it was a goal of genius, miss and it was ridiculed. Alas, Lafferty was no genius.

Graham Alexander the Clarets captain assessed the new manager. 'He's a confident fellow and a breath of fresh air. The ability and work-rate just needed channelling. He wants us to express ourselves.' There was no mention of the previous manager but the inference was clear. These players were enjoying a different regime and a new mindset.

Two consecutive home defeats and a run of five games without a win burst the bubble:

> As every long suffering football fan knows, when things are looking good, there's inevitably going to be something, or someone looking on the horizon and preparing to dampen our spirits. And as every Burnley fan knows, when we've recently destroyed the best teams in the Division, the last fixture we want is a home match against the bottom club.
>
> So a couple of weeks before Christmas we had a Tuesday night home fixture against QPR and as tradition dictates this was the match that was sure to kickstart our poor run. To be fair it's usually Boxing Day when our early season promise begins to disappear. I'd like to hear from any Burnley fan who has eaten a turkey curry and a selection box on the same day as we've picked up three points. Anyway we duly managed to lose to QPR 2–1 which had the effect of lifting them off the bottom of the table to be replaced by Preston North End of all teams, who we happened to be playing at home the following Saturday. This was another chance for us to lose to a lowly team. If it wasn't so tragic it would be funny.
>
> So, our players lined up against Preston, desperate to right the wrongs of the previous Tuesday, and blissfully unaware of what was to follow. The referee gave us a hint in the first minute when he denied us a clear penalty right in front of the two thousand astonished Preston fans. You wonder if you are suffering from some form of neurosis when you are convinced that we always get a bizarre refereeing performance when we play Preston North End. The Turf Moor choir adopted the chant 'We only get shit refs' as a protest. But anyway, we had come out all guns blazing and I thought that surely it would be just a matter of time before we got on top.
>
> So, it was hardly surprising that after 96 topsy-turvy minutes we left the field with nine men and an excruciating 3–2 defeat. That was bad news, and around the town expectations had already started to fall as people began to accept that this was part of the usual seasonal bad run.
>
> For Owen's part, he was getting used to the Championship and the level of competition. For us, a top half team, to lose to the two bottom teams was a realisation that all the teams in the Championship were capable of beating each other. (Courtesy of Brendan Flood)

There was a horrible 0–3 defeat at Blackpool. It was another shocking display to add to those away at Hull City and home to QPR. Tony Scholes reported that he had never seen as many supporters walk away and leave so early. Owen Coyle had certainly not yet found the elixir. Kyle Lafferty responded badly to taunts from the away supporters. He would be sold to Rangers and few were sorry to see him go especially at the inflated price for which he left.

A run of three consecutive wins restored confidence. The 4–2 win away at QPR was simply stunning. Andy Cole had enough money in the bank to put his feet up for the rest of his life. His house in Cheshire stood alongside several other millionaires. Transfer fees for his services had totalled £17million. He couldn't remember the last goal he had scored prior to arriving at Burnley but Coyle had persuaded him with the words that all footballers want to hear. 'Come in and enjoy yourself.'

At QPR he did just that:

> I am very pleased not just by the hat-trick but by the way the lads came back from 2–0 down to win. That gave me great pleasure because when they went 2–0 up, they were giving it the big 'ole'. But the game is not over until it's over and this was a big performance. Maybe the first goal was the turning point because it knocked the wind out of their sails a little bit. We came out and cracked on in the second half and I thought we dominated. Every goal feels good. I have not played too many games this season, but to score goals now gives the same feeling as it did when I was a kid. I still have the same appetite to play and win games. The manager played a big part in getting me to the club. He said he thought I could bring a lot to the club playing week in and week out and helping others. When managers have that belief it makes you feel really good and he has that belief in me. We are all playing for the manager. He gives us the enthusiasm to want to carry on playing and he makes me feel as though I am 21 again.

In truth the 4–2 win was the last of the 'big' performances. The defeat at Sheffield United prompted Coyle to announce, 'We'll freshen up this summer, we'll bring the right personnel in to complement the quality we have and if we do that we'll be a force to be reckoned with. The search has already started. We knew we were papering over the cracks. It's fair to say every area of the park needs strengthening.'

The one glamour game of the season came in the FA Cup when Burnley were drawn at home to Arsenal. Lafferty distinguished himself for two things. He missed a golden heading opportunity with the goal at his mercy. It would have put Burnley 1–0 up. And then he was sent off for what the referee judged to be an over the top tackle.

Burnley had not won at home since 23 October and they lost again, 0–2. It was a real damp squib, the proverbial anti-climax to the build-up. But, at least the Arsenal game was the last of that streak of poor results. Plymouth was the next game at Turf Moor and were beaten 1–0. It is a peculiar fact of life at Turf Moor that Plymouth can always be relied upon to lose at Burnley when points are desperately needed. If by some fixture mix-up Burnley could play Plymouth every week, promotion would be a certainty.

At the beginning of March the play-offs were still just an optimistic point away when Watford arrived. All thoughts of top-six places and possible promotion had long vanished while Steve Cotterill was manager but even though this side was inconsistent and far from the finished article, in fact still mostly Cotterill's players, Coyle had established grounds for positive and hopeful thinking. Alan Nixon reported on the game that ended 2–2:

Burnley hero Robbie Blake believes his vintage Clarets could be popping the promotion champagne corks at the climax of a remarkable season. Blake came off the bench to score two memorable equalisers in an explosive game and knows a thing or two about going up, in his long career. The seasoned striker has spent much of his time at Turf Moor of late and thinks this bunch may be about to hit the top six at the right time—with quality and experience to spare.

This is the best squad of players they have had since I've been here. It's showing in our performances. We play the ball down and do it the right way. We're just a point off the play-offs and we're going in the right direction. It's just there to be done, we've just got to keep our heads down and get on with it. Most people will look at Burnley and think we will fade away before the end. But we believe we can get there with the ability we've got here.

This side has the feel of a useful combination, their spirit is remarkable and they are finishing games strongly. That is the sign of a side that can last the course. (Courtesy of Alan Nixon)

But, even though a play-off place had come tantalisingly close on one or two occasions, the season petered out with certainly no sign at all of what was to come in 2008–09. Defeats had come with monotonous regularity. The last home game of the season against Cardiff City, however, had Burnley fans in stitches. But then leaving the ground at Crystal Palace after the final away game they feared the worst for the coming season.

The Cardiff game ended 3–3. Twice Burnley had the lead but Cardiff came back to make it 2–2. Then they pegged it level at 3–3 after Burnley had gone 3–2 up. But what caused the merriment was the Keystone Cops routine towards the end of the game.

Out came Cardiff and I thought, just how on earth have this lot reached an FA Cup Final. As for gifting goals to the opposition today was as good a day as any to witness the Burnley way of throwing leads away. We are so good at it you have to be impressed. Three all the final score and what good value it was I have to say. It had a sleepy first period when some nice tippy-tappy passing, some bouts of head tennis and an occasional burst through by a Burnley forward, was just enough to stop us all going to sleep, but only just. It gave me the chance to read the programme and the fanzine. And then just when you thought this might be a dull 0–0 draw we scored. Then we fashioned a superb second and you might have been forgiven for thinking this game is now won. Oh dear no, it then became 2–2. Cue delirium as late on we scored a third. This must be it we thought, a nice win to end the home programme. You are joking of course for then we had an own goal to make it 3–3.

As if all that wasn't enough and just to show that even the most meaningless of end of season games can provide real sparks and drama, we had the 'Cole Incident'. Surely this will be remembered for years. Purse and Cole clashed for the ball. It looked X-certificate stuff. Cole emerged from the heap pointing to his leg. Purse stayed down. Cole was livid. Purse got a straight red and walked off. Cole, still livid, picked up his leg and showed it to management, the referee and anyone else who was interested. The leg was examined by all and sundry and forensics. Suddenly Cole took off and hared off the field vanishing up his own tunnel. We all cottoned on. He was chasing Purse and hell bent on lamping him we guessed. Next thing, the Cardiff bench realised what his intent was. They all jumped up and chased across the field as well to lamp Cole. Next thing, police and stewards raced up the tunnel after the Cardiff lads. All of us waited for the tell-tale sounds of biff, bang, wallop from the dressing rooms. By now the game had re-started, but none of us cared any more. It was more fun waiting for everyone who had disappeared up the tunnel to come back out. Everyone did; but not Cole, who was nowhere to be seen. Spectators were all in agreement. When Cole ran off the pitch it was the fastest anyone had seen him run all season.

Cole later announced that there were just two games he wanted to play the next season—both against Cardiff City. Sadly, much as we wanted him to, he did not re-sign in the summer. There would be no more fireworks. (Personal Diary Saturday 26 April 2008)

The very last game was away to Crystal Palace. There had been hopes at various points in the season that this might have been a sort of mini-play-off game for sixth place. It was not to be. Carlisle was sent off. It was an embarrassing horror show, reported Clarets fan Tony Scholes on the Claretsmad website, without pride, effort or interest. This was the fifth defeat of the final eight games. Only Robbie Blake showed any level of effort with the defence sliced open repeatedly.

Owen Coyle's final team of the season was: Jensen, Duff, Carlisle, Caldwell, Harley; Elliott, O'Connor, Alexander, McCann; Randall and Blake. Eight of them would form the bedrock of the next amazing season and play at Wembley. Harley, O'Connor and Randall would not be retained. That eight players from a side that played so ineffectively and embarrassingly at Crystal Palace could be transformed in the way that they were into a fighting force that would enact a football fairy tale, was a tribute to one man—Owen Coyle. Jensen had been at Burnley since signed by Stan Ternent. The other seven were all Steve Cotterill signings. It made the achievements to come all the more remarkable. It begs the question, who wins Championships, players or the manager? Of course the players did the deeds on the field, but they were galvanised and liberated by the manager.

6

PRELUDE TO THE IMPOSSIBLE

Burnley fans are a phlegmatic and long suffering lot. Over the years there have been so many promises, new dawns, dashed hopes and what feels like more downs than ups. Seven years in the Fourth Division felt like an eternity. If every summer over the years had been optimistic; most new seasons had been disappointing or just centring on survival. No Burnley fans could ever remember a time when the club had been awash with money. It had always been a selling club. In recent times Blake, Akinbiyi and Gray had all gone for one reason or another, continuing the tradition started by Bob Lord 50 years earlier that survival depended on player-sales. The mantra from the top was always one of 'punching above our weight'. Directors' loans propped up the creaking finances, in fact administration had been close more than once and not that long ago the club had gone to fans themselves to ask for donations. The last success was in 1999–2000 when Stan Ternent won promotion to the Championship and even that, it could be argued, was done on a shoestring, with Chairman Barry Kilby using his own money to fund player purchases. Further progress after that was curtailed by lack of the funding that Ternent wished for.

In short, Burnley Football Club was like most others, creaking along, the 'jar on the mantelpiece empty', as Chairman Kilby once famously said, lurching from season to season with money too tight to mention; and yet, everybody wanting success and something to look forward to. It is no joke being a fan of any football club, let alone Burnley, for do all supporters not want the same end result? And yet only a select few can find that elusive happy season with a jackpot ending. Burnley fans were therefore conditioned into a firm mindset. We will not get excited. We are conditioned to disappointment.

The immediate end to season 2007–08 was therefore like so many others at Turf Moor, one of dashed hopes and a placid shrug of the shoulders. The 0–5 defeat at Crystal Palace confirmation that this had been another of those ultimately weary, let-down seasons. The London Clarets at that game wandering off to the nearest pub after the third goal went in, as is their tradition and rule. The new man, we thought, had changed nothing; as usual it had all faded away, and the next season would be just the same. Promises, promises, promises, the football and entertainment might have been just a little improved but defeats still came along regularly and painfully. And there was still no money. The next glum news was a projected £4million loss.

So, not a single supporter could have contemplated the flurry of activity in the summer of 2008, the money that would be spent, the record transfer deals and a player being sold for an astonishing £4million. That player was Lafferty who went to Rangers and the Burnley accountant must have laughed his way to the bank at this inflated fee for a very average player. Lafferty had made it clear that he wanted to leave, 'desperate to end his hell at Turf Moor'. He had given his views to a Belfast newspaper:

> I've given my all to Burnley but don't feel wanted. No player is going to stay where he is not happy. I need a fresh challenge at this stage of my career. I was happy under the previous manager Steve Cotterill. Things have changed though and to be honest I don't feel the same way. If I had been given the opportunity to leave during those last two transfer windows I would have left—however those bids were turned away by the club. I understand Wolves and Rangers want to sign me and I would be thrilled to move to either club. I feel the sooner a deal is done the better for everybody concerned.

Most supporters echoed Lafferty's final sentiment. It would be reasonable to suppose that Coyle too, privately rubbed his hands at the £4million sale, with the latter feeling that he 'had been backed into a corner'. Publicly he made all the right noises; didn't want to lose him and so on. Lafferty was described as a striker but had scored just 10 goals in something like 80 games.

Excitingly, players came in one after the other and when the news broke that Chris Eagles was to sign from Manchester United, and supporters looked at the back page of the breakfast newspaper, many a spoon was dropped in wonder into the cornflakes. It was the incomings that took supporters' breath away. Steve Corrigan wrote that he couldn't remember a summer like it and that it had left him, two days before the start of the season feeling like a small child waiting for Christmas. It wasn't that Burnley had bought thrilling young players, they had bought not just one, but two players for over a million pounds each, smashing the incoming and outgoing player transfer records. On top of all that Corrigan knew he was going to see a style of football that would win friends and be pleasing to watch.

For a long time supporters had wanted to see a defensive and aggressive midfielder of the calibre of Kevin Ball way back in the Ternent seasons. Their wish was granted (they thought) in the acquisition of Remco Van Der Schaaf. Here was a player who would protect the back four, break up attacks and then prompt ours. As it turned out, he was a dud, but nevertheless, in the pre-season his arrival was welcomed, before his limitations and injuries emerged. Coyle had identified a need and addressed it.

In came a Scottish youngster, the highly rated Kevin McDonald for £500,000. He fitted the profile of young and hungry players, lads who could grow and develop at the club at a reasonable price. The selling club bemoaned his departure to a 'small' club at a price lower than they would have got from a bigger club. But Coyle pursued the lad, and shades of Harry Potts, personally travelled to meet the parents, employ his charm and gifted tongue, and persuade them Burnley was the best place. McDonald already had Scottish under-19 and 21 caps and had been voted Dundee's player of the season. Coyle had known him since the lad was 16, but McDonald chose Burnley in preference to Celtic and Liverpool who were also interested.

'Owen talked me into coming here,' said McDonald. 'I like the way he has been. He has been good for me and has seen me all the way through the years.'

Next up was the goalkeeper problem. Brian Jensen had been at Burnley since the Ternent days. On his day he was brilliant but there had been a number of gaffes over the years. New goalkeeper replacements had come and been seen off. The next one to come was international 'keeper Peruvian Diego Penny. 'Peru', supporters blinked, 'an international, good Lord.' This was extending the boundaries, raising the bar, making people smile. Once his work permit problems had been solved, he was given a three-year contract. He too would turn out to be a dud but at the time of the signing supporters were delighted to think another problem had been solved. Ironically, no-one knew that Jensen was about to have his greatest ever season.

The next to arrive was another Scottish player, Norwegian to be exact, Christian Kalvenes. He ditched his plans to return to Norway in exchange for a two-year contract at Burnley. At 31, he was hardly one for the future, but was brought in to solve the inconsistent left back slot and the recognised defensive frailties. If slow, he was tough, hard-tackling and at his own pace could make forays into the opposition final third. Pace would have made him a superb addition and the complete full back.

The signing of striker Martin Paterson was wrapped up and then came the news that glamour-boy Chris Eagles was the next target. Both of them involved fees far in excess of anything previously experienced at the club. Supporters looked at each other astonished. Here was a player who could easily feature in a fashion magazine. The hair, Alice band, healthy tan, plucked eyebrows some said, good looking—nothing like it since the days of Willie Morgan and his boutique—and a year later a Ferrari for heaven's sake rolled into the players' car park one morning. Was this really happening? After Eagles signed Coyle said:

> To get a player of his stature on board shows what we're trying to do. He can play anywhere but I see him playing in a very attacking role for us, to get forward at every opportunity. He's a creative player, he scores goals,

and he's capable of taking players on. He has an array of talent and we're just delighted to get him at the football club.

Brendan Flood played a large part in the new signings:

Owen and I had been discussing how to improve the playing squad from the Monday after our last game of the season. Locked in the Chairman's lounge we had pondered over the various player issues to decide who we wanted to retain and started by looking at the squad that had collapsed 5–0 at Crystal Palace. It had been Owen's first season and I think he felt inclined to keep Jon Harley and James O'Connor because they had both given their all for the club and he was reluctant to make the tough decision of letting them go. Having had the benefit of watching them from the stands for the last three years I felt they weren't top-six players and we needed to get better. Owen agreed and decided to offer them both a shorter new contract and if they didn't take it up they could go. They both found clubs quickly. Jon went to Watford and James to Sheffield Wednesday. We talked about Alan Mahon but Owen didn't see him as a regular as his form had been indifferent. Owen had brought with him a list of players that he wanted to pursue and at the top was Martin Paterson, the promising striker who had scored 15 goals for Scunthorpe as they were relegated from the Championship. He had Kaspars Gorkss the Blackpool centre half, Chris Eagles at Manchester United, Andrew Driver at Hearts and a keeper called Diego Penny from Peru. I'd never heard of Penny but then I'd never heard of Owen Coyle a year ago. But Owen thought that he'd be adequate for the first-team, he'd played a blinder for Peru against Brazil and Owen had seen enough evidence to suggest he had a future with us.

We were determined to do everything possible to get our target list of players. The top priority was a faster striker and Martin Paterson was certainly that. Both Owen and I thought he was the best young striker in the Championship. When we played Scunthorpe I had got on well with their Chairman, Steve Wharton, and so I said I'd chat over the summer. And, Martin Paterson's agent is Gary Mellor so I alerted Gary to the fact that we might be interested in going for Martin. But Scunthorpe, being Lincolnshire country boys certainly knew the value of a pound and they wanted £2million for him. Owen had put nominal values against his targets on the list and had Martin at £500k. So we went round and round for a while, starting at £500k, then £650k, then £720k. I don't think they were getting fed up of me but Owen didn't want to go above £750k. He was naturally nervous of spending too much money, which isn't always a bad quality in a manager. Most managers are wary of spending too much money. If it doesn't work out you may lose your job.

By the third week in June I received a call from a contact telling me that Ipswich were about to make a deal and that if we wanted to do a deal we should get a move on. It was a Saturday morning and I said to Ellen that I needed to spend most of the day sorting it out. From nine in the morning to seven in the evening I was on the phone to two Scunthorpe directors. In the end I got to £1million, with £300k on appearances and a bonus if we got promoted. I was keeping Owen informed as I went on and by teatime he said:

'Well you know Brendan; I don't want to pay more than a million.'

'What's he worth if he scores twenty goals for us next season what's he worth? Just stand back and think about it.'

'Three million,' he replied.

'Is he going to score twenty goals do you think?'

'Yeah.'

In the end Owen agreed to go with it. We had confidence in the player and to me we were more than likely paying £1.3million for a player who'd be worth £3million at the end of the season.

So we moved on to Chris Eagles. I agreed that I'd try to progress this because I have a business relationship with Gary Neville and Ryan Giggs. They're both super lads and for all their unbelievable success they have life in good perspective. When we're together we talk football for a good forty five minutes before we move on to business. I hoped that they would reference Burnley for me to Chris and tell him that we had big plans for promotion. Hopefully this would set the scene for Chris and give us a chance to sign him.

In due course Owen contacted Sir Alex to agree a transfer fee and then he arranged a meeting with Chris before he went on United's tour of South Africa. Owen was delighted with the meeting because Chris wanted to talk about football and not about the contract details. You know a player of his calibre will ultimately want to be looked after but that discussion came later. He had his priorities in the same order as Owen's. But the deal hadn't been cemented and on the South Africa tour Chris was top scorer for United. Then one evening I received a text from Gary Neville saying, 'I'm sat next to Chris Eagles at dinner and I've put in another good word for you'. It was all I could ask for I guess.

Owen had got his agent to make sure Chris could come up to the club the day after he returned from South Africa and after a bit more reassurance from Owen he signed. Sunderland had been interested in Chris but I think it helped us that Roy Keane had said some things in the Press that Manchester United hadn't liked.

It was a huge coup for us to get these two players, both young with bags of potential and both desperate to play football. We'd secured them for less than £3million and were sure we'd got great value. The one player we missed was Kaspars Gorkss. Owen met his agent who is his father a couple of times but he went to QPR, probably with different priorities to Paterson and Eagles. (Courtesy of Brendan Flood)

The scene was set. Pre-season anticipation had risen as a result of all this activity. The pre-season training and games had gone well—even as far as games in the USA where there was imaginative hope (eventually doomed) of setting up links with US clubs. Not even a projected £4million loss for the coming year put a damper on supporters though it would understandably bother the Chairman and directors. It would later impact on Owen Coyle and any plans in mid-season to freshen the team. In truth the finances at the end of the season would be at breaking point.

The *Guardian*'s John Ashdown wrote: 'There's usually one surprise thrown up during the course of the season, and Burnley could well be the Hull–Stoke of 2008–09.'

The first game was coming up, away at Sheffield Wednesday, still managed by Brian Laws the original target as Steve Cotterill's replacement. If Wednesday had agreed to let Burnley talk to Laws, Coyle might never have arrived. The away support was huge. Burnley fans travel in their hundreds to all away games and for a game as near as Sheffield they were out in their thousands. They, chairman, directors, management, staff and most of all the players were in for a huge and totally unexpected shock. They came back ashen. They were thrashed 4–1.

'Oh Jaysus,' groaned Phil Whalley in the *London Clarets* magazine. 'We can forget the play-offs if we continue to defend like this.'

A fuming Coyle announced after the game:

> The defending was nothing short of naïve. We lost a goal from a throw in, it looked like schoolboy defending. I can accept being beaten and I can accept somebody working really hard to score a goal against you but I don't think Sheffield Wednesday had to work particularly hard for any of their goals. I left the players in no uncertain terms about that. What we need are players with a real desire and hunger at 3–1 to right the wrong.

He had been hoping his side would get off to a flyer and underline their potential with a good display and three points. Only three players were spared the criticism. 'Martin Paterson did well, Stephen Jordan and Wade Elliott but you're not going to win in the Championship with only three players.'

The limitations of new goalkeeper Diego Penny and new midfielder Remco Van Der Schaaf were cruelly exposed. After this game Penny was consigned to the bench for the remainder of his Burnley career, and Van Der Schaaf never featured again having been replaced during the game. They say you shouldn't start looking at League tables until 10 games have passed by. But after the second League game of the season Burnley fans could be forgiven for looking at them already and thinking that this was going to be a horrendous season.

The first home game of the season began in farcical conditions. Brendan Flood had decided he wanted to excite the fans with a carnival atmosphere. Accordingly he booked a parachute team to land in the centre-circle. He said he'd learned that anything coming in from above is 'apparently spectacular' to fans because you're looking up, which you don't often do at football grounds.

Obviously Brendan had forgotten fans at Burnley had spent a lot of time looking up at goalkeeper Jensen's stratospheric goalkicks and during the Cotterill period had become keen ornithologists watching the pigeons when boredom had set in.

Unfortunately the fifth parachutist landed not in the centre circle but on the stand roof behind one of the goals. He lay inert on the top of the roof before gingerly making a move to see if he was still in one piece. Meanwhile Owen Coyle plus teams were stuck in the claustrophobic dressing rooms waiting until the situation was sorted. Asbestos sheets began to drop down from the roof into the stand below. The small number of Ipswich fans were seated away from the drop zone at the other end of the stand, otherwise things could have been nasty. Health and Safety swung into action. Until this guy was off the roof the game could not begin. For 50 minutes the words 'faff about' and 'does anyone have a fire engine' just about summed things up until an announcement was made that he was off the roof and the game could start.

'Oh no he isn't,' the crowd roared. He was still on the roof as the game started.

Jeff Stelling on Sky Soccer Saturday had a field day announcing to the nation that at Burnley a parachutist who had missed the target would be booked for descent. Supporters joked about parachute payments.

Only 11,000 fans turned up for this game and in truth the mood as the game was delayed was one of increasing irritation. It was funny for just ten minutes or so. 'You don't know what you're doing,' sang the crowd. By full-time it was another feeling of utter let-down as Burnley trooped off having lost 0–3 to add to the ignominy.

A despairing Owen Coyle told the Press after the game:

Goals change games, there's no doubt about that. I thought we had total control of the game and probably had three or four real opportunities. It just looked like a matter of time until we'd score and go on to win it. But we really shot ourselves in the foot. We just needed that spark to get the goal and give us a lift but we never got it. The players do one of two things. If they want to go away and feel sorry for themselves then they're no good to me. But if they're prepared to come in on Monday, roll their sleeves up and get some hard work done, then that's the type we need. Ultimately I take responsibility because I pick the team.

Diego Penny and Remco Van Der Schaaf had already lost their places after just the one opening game and after the Ipswich debacle it was back to the drawing board. A move was made that stayed in place for the rest of the season. Full back Graham Alexander was moved to a holding and protective role in front of the back four and Duff and Kalvenes were the new full backs. Excessive talk of formations is boring but a new line-up of 4–1–4–1 was adopted. It was back to basics and centre half Steve Caldwell later recalled that the sole objective was not to concede and that they were almost frightened to go over the halfway line. It worked, but neither did they score even though Palace were reduced to nine players for most of the second half. Nevertheless it was a clean sheet as would be the next game so that including a Carling Cup game at Bury (won 2–0), there would be four clean sheets in five games, by the end of August.

The rot was stopped and a foundation was laid. Coyle's move of Alexander to midfield was crucial and he would stay there indefinitely. Added to his natural skill, he was a born leader, tough, uncompromising, shrewd and one of those canny players who could read a game and anticipate trouble. He won the ball in tackles, or he intercepted it, and then made the short pass. His penalty taking skills were legendary and became crucial to the season. And this, a player already in his middle thirties.

On the eve of the Crystal Palace game Coyle admitted the setbacks had been a jolt. 'But I think it's been a test of people's character. It's been self inflicted, not because we've been massively outplayed, there's not been a good goal scored against us.' He remained convinced his team could beat anyone in the Championship.

Another Carling Cup game afforded the opportunity for a win and some confidence building. The team at last clicked, 3–0, against Oldham Athletic. If only people had known that these Carling wins were mounting up and would lead to fame for the club, glory and limelight for the players, but then last minute heartache and despair for everyone. 'A pleasing night's work,' commented Coyle, 'We scored three very good goals.'

Things then happened that had major effects on the season and team. If the first was the shrewd move of Alexander to midfield; the second was the sending off of Chris Eagles in the Plymouth game. And the third was the acquisition of Steve Thompson from Cardiff City:

> Ade Akinbiyi didn't look like he was having the best season with himself and we needed somebody younger to work with Martin Paterson up front. Owen had looked around at different options and on the Sunday he rang me up before the last day of the transfer window and suggested Steve Thompson at Cardiff City. I knew that we were over our wages budget at seven and a half million pounds and we'd be heading towards eight, but we did need a bigger presence. So we decided to try and get him on loan but when Owen talked to Cardiff on the following Monday they wouldn't agree to a loan. They were happy for us to speak to Steve in the hope of coming to an agreement with the player before the end of the business. Owen and I agreed that I would be unavailable to take calls on the Monday afternoon. So as Cardiff were ringing up to see if they could get a fee out of us, they were asking for £300,000, Owen was doing his best to agree terms with Steve Thompson and his agent. Peter Ridsdale called me twice but before I rang him back I called Owen to see if he'd agreed terms with Steve, which he had. Owen was very happy, Steve's a 'good type' as Owen would say and he thought he would fit in well. He's a good strong player and Owen was convinced he would fit in well. We were going beyond our comfort level to get Steve in but we desperately needed a quality target man. As luck would have it, Cardiff appeared to be so desperate to reduce their own wage bill that just by avoiding Ridsdale's phone calls through the afternoon we managed to sign Steve on a free. (Courtesy of Brendan Flood)

Eagles had not been firing on all cylinders and his sending off and three games enforced absence prompted another re-think. From that point on, although he played many games, he could never be assured of his place or be one of the first names on the team sheet. But, it was maybe the arrival of big bustling, and not unskilful Steve Thompson that was the catalyst for much of what happened in the coming months. Here was a player who could win the ball in the air from Jensen's punts. He was a focal point, could hold the ball, lay it off, bring others into play, worry defenders and he scored some critical goals. As a young lad he had once cleaned Coyle's boots at Dundee United.

Coyle commented:

> I'm delighted. Steven is a player we've been tracking for some time. We have managed to persevere and bring him in and it was very attractive because there was no fee involved. I have known Steven since he was a YTS lad at Dundee United. The competition we have now in the striking department is brilliant and gives us a new dimension when we need it.

At this point Wade Elliott made some interesting and revealing comments suggesting that pre-season games had been too successful, especially the game against Inverness, and lulled them into thinking they were better than they were, ill prepared for real competitive football in the opening games.

> It all came too easily. I don't know whether we thought it was going to happen again for us at Sheffield Wednesday but it was a completely different game. It was a shock to everyone . . . we've learned our lesson. We went back to basics against Crystal Palace and Plymouth. To come off the back of a 4–1 and a 3–0 defeat, you're never going to stroll around and play brilliant football. You do it in small steps.

The small steps led to a brilliant month. It was in September that the real road to promotion began. As a result Coyle was named manager of the month. The first game of the month was not until 13th September. By the end there had been five wins and a draw. One of the wins was against Fulham in the Carling Cup. Was there any secret complicated method of management to explain this transformation? Not according to Brian Jensen who months later explained it was the simple things that Coyle brought:

> Everybody thought he was a magician. Not at all; the main thing he did was to tell you that you were good enough. He gave us so much self-confidence and belief and that's 90% of football. There wasn't a day when he didn't come in with a smile on his face. That was his philosophy, have good banter, crack jokes, work hard, but at the same time enjoy yourself. What he was doing wasn't rocket science. It was basic stuff, really quite simple. He was just being human.

If Brendan Flood had made a comparison with Shankly, Jensen's summary of Coyle's skills made him more like Harry Potts.

The breakthrough came at Nottingham, a rare victory at this ground. Burnley deserved the win with neat, attacking football. Graham Alexander was pivotal with two goals as well as his screening role. The first goal was a curling free kick, and the second a trademark bullet penalty. It was the first penalty Burnley had been awarded in 35 games. The win took them out of the bottom three.

Coyle was quick to praise Alexander. 'We know what we get with him; he acted as defensive screener for us. We've moved him into that role which we felt we had to after losing the first two games and the one thing we know is that when he gets the ball he is capable of passing it.'

Blackpool were next up and were soundly beaten at 2–0, the score no reflection at all of the Burnley dominance. I wrote in my personal diary:

> Tonight was a match to remember. The game was outstanding. First half the most one sided game I've seen in years; new centre forward Thompson, excellent—strong and good header of the ball. Elliott was on form again. Paterson was electric; Alexander in midfield mopping everything up. McDonald and McCann could be the best duo since Harris and O'Neil back in the 60s. Duff was solid and calm. This was a superb team performance. And then when you can bring Blake on for the last 15 minutes it was the icing on the cake. Eagles was out of the team and it was back to a basic, uncomplicated formation. (Personal Diary September 16th 2008)

'We're delighted to get back on track because we were certainly hurt by the first two games. So to bounce back with the two draws and then the two wins on the back of that, it's been a good bit of work,' said Coyle after the game with every reason to be well pleased. He was less pleased after the next one away to Swansea when deep into injury time Swansea got an equaliser and three points were reduced to one. There surely isn't a worse feeling in football than conceding a last minute goal that prevents the win. 'I don't know where the referee found the extra-time,' grumbled Coyle. 'My watch isn't the greatest in the world but it doesn't account for that amount of time.' There were stories that his watch had cost him a tenner from Woolworths. 'But, it's now six games unbeaten and we are heading in the right direction.'

They certainly were heading in the right direction with three consecutive home wins. From in the bottom three at the beginning of the month Burnley were now a stunning fourth. The first of the three wins was against Fulham in the Carling Cup. It was a strange kind of game as my diary revealed:

> Not entirely dull, not entirely lifeless, but almost like a practice game. Both sides played nice tippy tappy football without getting anywhere. Just when extra-time looked likely, the most extraordinary thing happened. Out of nothing the rookie Rodriguez was played through in the clear by Eagles and slotted home with the aplomb of a veteran. It was so unexpected, such a surprise there was a nano second of total silence and disbelief before the cheers of relief. It was doubtful that anybody would have wanted another 30 minutes. The final whistle was almost immediate leaving a mild incredulity and then; exit 7,000 pleasantly surprised supporters. Late at night on empty roads it takes an hour to get home. We were still just as surprised when we unlocked the front door. (Personal Diary September 24th)

Preston arrived at Turf Moor with an unbeaten away record and in third place. They left, tails between their legs, after a 3–1 defeat inflicted by what was now becoming a fast, attractive and very attacking Burnley side. The pundits were taking note. The key moment was a screamer of a 35 yards dipping, swerving shot from Gudjonnson that must have changed direction six times. Most of his shots usually hit the roof of the stand but this one was a fantastic strike. Eagles in this game showed his skill and class with the final goal moving onto a McCann through ball and placing it home without breaking stride; and Alexander's move to the defensive role was again a foundation.

'I thought we deserved it from start to finish,' said Coyle. 'We dominated the game. The lads showed the hunger and desire to win the game and Joey's goal was very special.'

'That's a magnificent three points for us,' Coyle beamed after a terrific 3–2 win over Watford. It was a game that ebbed and flowed; confrontation, in yer face, cynical and physical football against the more refined gifted Burnley style. Power and physical strength is often the key to Championship success but it was not Coyle's way. It would be way over the top to say this was a win for good over evil but it was nearly something like that. 'We had one or two words with the players at half-time and they were under no illusions what was required. In the second half we really went for it. The second half fight-back sums up the spirit and desire this group have got.'

On Sky, pundit Chris Kamara was one of the experts who had noted Burnley's rise and the influence of Coyle:

> A month ago the talk around Burnley was not so much of the Coyle they had, as the noose they would be needing. Two games gone, two heavy defeats and suddenly a few murmurings were starting to be heard about manager Owen Coyle. This morning, seven games and just three goals conceded later, the Turf Moor boss can do no wrong again. So, a big well done to Coylie for turning things around after those dismal losses to Sheffield Wednesday and Ipswich. And on Tuesday he claimed the biggest scalp of his 11-month reign with a marvellous League Cup win over Fulham.
>
> When things were not looking too clever after those first two games, Owen responded in the way you'd expect—by taking his squad back to basics. They repaid him with three clean sheets on the bounce followed with another against Premier League opponents in midweek. I know Coylie started the season with high hopes of at least the play-offs—and in his mind none of that has changed.
>
> Don't forget Burnley are now missing two of their finest after Kyle Lafferty was sold in the summer, following Andy Gray's departure in January. That brought the club a combined £4.5million but there were no complaints or moans from the manager at losing a couple of prize assets. He knows the economics of working at a club like Burnley, where buying and selling has been the order of the day for a long while. It's a remit which previous bosses like Steve Cotterill and Stan Ternent both had to work under—and nothing's changed in that department.

But Coylie has certainly bought well, bringing in Martin Paterson from Scunthorpe and Chris Eagles from Manchester United. The club will certainly reap another handsome reward should they decide to cash in on the pair of them somewhere down the line. The question, now, on all fans' lips is whether Burnley can keep their resurgence going and force their way into the promotion battle. The confidence they will have taken from beating Fulham will definitely help them along the way, even though no-one needs to tell them it won't be easy. Yet the way Coylie has got them playing, you wouldn't put anything past him at the moment and he is rightfully earning a reputation as one of the best young bosses in the game. He also has that crucial ability of being able to pull a rabbit or two out of the hat when it's needed—and with that magic touch anything's possible.

Pundits are paid to talk and much of their talk is waffle but Kamara's words would be prophetic. With Coyle at Burnley things were definitely possible. There was a serious blip over the Christmas period but back came Burnley to maintain an unlikely promotion push. Not only that, but the Carling Cup was destined to bring a level of fame and exposure to this little club that it had never experienced before.

It is a well worn cliché, but things were indeed about to take off.

7

UP FOR THE CUP

When Burnley disposed of Bury at Gigg Lane in the Carling Cup in August, 2008, it is doubtful that anyone could have predicted the run they would have that would take them to the semi-finals and to within just two minutes of Wembley itself. Bearing in mind how Burnley made heavy weather of the Bury win, it was even more remarkable.

The game belonged to two people, old boy Brian Jensen and new boy Martin Paterson, described by one fan as 'raggy-arsed, in a kit that looked two sizes too big'. It wasn't really supposed to happen that Jensen would have an absolute blinder and reclaim the number one jersey. But it did. Brian was supposed only to appear for Carling games but after this game he was number one again. He shone throughout the game making point blank saves, fending off swerving volleys, turning away dipping screamers, and generally sorting out all the defensive messes and penalty area confusion.

Bury must have trooped off the field wondering just how they had lost. They lost because Paterson scored twice whilst they failed all night. A relieved Owen Coyle praised Paterson. 'Three goals in two games shows one of the reasons why we brought him to the football club. He'll be a tremendous asset and we're delighted to have him. He's a great lad. He knows where the goals are and his work-rate is terrific. You can never fault the work-rate he's got and that's what I want to see in the Burnley jersey and hopefully that rubs off on other players and we get the same passion and work-rate from everybody. Tonight we had to stand up and be counted.'

The modest raggy-arsed Paterson deflected the praise onto Brian Jensen. The Beast was back.

When Burnley met Oldham at Turf Moor in the next round, they had still to win a League game. Oldham came as the Division One leaders and in tremendous form whilst Burnley at this point were in the bottom three of the Championship. Strictly speaking then there was little to separate them. With attendances such as the 5,528 that night, there is always the question is anybody really interested in the Carling Cup? Very soon football fans everywhere would be enthralled by Burnley's Cup exploits.

The new 4–1–4–1 formation took the field and with just a small squad to choose from, there was no room for the 'second' team to be put out.

There was no 'second' team. At Crystal Palace the new tactics had kept a clean sheet. If it ain't broke don't fix it. That mantra might have been written for Owen Coyle whereas too many other managers tinker and fiddle and send out different players for different games using different tactics for different occasions. If Coyle did have a secret it was that of simplicity. Keep it simple, work hard and do it well. It was beginning to work.

The possible banana skin game was won 3–0. Oldham played well and their good football showed why they were top of their Division. Any early goal always settles the nerves and boosts the adrenalin. It came in the 12th minute. Paterson poached Burnley's second goal, then his own second, 10 minutes from the end. At this stage of the competition fans might say ah well it's only the Carling Cup, but a win and a clean sheet was just what was needed at the club. Coyle, simply by moving Alexander to the midfield defensive role, had paved the way for a season to remember.

'We scored three very good goals,' said Coyle after the match, adding:

> And all in all it's a pleasing night's work. It was always going to be a tricky tie—and Oldham are flying at the top of their Division and you could see there was a confidence within them. But I think we merited the victory on the night. Martin has shown he is a natural goalscorer who will get his share of goals. For him to go and get two more goals on the night will give him a terrific lift.

In the mid-fifties it had taken five games to settle an FA Cup tie between Burnley and Chelsea. In the next Carling game coming up, it would not be five games, but five penalties, that decided the result on a night of drama, excitement, shock and elation that shook the football world. The next round was in November away at Stamford Bridge. Fans smiled; of course they'd go down in numbers to support the club. Of course they'd make a night of it, enjoy the occasion, make the most of it, sing their hearts out . . . and then come back after a happy defeat. How on earth could mighty money-bags Chelsea lose to Burnley? Surely it was just a formality?

'We've got a nice easy week now, with Wolves away, Chelsea away and QPR away,' Coyle grinned. 'These will be real tests and it's a great week for those players to be looking forward to.'

If someone had said that two of them would be Burnley wins you'd never have said Chelsea would be one of them. But that is what happened. 'We'll respect Burnley,' said Chelsea's Frank Lampard. How hollow was that Burnley fans wondered. Routine words of course before the game, a tad condescending perhaps, they thought. Lampard probably never gave Burnley a second thought. After all, were Chelsea not invincible with an amazing home record stretching back over 86 games?

And so they set off, all 6,100 of them to the bright lights of London, essentially for nothing more than just a good night out on the town, and come what may the chance to see their team at a Premier ground. But God damnit they won and those who were there will never forget it as long as they live.

Chelsea 1 Burnley 1 was the highly creditable result of 120 minutes of League Cup football but the mile-thick icing on the cake was the bit that follows: Burnley won 5–4 on penalties. There was the familiar we'll give it a go expressions of knowing pluckiness from the players, but who were they kidding? The opening period of the game saw Chelsea imperious, and when Drogba struck with daunting efficiency just before half-time every Burnley fan in the ground could be forgiven for thinking this great occasion was going to turn sour. But the clarets hung on till half-time and in the second half began to dig themselves more firmly in the game, enjoying possession, passing crisply, moving sharply and growing in confidence all the while.

Burnley were hardly besieging the Chelsea goal but their focus on possession and movement did finally open up the home defence and crucially the Clarets made it count. Coyle had rung the first change on the hour and it was Akinbiyi on for Paterson. Akinbiyi executed his role to perfection running tirelessly and treading on a few Chelsea toes in the process. Eagles and Blake then combined in a moment of telepathic brilliance. Eagles darted for a gap through the inside-left channel that Blake had already seen. Robbie found him with a perfectly timed, weighted ball. Eagles swivelled and unleashed a stinging shot that Cudicini could only parry straight into the path of the oncoming Akinbiyi. The shed end held its breath as Akinbiyi took aim, but the big man was composure itself, calmly stroking the ball home to spark scenes of unhinged celebration.

The game became a battle of attrition between two equals; Burnley looked the side who wanted to play football, Chelsea the purveyors of a less sophisticated, direct approach. There was time for Alex to miss another gilt-edged opportunity before the referee blew time on open play.

As seems to be the convention the penalties were taken at the home end. The ever reliable Alexander slotted home. Lampard did likewise. Mahon who had come on for Blake netted with little fuss. Now the Beast made his presence felt. Wayne Bridge stepped up and placed his shot to Jensen's left but the Dane had read his intentions perfectly and he pawed away the shot with a firm hand. Chris Eagles cemented Burnley's advantage with a classy, top corner finish. Chelsea scored. Kevin McDonald stroked home with ease. Chelsea scored. Wade Elliott stepped up for the decisive kick to win the game but disastrously skied his effort. Aghast he walked back. Malouda levelled it at 4–4. Who would take the sudden death penalties? Duff stepped up and slammed it straight down the middle. 5–4. Kalou trudged forward and quickly set up his kick. He hit it firmly to Jensen's right but once again the Beast proved equal to the task athletically springing across and tipping the ball onto the post. A famous victory had been secured. (Courtesy of Phil Whalley *London Clarets* Magazine)

If the Bury night belonged to Jensen and Paterson, this one belonged to Jensen and Akinbiyi. It was the latter's first appearance in 12 games since Thompson had arrived. He had been linked with loan moves but Coyle had kept him in his plans. It was Akinbiyi's first goal of the season and last goal for Burnley; what a place and occasion to do it. He ripped off his shirt in front of the jubilant Burnley end. It could not have been better. He agreed afterwards that this had been one of the best nights of his career, but he had dreaded being called on to take a penalty in the sudden death phase. He stayed in the huddle of players in the middle looking at his feet dreading the tap on the shoulder and the words 'you're next'.

If Akinbiyi was a bag of nerves in the shoot-out, Jensen claimed he was not:

> I started to think about it five minutes before the end. It's big pressure but we had nothing to lose. I haven't lost a penalty shoot-out yet. We said beforehand just concentrate on putting the ball in the net and not change your mind—everyone said I would do the rest. No pressure then. Chelsea are probably the best side in the world but the longer we went into the game the more we started to feel we might have a chance. It's a big scalp, probably the biggest achievement in my career. Chelsea had lost one game in '86 and then we come here and turn them over. It was just a magnificent effort from everybody. When we see our name in the draw again, that will be absolutely unbelievable. Anything can happen in football. But we know the Championship is hard work, and that is our priority.

Of course Alastair Campbell was there:

> As Chelsea's Alex missed a total sitter towards the end of Wednesday's match, the fan standing in front of me turned and said, 'I know you don't do God, but He is playing for us tonight.' Then, when later we had beaten the multi-millionaires I thought I had died and gone to heaven. I have been to hundreds of Burnley games in the 47 years since I first saw them—when we were League Champions. So Wednesday night was a reminder of those great days when we took on, and beat, the best in the land. But it was sweet because we have had so many bad times in between. Sweeter than anything the new generation of Chelsea fan has ever known, or likely ever will. You need to suffer before you know real joy. We did something very few teams ever do at Chelsea, we went to attack. We didn't look scared. All of our players, some of them out of position, played well. Our Danish goalkeeper played out of his skin, and not just when saving penalties. And the fans played a part. Maybe now more of them will start going to games regularly and giving the team that bit of support every week.
>
> I don't condone the coin throwing at Drogba. But he was a bit daft to celebrate his goal how and where he did. And even dafter to throw the coin back into the crowd. 'More money than sense,' said my Believer in front of me.
>
> When Ade Akinbiyi equalised, I thought I was going to have a heart attack as fans piled on top of each other. And when it came to the penalties I discovered that the woman standing behind us was the mother of Michael Duff, taker of our first sudden-death spot-kick. I have never seen anyone looking as nervous as she did, as he walked up to take it, nor as relieved when it went in.
>
> By now the whole place just knew for sure that The Beast was going to

save the next one from Jon Obi Mikel. And so began a night of celebration and a million text messages. I know believers in God get a lot out of it. But on nights like Wednesday, by God, you know why people say football is the new religion. (Courtesy of Alastair Campbell)

Owen Coyle was ecstatic.

To come to Chelsea who are top of the League on merit and one of the favourites for the Champions League, and in terms of world football one of the elite clubs, to win the game, albeit on penalties, I think it shows you the magnitude of the effort the players have put in. And I think we've deserved it. I know that sometimes you ride your luck, but at 1–0 down it would have been very easy to feel sorry for ourselves and hide, but nothing could be further from the truth. I said before the game that we'd try to commit players forward at every opportunity and I think that we did that. We went down to a quality goal but we felt at half-time if we could stay in the game and retain a belief in what we could do individually that we had a real opportunity and that would give us a platform to mount a real challenge in the game. We did that and scored a very good goal. Brian has been outstanding all season and we said that if it got to a penalty shoot-out we felt he'd save a minimum of one. I've been there a few times myself and missed a few so I asked the players to stay true to where they they'd chosen to place the ball and not change their mind. I'm delighted for him because it's a reward for how hard he's been working in the games and training. The lads practise a bit every now and then for a bit of fun. Wade Elliott took one at the end of training on Tuesday and it ended up in the same place.

Aside from scoring the goal, Ade led the line, brought us up the park to get others on the ball, and that was a big turning point in the game. The backing we got from 6,100, you'd have thought there were 30,000 there. From a population of 70,000 to bring over 6,100 to London, with what's going on in the world economy when money's tight for everybody, to come and give that level of support I'm absolutely thrilled and delighted for them. People would have missed a day's work and there's lots of travel and cost. Hopefully it gives everyone in the town a lift.

It gave more than the town a lift. It struck a blow for the football little-guy everywhere. If Frank Lampard's words before the game about respecting Burnley rang a little hollow and were probably nothing more than just 'words' then he and his team certainly respected Burnley after that result.

By and large Owen Coyle had been getting his substitutions spot-on and the appearance of Akinbiyi changed the game. Coyle's respect for him shone through after the Chelsea game.

He's had an unbelievable career and moved for an awful lot of money. He's been out of the team due to the emergence of young Jay Rodriguez, and he's been nothing but a model professional. Every day he's in here, the team spirit is so important to him and he's there wishing the boys all the best and encouraging them.

85

Akinbiyi got his wish. It was Arsenal in the next round and the bonus of a home tie.

Capital Punishment 111 was the promotional spin and just along the road from the ground at one of the main traffic junctions a billboard advertised the forthcoming attraction. The names of Fulham and Chelsea were boldly crossed out beneath the heading. The accolades and attention were by now raining down on Coyle with newspaper features and articles in all the dailies. Cup shocks were nothing new for the 'mischievous manager', said one. 'Find a scalp or two by the wayside and it's a fair bet the wiry Scot has been thereabouts. As a whippet-like striker, he helped the Beastie Boys of Airdrie to the 1992 Scottish Cup Final.' Now, having outwitted Roy Hodgson and Luiz Felipe Scolari, he was gunning for Arsene Wenger and the kids he lets loose on nights like this.

As the game approached Coyle explained what he was trying to embrace. 'We have a couple of big new stands, but there are still some old seats in the main one. When we are close to filling the place it feels like a genuine football environment. When we play Arsenal the atmosphere will be brilliant.'

If Wenger had his youngsters, Coyle was equally proud of his— McCann, Rodriguez, McDonald and Paterson. 'I've some great young players and we'll take Arsenal on. I hope my lads want to play in the Premier League because I think they can.'

Ade Akinbiyi said what many were thinking. 'They are probably the best young kids that most people have seen. But they are not going to like coming to Turf Moor on a cold Tuesday night. We've come this far, we have nothing to lose and everyone has confidence in themselves. When we went to Chelsea we didn't lie back and we're not going to do that against Arsenal.' Martin Paterson too was determined that the visit of Arsenal was not just an occasion to rub shoulders and swap shirts.

December: a cold, thoroughly unpleasant Tuesday night in Burnley. It was bitter, icy, snow had fallen. Added to that there was a hostile, vocal crowd, baying for the defeat of these Arsenal upstarts. Before they even set foot on the pitch, they had to experience the spartan, cramped dressing rooms where the nearest thing to luxury was a coat hook—a million miles away from the five-star surroundings and comfort of the Arsenal dressing rooms. 'They haven't changed since the 70s,' quipped Chief Executive Paul Fletcher later. 'This isn't a hotel. They'll get a chair and a peg.'

And Burnley won.

The view from cloud nine looks pretty good and I don't want to come down yet. We DID beat Arsenal. I went out and bought five newspapers the next day and wasn't Wenger thoroughly ungracious. He was stunned to have lost and it was difficult to find anything complimentary he said about Burnley. How do you get the images of such a night to people who weren't there, or strangers in a pub or pals on the end of an email? For starters there has always been something special about big games at Turf Moor under the floodlights. Everything is sharper, brighter; it's theatrical, more urgent and vivid. Add to that a packed house, expectation and palpable apprehension, plus the growing belief as we scored one quite early on, kept them out, scored again in the second half and then thanks to Jensen almost coasted home. Our kids, McCann, McDonald and Paterson outshone their kids; it's as simple as that.

All through the game, the noise was awesome, the shouts, chants and songs never-ending. I know it's easy to say but I had the feeling all day that Burnley would win. The Arsenal kids must lose a game sometime, I thought, and the way things are going at the moment, it's on the cards that it will happen at Turf Moor. At the end of the day, that's all they are, kids. Sure they play lovely tippy-tappy football, delicate and intricate as lace embroidery. The patterns they weave are delightful but on this night the Burnley patterns had that bit of grit; that extra know-how, power and determination, plus Coyle's spirit and belief, notwithstanding the constant one-on-ones that Jensen had to keep out. At the moment he seems to be Superman in disguise. He was man of the match, but what about Alexander and his faultless display? McDonald with his two goals was a giant, Blake all guile and cunning; and Eagles, our very own Bambi, in the thick of everything. Paterson had them chasing shadows. McCann's surges must terrify retreating defenders. (Personal Diary December 3rd 2008)

The best bits from all the hacks made great reading:

A thrilling Cup upset on a cold northern night with the goalkeeper emerging as one of the heroes. Wasn't this how football used to be? Before the days of foreign owners, £5 hot dogs, and players with unpronounceable names, English football built its reputation on theatre such as that witnessed by 19,000 hardy souls at Turf Moor last night. Burnley's choice of pre-match music provided something of a throwback to times when they were rather more fashionable, as early arrivals to Turf Moor were treated to sounds from Talk Talk, Dexy's Midnight Runners and Tenpole Tudor. Heaven knows what Wenger's young players made of it in the away dressing room.

Arsenal's kids were simply outplayed by a Burnley team whose football was as splendid as anything that their illustrious rivals had produced in the Carling Cup this season and there cannot be a side more deserving of a place in the semi-finals of a competition that continues to rediscover itself after a long malaise . . .

Turf Moor is an intimidating place at the best of times. When a cosmopolitan bunch of kids plucked from around the world and brought to a finishing school at Arsenal constitute the opposition, however, the atmosphere turns positively hostile. As the cold bit and the crowd roared it almost felt as though lambs were being fed to bloodthirsty lions. . . .

Arsene Wenger can now add another grim northern town to his list of places not to visit. When he reflects on this chastening evening he will only recall a night when his stars of the future were given a footballing lesson by Owen Coyle's mixture of veterans, cast-offs and youngsters with a point to prove. But while Arsenal have often complained, sometimes with justification, of being kicked off the pitch, they can level no such accusations at Burnley.

Anchoring the midfield quintet was Graham Alexander. Old enough to have sired several of the striplings in the visitor's XI, the Scotland defender was quietly outstanding in the polyfilla role, plugging holes and closing down the gaps . . . .

Most of our time is spent enduring the cantankerous cynicism of the Premier League, but there's nowt as enriching as watching a team of fearless young players rejecting the joylessness of professional football and actually having fun. Burnley are a better side than some people realise and because of Didier Drogba's coin-throwing tendencies, they didn't get anywhere near the credit they deserved for beating a strong Chelsea side in the previous round.

The Emirates youngsters were supposed to deal with Burnley, fourth in the Championship, having already despatched Sheffield United 6–0 and Wigan 3–0. The full-time whistle brought the loudest roar of all. Little wonder the crowd chanted Coyle's name all night. After a year at the helm, he had got them dreaming of the double of promotion and a major trophy. Few better fairytales will be told this Christmas.

There was a time, of course, when this famous old stadium used to reverberate to the clamour of packed houses every week. Coyle and his players should be proud that they brought their own taste of it once more last night.

Burnley are into their first semi-final since 1983 and deservedly so. They needed their keeper Jensen to make no fewer than five one-on-ones but they played some superb, brainy football on the counter attack, scoring twice through the excellent McDonald and testing Fabianski on many occasions. Arsenal's kids were brilliant at times, impotent at others, but the Bible-sized Book of Football Clichés says they will have learned ten times more from this than they did while tonking Wigan and Sheffield United. All told a thoroughly enjoyable evening.

Owen Coyle told the Press after the game, looking calm, though inwardly no doubt well pleased:

All credit to the players because they are producing the goods. People will talk about individual players, but each and every one of them was magnificent from start to finish. We knew Arsenal were going to get chances. When they did, Brian produced great saves, but it wasn't about us scoring two goals. We had numerous chances and I knew if we stayed brave, in terms of passing and moving and committing players forward, we would have chances and so it proved. The last thing I said to them before they went out for the second half was to come back in with no regrets and that if we got to our maximum but were beaten by a better team we could accept that. We just didn't want to feel we let ourselves down, but with this group of players there was no chance of that happening, and from start to finish they gave everything they had to secure a magnificent night for this football club. People will talk about individual players but it was a team effort. From start to finish the players did everything I asked of them. We try to play in the right manner by getting the ball down and passing it. I like to think we are competitive but not over-physical and we try to play. Arsenal are the yardstick for all other clubs that want to play with freedom and terrific interplay and we had all those things.

Chairman Barry Kilby was ecstatic, but clear-thinking as ever put his cautious hat back on after the late-night Boardroom celebrations had subsided.

> We've had two fabulous Cup wins against Chelsea and Arsenal back-to-back, which have lifted everyone's spirits and gives you faith. The absolute thing we want to achieve is to get into the Premier League. It can work both ways. I've seen Cup runs act as a distraction but I've also seen them galvanise sides, and we've got to make sure it has a positive effect on our League performances. After all these years out of the top flight, promotion is still our major aim.

Capital Punishment 1V paired Burnley with Tottenham.

And Tottenham were a struggling side at the bottom end of the table, with Harry Redknapp the newest manager trying to bring some stability and better results. The semi-final was a two-legged affair. The first 45 minutes at White Hart Lane would see Burnley give one of the most dazzling displays of one-touch football seen at any ground. The return game at Turf Moor would provide one of the finest and most dramatic games in the club's history.

Alan Nixon in The *Daily Mirror* previewed the game, focussing on Owen Coyle:

> Burnley boss Owen Coyle has revealed how his own Wembley League Cup Final heartache made him a better manager and person. Coyle will have to upset a few of the Clarets' Carling Cup hopefuls tonight when he names the side to face Tottenham in the biggest game in the club's modern history. But he plans to handle it the right way after missing out on Bolton's Twin Towers date against Liverpool when omitted from the squad by Bruce Rioch—who left it to assistant Colin Todd to tell him. Coyle learned from that pain and sees it as a turning point in his life.
>
> He said: 'I played in every round for Bolton, but in his wisdom Bruce left me out of the Final. I laugh about it now but it helped me enormously in terms of my own development as a player and a coach. I remember Bruce went down to his home down south before the game and left Toddy to name the subs. Gudni Bergsson who had never even played for the club, was in ahead of me. I felt like walking out there and then but that would have let down my team-mates. Instead I put my suit and a smile on. I had to be mentally strong and that took me on ten-fold. I got back; I worked hard and a few weeks later was in the team and scored a winning goal at Wembley when Bolton won the promotion play-offs. Bruce later offered me a medal for the Final. He said it was because I had played in every game. I said apart from the one that mattered. I took the medal as it would have been dishonouring my pals if I had left it. It's in the house somewhere now. Nobody has to tell me how difficult it is to leave players out. I know that feeling. I have always been straight with my players when I leave them out.'
>
> Coyle's main selection problem at Spurs will be getting a side out. Kevin McDonald whose goals knocked out Arsenal, is a doubt, while Chris McCann could miss out at White Hart Lane. And, Coyle is without his skipper Steven Caldwell. (Courtesy of Alan Nixon)

Owen Coyle was pragmatic:

> We're under no illusions on Tuesday night, we're massive underdogs. If Tottenham Hotspur play to their maximum, and we play to our maximum, then you'd think they've got the better players. But what I do know is the group I've got will give you everything they've got to try to get a result so, hopefully, home advantage would play a part in the second leg. We have to make sure we give an accomplished performance and we keep ourselves right in that game; having said that—we've no designs on being negative. I think Harry will recognise we've got some very good offensive players and we like to try to get forward. That won't change.

Phil Whalley felt the result was slightly unfair:

> What was that about keeping ourselves in the home leg? Tottenham 4 Burnley 1 all but puts us out of the competition. The result appears to signal a one-sided affair, but frustratingly, this was not the reality as the Clarets took the game to Spurs and went in at the interval a goal to the good and well worth their lead. A second would have put the Clarets in an utterly dominant position. The chance arrived when Eagles found Blake on the penalty spot but his glancing header drifted just wide of the far post. Burnley were to rue that opportunity missed for Spurs came out in the second half and forced the Clarets back. The Clarets were left to contemplate the perils of switching off defensively in the face of international strikers. (Courtesy of Phil Whalley *London Clarets* magazine)

'Just blown away by a virtuoso second half performance,' said the Sky commentator: 'Jensen of all people gifting the second, poor marking from a deep corner, the first; statuesque defending gave them the third and an own goal the fourth—and all in 20 minutes. It doesn't get much worse than that.'

A deflated Owen Coyle faced the Press. He had seen a wonderful first half performance witnessed live on TV by millions. It had ex-players like England international Dave Thomas absolutely purring and quite unable to believe how good Burnley had been. 'This is how football should be played,' he said. Thomas had spoken to Redknapp in the morning and Redknapp knew that Burnley were good. But what followed in the second half was a team's worst nightmare when the opposition equalises almost immediately and then in a blistering spell, but aided by calamitous defending, then rams in three more goals. The wily Redknapp, as well as giving his team an absolute roasting at half-time, had made one significant change bringing on O'Hara. 'Triffic,' said Harry. 'It changed the game.'

The second leg night came and Burnley fans consoled themselves with the thought that they were at least in the last three of the Carling Cup. Manchester United versus Burnley or Tottenham Hotspur looked good up there on the giant TV screens. 'There's more chance of scaling Everest than overturning a 4–1 scoreline. We're a Championship team facing a three-goal deficit against a Premier League team. It's not even Everest, it's probably beyond that,' said Coyle. Nor was League form good. The last four games had all been defeats.

Conditions were atrocious, bitterly cold yet again, with swirling, gusting rain that battered the ground and soaked everyone to the skin as they queued to get in. It couldn't have been worse on the decks of a deep-sea trawler in the North Atlantic. It was a night so bad you wouldn't have put a dog in the back yard. And yet there was a game that was truly astonishing, filled with the magic of Cup football and the endeavour of a Burnley team whipped up by Owen Coyle that gave absolutely everything as one by one three goals went in.

Goal one: a devastating, Blake curling free kick from 30 yards that had everyone expecting the cross and left the keeper clutching at thin air. Goal two: a twisting, turning run by Blake into the penalty box that left defenders trailing in his wake and on their backsides before he slipped the ball across the area and there was McCann to slam it home. 2–0 and yes it was game on with time to spare to get the third. With just minutes remaining Blake sent over a long free kick, Carlisle powered in, the goalkeeper fumbled and there was young Rodriguez instinctively volleying it home. Turf Moor went utterly wild, the Theatre of Dreams and the Theatre of Ecstasy all rolled into one. It might have been a volcano erupting as three sides of the ground went berserk, and the noise must have reached the heavens. The impossible had suddenly become possible.

Burnley had needed three goals and they had scored three goals. It was now a matter of hanging on in extra-time. Burnley's away goal at Tottenham did not count double. Tottenham would have to score, would have to play better and the absurd rules of the competition gave them an extra 30 minutes to do just that. Over the two games Burnley had won, but rules are seldom based on fairness and common sense in this unjust world.

Previously as good as invisible with some abject individual performances, Tottenham would now have to make some effort. And they did, beginning to exploit the spaces left by a tiring Burnley. The heart and will remained, but legs and stamina by the end had gone. The crowd could see it happening. Chris Eagles was out on his feet. They could not hold on in extra-time and Coyle had made a rare mistake sending on the ineffective Akinbiyi to replace the younger Paterson who had thus far led Spurs a merry dance and kept the back four fully occupied. The ability to retain possession up front was gone and as the final minutes ticked by the ball came back at Burnley with increasing regularity.

In the final minutes as they ticked away so slowly, supporters seemed to sense that to hang on was just too much. Somehow Burnley contrived to lose possession on the Spurs left and they advanced swiftly leaving Pavlyuchenko in the middle to casually stroke the ball home. Defoe added a second almost as the whistle blew. At that moment fans knew the game was up and God knows how the players must have felt. The football gods make sure sometimes that heroics count for nothing and what one deserves and what one gets are two entirely separate things. Just three minutes away from a Wembley Cup Final, from lasting fame, that's all that remained until the Russian scored from the one and only flowing football move that Tottenham managed all night. Defoe, a living metaphor for the overpaid, modern player, who had done nothing all night, then scored an irrelevant second as Burnley players were close to collapse. Eagles in particular had run himself into the ground. The final whistle went, the Theatre of Dreams now the Theatre of Broken Hearts. Football can be so cruel filling people with joy on some days but despair on others.

The game will be remembered in Burnley for years to come, but cruelly the record books will simply say that Tottenham won 6–4 on aggregate. They will say nothing of how brave Burnley came so close with players and supporters alike leaving the ground distraught and heartbroken, stunned by those last three minutes and drained by the whole experience. The record books won't say how Eagles' name was chanted to support him in the final minutes when he was totally spent. They won't tell of little Robbie's masterclass, for that, truly, is what it was. They won't tell of heroic defending, the tireless running, the grit, passion and determination of every single Burnley player. They won't record that Jensen, in fact, came so close to saving Pavlyuchenko's shot with a fingertip. They won't record manager Redknapp's after-match words that this was the most uncomfortable night of his football life and that after the third goal went in, he thought they were dead and buried.

The editor of one of the main Spurs fans' websites wrote:

> Tonight's 6–4 aggregate win over Burnley was less a case of daylight—or moonlight—robbery, more one of the greatest, shameful heists in the history of British Football. This evening, in a pulsating Turf Moor, we didn't just steal our way to the Final, we made off with Burnley's most prized possessions, before sleeping with his wife, nabbing his job and scratching his brand new car. All of this in front of the local copper. It was that cheeky, it was embarrassingly undeserved.

'Pavlyuchenko and Defoe leave it late to break Burnley hearts' was the heading by Henry Winter in the *Telegraph*:

> As Burnley's magnificent fans made their way out of Turf Moor, muttering about how lucky Spurs had been and how proud they were of their claret and blue idols, a father tried to console his son. The lad's hair was damp from the rain and his face moist from the tears, 'Their legs went,' the father kept saying to the boy. 'They'd given everything.'
>
> The lad was heartbroken, his mind too confused to take in the reasons for Burnley's late collapse. He had seen Owen Coyle's Burnley players 'climb Everest' in the manager's opinion, overturning a 4–1 first-leg deficit through goals from Robbie Blake, Chris McCann and Jay Rodriguez. He had thrilled

to see Blake give one of those games of his life, a masterclass of enterprising wing-play. He had watched Joey Gudjonnson, Wade Elliott and McCann hand the atrocious midfield pair of Tom Huddlestone and Didier Zokora a lesson in possession.

The Carling Cup Final was within touching distance, three minutes away but exhaustion was invading Burnley legs, the game was stretching and suddenly the Premier League visitors finally awoke. Barring honourable exceptions like the disciplined and determined Michael Dawson, who battled on with an injury, Tottenham were a disgrace for 117 minutes. Most of the players were unworthy of wearing that famous shirt or taking home their fabulous wage-packets. Luka Mosric resembled a hiker who had wandered in off Pendle Hill, attracted by the bright lights. Chris Gunter was constantly bypassed by Blake. Ben Alnwick, a promising keeper, was a bundle of nerves. Spurs were a mess. Sandra Redknapp could have played a number of positions and been an improvement.

'I was stood there with a couple of minutes to go, thinking it could be the most embarrassing moment of my football life,' reflected Harry Redknapp. As he peered through the rain, Roman Pavlyuchenko pounced, making up for a dreadful earlier miss with a neat finish. Seconds later, Jermain Defoe raced in and Burnley's dream was truly destroyed by a strike-force that cost nearly £30million. Burnley never deserved this denouement and if the sporting fates have any conscience they will guide Coyle's side to Wembley in the play-offs.

'It was cruel,' said Coyle of the way Burnley were so brutally denied. 'It is twists and turns that make us all love football, although I don't love it tonight. The lads are distraught in the dressing room but I told them to go out with their heads held high.'

Quite right. Arriving with such a comfortable-looking advantage, Spurs had known Burnley would throw everything at them. On a magical night of Cup football when Burnley did the Championship proud, Turf Moor was rocking as Coyle's men dismantled Redknapp's side. Even the weather played its part in scripting some of the drama, a raw wind biting into Tottenham's faces in the first half. Within a minute all the players were soaked, the chill wind lowering body temperatures. This was a rain-hit, flood-lit night when players' characters, strong or meek, shone through and Harry Redknapp will worry about the competitive instincts of certain players in contrast to Coyle's. David Bentley never imposed his undoubted talent. The former Blackburn Rovers player was venomously booed when he dared clatter Chris Eagles, the Ronaldo of Turf Moor.

Tottenham were poor. When the sluggish Benoit Assou-Ekotto overhit a back pass, Alnwick managed to scramble back and push the ball away. The Spurs fans in the cricket field end were horrified, screaming at the players to raise their game, a request ignored until late on. Coyle had told his players to be patient, to keep pushing, keep probing, because chances would come. When Jonathan Woodgate fouled Marin Paterson 25 yards out to the right of Alnwick's goal, Burnley were granted a prime opportunity. Blake placed the ball down while the inexperienced Alnwick demanded a two-man wall. Modric and O'Hara hardly represented the most formidable of obstacles, even combined, and Blake almost nonchalantly curled his free kick around them, the ball easily beating Alnwick at his left-hand upright.

As Blake sped away in celebration, both Modric and O'Hara turned and gave Alnwick withering looks. Having organised the wall, the keeper really should not have been beaten at his near-post but Blake's brilliance also needed applauding. Alnwick has real potential but it was little surprise to find Spurs being linked with Chelsea's Carlo Cudicini and Newcastle's Steve Harper, although Redknapp said he knew nothing of interest.

Redknapp gave his players a rocket at the break, a theme that continued in the 50th minute when a firework launched from the Jimmy McIlroy Stand landed on the pitch and will doubtless be mentioned in Mark Halsey's report to the Football Association. A moment of profligacy from Gareth Bale, the Welshman skewing his shot wide, did not appear too costly but then came McCann. Turf Moor has seen some drama down the years, has seen the roof raised on many an emotional occasion but the noise in the 73rd minute was unbelievable. Blake began the move, twisting Spurs defenders into the ground, leaving Chris Gunter and Dawson totally bemused before crossing for McCann to make it 4–3 on aggregate and Turf Moor screaming itself hoarse.

Spurs were shell-shocked, riddled with errors and uncertainty, allowing Burnley back in again. When Alnwick fumbled another free kick from Blake, Rodriguez calmly swept the ball into the net to force extra-time. But then came Pavlyuchenko and Defoe. The tears began to flow for Burnley but really their eyes should glisten with pride. (Courtesy of Henry Winter)

Alastair Campbell wrote:

Our Wembley dream was dashed by daft rules. There are few more numbing feelings than one that wakes up with you in the morning after an experience of punctured euphoria. Text messages can ping in their consolatory clichés about feeling for you, better team lost, so close, blah, blah, but they cannot erase the reality. Burnley lost, Spurs won; they're going to Wembley, we're not.

Our manager, Owen Coyle, said that for Burnley to turn round the three-goal deficit after losing the first leg 4–1 was football's Mount Everest. We went and climbed it, leading 3–0 after 90 minutes; this, having already scaled Ben Nevis, then K2 and Kilimanjaro in the form of wins against Fulham and Chelsea away and Arsenal at home. And what happened as we stood at the summit? Up pops the bizarre rule, seemingly unique to the Carling Cup, that away goals only count double after extra-time, and penalties come into play only in the event of both ties being identical, reversed scores. Logicians please advise.

Sky's Andy Gray must be paid to be neutral, but his messages suggest that he was far from it once our third goal went in. Other than diehard Spurs fans, I don't think there was a neutral left as extra-time neared its end, Wembley beckoned and the thousands at Turf Moor felt a beautiful, rain-lashed joy descend to recall glory days of old and push away all thoughts of economic pain today. Even Sam Allardyce, manager of our closest rivals, Blackburn, was rooting for us.

'Keep playing as you have been and you're there,' texted Alex Ferguson, who will now line up against Harry Redknapp in the Final. Oh how our players tried, but tired legs and, finally, a bit of multisquillion-pound class from the Spurs strikers, saw the dream snatched as quickly, and as dramatically, as it had arrived. Even as the players trudged off, Burnley fans continued to roar their support, but it was a roar of pain and pride, bereft of the euphoria of victory.

Redknapp at least had the good grace to look embarrassed as he shook Coyle's hand and the post-match phone-ins were flooded with Spurs supporters saying that they didn't deserve to win. In which case all that remains to be done—a long shot I know—is to appeal to their sense of fairness. If Harry truly wants to concentrate on avoiding relegation, if he really is a man of the people, surely he has to do the decent thing. Stand aside. Let Burnley take their rightful place in the Final, where the people want us. Take his overpaid, underperforming superstars on a sabbatical—and take the numpty who invented the Carling Cup away-goals rule with them. (Courtesy of Alastair Campbell)

Burnley might have been forgiven for slipping into despondency after the game. The fairy tale had ended. There were tears in the dressing room as they dragged themselves inside from the raging weather and the cruel destruction of what they deserved. The close-ups of their faces on Sky said it all. Next up was Premier side West Brom away in the FA Cup. If an exhausted, dejected Burnley, running on empty, had lost that game 6–0 it would have been no surprise. But this, the Band of Brothers, was made of sterner stuff. Burnley fans were there in their thousands again showing their feelings and loyalty. They were not disappointed.

'If the sporting fates have any conscience they will guide Coyle's side to Wembley in the play-offs,' wrote Henry Winter. The sporting fates, for once, looked down kindly, and eventually, did exactly that.

8

'HERE FOR AS LONG AS THE CLUB WANT ME'

Until two thirds of the way through December, it looked as though the Clarets were well established in the top six, notwithstanding the strange 2–3 defeat at Barnsley when officials' decisions ruined the night. But after that bizarre night at Oakwell a run of four wins and a draw restored confidence and optimism. One of those wins had been a superb 3–1 result away at Coventry where Robbie Blake, after scoring, revealed a pair of bright red underpants with the words Bad Beat Bob inscribed on the back; a reference to his poor card playing. At Sheffield United, usually an absolute graveyard for Burnley, Eagles had a brilliant game, scored, and there was a terrific 3–2 win.

Prior to the Sheffield win Owen Coyle had been particularly pleased by a win at QPR immediately after the amazing night at Chelsea. In fact the QPR win gave him more satisfaction than the victory at Stamford Bridge. It was where Mahon scored a rare Burnley goal. Cotterill had bought him and referred to him as 'the jewel in the crown'. Fans had waited to see sustained polished performances from this hugely skilled player but alas there was always less to actual Mahon performances than the hype suggested. Injuries had blighted his career. It was another game when manager Coyle brought on attackers not defenders when making substitutions, and as often as not the substitute would score a key goal.

Three points looked unlikely on the half hour as Burnley trailed to Dexter Blackstock's opener and were having to defend stubbornly to keep the deficit to just the one. At this moment Blake latched onto a Gudjonnson pass. It looked at first as though Blake was being shepherded out to the left, but with little backlift he hit a left-foot shot from the edge of the box that flew into the corner with such power and precision that Cerny in the QPR goal was motionless. Rarely can Robbie have connected so sweetly. That was the cue for a complete change in the game's pattern. Suddenly the Clarets were the fluent, footballing side that had become the talk of the Division and beyond. The half-time break did nothing to interrupt the flow of the Clarets. Between themselves, Eagles and Blake were speaking a football language of a higher order before Eagles himself was crocked by a jealous QPR boot. No matter, Mahon, once himself a cultured young starlet tipped for great things, replaced Eagles and almost immediately won the game, instinctively firing a half-volley home from the edge of the box after Blake's effort had been charged down. Owen Coyle emphasised the importance of this result over that of Wednesday. (Courtesy of Phil Whalley, *London Clarets* magazine)

Commented Coyle:

This might sound bizarre but I'll take more enjoyment and pleasure from this. When I was manager at St Johnstone, we beat Rangers in a quarter-final and on the Saturday we had a poor result. It would have probably left a sour taste if we hadn't won after the result and performance we had during the week. I certainly tried to get the point across to my players how important it was, because if we'd lost there's every chance we could have fallen out of the top six. By winning, it helps you enjoy even more what you did during the week.

A little later in the week, in a rare moment of almost self-congratulation, he added:

I took a gamble in the summer because the Championship is known for churning managers out for fun. We spent the money on younger players who we think can grow within the team. We make no claims about it. There are far bigger clubs with financial clout, but we're very positive in our outlook. We try to win each game, and we'll see where that takes us come the end of the season. I don't think in pre-season that Burnley would have been one of the names you'd have put in there. But we certainly had belief. We know we have a group of players with honesty and integrity, and ability to go with that.

The younger players had been Eagles and Paterson at over a million each, yet in fact, it had been the arrival of the older Steve Thompson that had provided the missing piece of the jigsaw. Thompson was by no means individually brilliant but he had a range of skills, and he provided something up front that had been lacking—the bustling, mobile front-line man who could win the ball in the air and disturb bigger defenders. And he could score goals at crucial times. Cardiff City, his previous club, came to Turf Moor on a cold December night and played Burnley off the park but thanks to Thompson Burnley somehow came out of it with a 2–2 draw.

Coyle was livid after the defeat at Barnsley, another place where Burnley wins were hard to remember:

There's no getting away from how big a turning point the second goal was. I knew during the game and I've seen it since on TV, that they have three players at least two yards in advance of our back line. Then it hits his arm as he puts it in. They can't tell me he wasn't interfering because he scored and he's at least two yards offside. It's just a bad, bad decision, and it's a hard one to take because we certainly merited a result out of it. When all's said and done, we should certainly have achieved a result out of that game, even being 3–0 down, because I thought the last half hour we were absolutely magnificent. This group of players don't know defeat.

Another result that infuriated him was the 1–1 at Charlton when a perfectly good Paterson goal was disallowed:

> For me it's very simple. When the ball was played through, Martin Paterson looked to be in an offside position in the first phase of play. But as we all know, the linesman didn't raise his flag until the ball reached that player. That never happened. The Charlton player then knocked it on, so in effect played Martin Paterson onside. The referee recognised that and over-ruled his linesman and gave the command to play on with the advantage. It seemed a bit bizarre to pull it back then and rule it out. I think it was a mistake.

Some games are defining. The 1–0 home win over Reading was one of them during the season. Affected by injuries, Burnley were outplayed for long stretches but Jensen was unbeatable. Injuries were such that midfielder McCann played centre half for a long spell in the second half. With home fans biting their fingernails and thinking it was a matter of time before Reading deservedly scored, with 9 minutes remaining Blake took possession from Elliott and moved to the edge of the box. He was surrounded by Reading players, but somehow threaded a low shot through a host of players and into the net. On this occasion Coyle was beaming (and also made a mental note of the outstanding Bikey in the Reading side).

> It's a magnificent three points I've got no doubts about it. Given the circumstances before the game and indeed during the game, it summed up everything I know about this group of players—about their desire and the spirit they've got for each other and how keen they are to do well for themselves and the football club. Brian made a couple of big saves in the second half and they hit the woodwork but I think on the balance of play we had as many chances as Reading had, and a sublime finish from Robbie, which we know he's capable of. We know the quality.

The smallness of Coyle's squad was well documented. That it accomplished so much in 2008–09 was, in short, miraculous. It was a season of 61 games and by and large it was a group of just 18 players who played the majority of them. The game at Sheffield United on December 6th was an illustration of just how stretched the squad was. It was a makeshift side that Coyle was forced to put out. Carlisle was unavailable so Duff was to play with Caldwell in the middle but in the warm-up he injured himself. It meant a left back went to centre back, a right back moved to left back and a midfielder played at right back. Added to which, key midfielder McCann was also missing. When Sheffield equalised Burnley's fortuitous first goal Burnley fans could be forgiven for thinking 'here we go, the usual defeat looms'. But, with just minutes of the first half remaining Eagles went down under a challenge and Alexander slammed home the penalty. Never one to make defensive substitutions Coyle replaced Blake of all people with the rookie forward Alex Macdonald. Gudjonsson headed a Sheffield effort off the line and then Eagles scored a delightful third with a low shot that went nicely into the far corner. A Sheffield second gave a few final anxious moments but Burnley held out for the first win at Bramall Lane since 1973. With the team that Coyle had cobbled together it was a remarkable win. But, Coyle was prompted to comment on the resources available:

> I don't know if the Board will look at it, and think we can soldier on with that, but I know that whenever they're asked to play they'll look to do their very best. That's the most satisfying result of the season. Before the game, everything that could conspire against us did, with Clarke Carlisle suspended, Chris McCann falling ill and being left at home to stop the bug spreading and then Michael Duff getting injured in the warm-up. In the end we had a right winger at right back, a right back at left back and a left back at centre half. But each and every one of them showed they can play against a side that will be there at the shake-up at the end of the season.'

The last part was prophetic. The long and winding Championship road was taking the club towards Wembley and the ultimate showdown with Sheffield United.

Eagles commented on Coyle after the game:

> I came here because myself and my agent thought he was the type of manager that would push me, and that's what I need. For a manager to encourage me and say the things he is saying about me is a dream, because without him playing me I wouldn't be making a name for myself. It's a win-win situation and I just love playing for the club at the moment.

Chris Eagles was an enigma, a player of undoubted skill, but inconsistent, brilliant one minute, losing the ball with a poor first touch the next. As a player who loved to take players on, there were inevitable occasions when he lost the ball, part and parcel of being a winger. In the old days of football that was accepted by a football crowd. In the modern game it induces groans of exasperation from a crowd and managers. And not being the most physical of players he frustrated spectators who wanted every player in the team to be able to win every fifty-fifty ball. On his day, he could be unplayable; on others critics would nod their heads and understand why he had been sent out on loan deals from Manchester United. So far he had never fulfilled the early glistening promise but nevertheless was a real asset with Coyle bringing out the best in him.

There were two more wins before the five-game rot set in. Burnley 3 Southampton 2 was on December 13th, followed by a 2–1 win away at Bristol City. The Southampton game was a strange one. Burnley raced into a 3–0 lead within 15 minutes and it looked like a cricket score was on the cards. By the end they were grateful for the points. It meant there had been four wins out of the last five games and Burnley sat in fourth place with a very impressive 43 points, six points clear of the side in sixth place. With the ongoing Carling Cup success this was a happy, buoyant club. The Press were singing Burnley's praises, and Eagles was coming in for a lot of attention. Burnley usually sold a player in January. Was all this leading up to a bid for him from a bigger club and a quick profit? He was giving match-winning performances, said Coyle, announcing that he was sure he could go back and play in the Premiership. Joey Gudjonnson was another player in the spotlight after some sterling performances and goals. Scouts were frequent visitors to Burnley games.

Coyle was philosophical: 'It's never a problem for me if other clubs admire our players. It's all hypothetical but we have invested in this group for years to come and we want to see them grow together.' These words were interesting, talking about 'years to come' and 'we want to see them grow together'. Burnley fans realised that Coyle was becoming a hot property and would not be at Burnley forever but words such as these gave fans reason to believe that here was a man who would give the club more than just the one further year that he would remain in office. Statements like this gave a belief that he saw a future for himself at Burnley, if not forever, at least for a reasonable period. There would be more words later which fans found pleasing, convincing them that the manager was genuinely binding himself to the club and town.

'The fans believed every word he uttered,' Paul Fletcher later wrote in the *Lancashire Telegraph*. If the Carling Cup had provided the glory before Christmas, in the League Burnley began to struggle, and spanning the Christmas period five consecutive defeats severely dented their position in the top six. Supporters groaned but were simultaneously philosophical. Did this not always happen at this time of year? How often had a promising start folded at the halfway stage? It was nothing new and was part of the burden of being a Burnley supporter.

The first shock lay round the corner on Boxing Day. It was a day for consolidation, a Christmas win, three more points and back home for turkey sandwiches and leftover Christmas Pud. Unfortunately Barnsley turned up with different ideas and a 2–1 win gave them the points. Coyle tinkered for once and Burnley included Blake, Eagles and Elliott, a combination that was doomed to failure. After all the praise and publicity that had come his way, fate being what it is, Eagles had a nightmare miss that might have changed the game had he scored.

Next was Doncaster away, another side that the previously rampant Burnley would have put away with anything like a normal performance. The performance was anything but, with a display that was simply dismal. To compound matters Caldwell was sent off for a rugby tackle and the Doncaster first goal was a giveaway when Carlisle and Jordan totally gifted Doncaster a simple goal. Doncaster thus far had spent most of the season in the bottom three. 3,000 baffled Burnley fans wondered what was going on and where was the Burnley that had been so impressive until now.

'This was an extremely disappointing performance and one that filled me with dread,' wrote Julian Booth. 'If we can't finish off weak opposition like this, then the play-off dreams will just disappear over the horizon. I just hope that Coyle can work his magic and invigorate the boys and get us back to winning ways.'

Coyle remained upbeat:

> It has not been an enjoyable few days. The players are annoyed with themselves because they never reached the standards they have set. We know that within our team we have potential match-winners, but we have to make sure that everyone individually is doing their job and collectively as a unit, we get to the standards we've set previously and are not gifting goals. I said to the players as disappointing as the last two games have been, you're in the top six coming to the end of the year, you're in the semi-finals of the Carling Cup, so they've got an unbelievable second half of the season coming up.

The League defeats continued to mount up however, and Barry Kilby had been correct in his earlier comments that Cup runs can be a distraction. It wasn't that Burnley were putting every effort into the Cup games at the expense of League games, but what was happening was that successful Cup games (now the FA Cup as well) were masking the impact of accumulated League defeats. Maybe after the fourth defeat it was sinking in and after the fifth, fans realised there was a crisis and that more of the same meant it was back to the days of disappointment. And, on top of all that, Brendan Flood's business empire, Modus Ventures, was in serious financial trouble. The days of Flood dipping into his and the Modus coffers to support a manager were ending, which meant that Coyle, desperate for new players to shore up the creaking squad, had no access to further funding. He would refer to it several times.

Flood described this early period of his declining fortunes:

> I had openly shared the fact that my fortunes were becoming negatively affected by the property market and informed the Board that they might not be able to rely on me for every cash call from here on . . . One or two of the directors were questioning the judgement in spending so much money on Chris Eagles and Martin Paterson. The implication was that if I'd known how the property market was turning, we should have stored the money we had received on the sale of Kyle Lafferty. So, when we met in November (2008) to discuss our cash requirements for January, economic conditions were bound to impinge negatively on our discussions. Cash was tight all round and I had the feeling that some of my colleagues were running for cover . . . I suggested that we may need a cash injection of one million pounds from existing directors and I saw it as my responsibility to find the balance . . . But we needed to look among ourselves to find £1million . . . As I passed the discussion round the table, to a large extent it was met with some reticence. One million pounds is a big ask at the best of times but in the middle of a ferocious economic downturn anybody would baulk at the prospect of taking any sort of risk.

Flood's measured account of the impending crisis in fact gives no real sense of how serious the financial situation was. Nor does it give the real picture of how some directors were dissatisfied with the decision making processes and their exclusion from them. This was a small club with a squad and wages in excess of income and for years this had been an extremely cautious Board. In truth the club was losing money badly, and to come was a debt-induced transfer embargo that was kept well quiet at the time but not before Coyle did manage to arrange the loan signing of Rhys Williams a full back from Middlesbrough. The income from the Carling Cup run and TV coverage therefore went not to the manager but to prop up the creaking bank account and by the end of April the club would be bordering on real problems.

The next defeat of the five was Burnley 0 Swansea 2. Duff conceded a penalty and was sent off. The general performance was lacklustre. The place in the top six was lost. Supporters were resigned to another mid-table finish at the end of the season and Owen Coyle was not best pleased with his players:

Coyle gave his favourite mantra about downcast players being no good to him:

> The penalty was a big moment in the game, but we never started well enough—I don't want to hide behind that. It's disappointing but if they want to feel sorry for themselves, as I've said before, they're no good to me. With the nature of football, we know you're always going to get that smack, and the sooner you get out of it the better. It's time to look for characters and who has got the mental strength to come through it. And when they do there's no doubt we'll be up and running, but we want that to be sooner rather than later. We've played a lot of games, but I don't want anyone hiding behind that because we've got Graham Alexander out there at 37 who I can hang my hat on every week because I know exactly what I'm going to get from him. It's far too easy in football to look for excuses. The bottom line is we've not had enough players in the last few games that have played to the standard we've previously set, and they have to look within themselves to resurrect that, otherwise maybe the boys who haven't had a chance, or the younger kids need to play.

A Cup win in a re-played game with QPR resulted in a 2–1 win, with a last minute winner in extra-time. 'It would have been a travesty if we hadn't got through,' said Coyle. Maybe the win would kickstart the faltering League programme. Unfortunately the next game was at Preston North End a place where Burnley had seldom done well or had the breaks in recent times. This time would be no different with two refereeing decisions going against Burnley both of which resulted in penalties. For the first, Jensen took the ball from the feet of the inrushing Elliott. The latter contrived a dive, trailing a foot that totally fooled the referee. Subsequent replays confirmed the choreography of the fall. Blake equalised with a stunning free kick, and then with just five minutes remaining another penalty was awarded. The burly Parkin, who had already had hold of Caldwell's shirt bustled and shoved into the defender. Off-balance his momentum caused the ball to strike his arm. To the fury of the away support the penalty was given. Two bad decisions thus caused defeat number four and Burnley stayed in 7th place.

Coyle was incensed. 'You guys have seen it,' he said, aiming his remark at the Press. He continued:

> Please report on it and call it the way you've seen. But if I start getting involved in it you end up just harming yourself and I think we've been punished enough today. Robbie Blake scored a wonder goal and we were in charge and looked all set to go on and win it. For that to happen with the second penalty award it really is beyond belief. Preston will know they've been fortunate today.

Steve Cotterill was on the Sky panel at the game and afterwards spoke to Brendan Flood, possibly tongue in cheek, to tell him that he thought it was a good Burnley team. 'Nine out of that team were mine you know,' he told him. Flood later mentioned this to coach Steve Davis. 'He wouldn't have said that if we were near the bottom,' commented Davis.

The games came thick and fast. Next up was the 'win' over Tottenham in the Cup immediately followed by the 2–2 FA Cup draw at West Brom. The problem was that the four League defeats in a row were forgotten, the seriousness buried by the agony and heartache of the Carling exit after such a wonderful performance, and then the great away day at The Hawthorns. Against the Premier sides Burnley were back to their best. A midweek game at Watford would surely halt the run of League defeats.

> Tonight was the Watford we all despise, consistent gamesmanship, time-wasting and (the only thing they do with some subtlety) incessant fouling. The evening started poorly when Burnley were caught flat-footed at the back with just two minutes on the clock. As the half progressed we became increasingly worried by the antics of Carlisle who seemed to be at a different game to anyone else. Burnley continued to chase the game hard but with 12 minutes to go Carlisle misdirected a routine headed clearance into the path of Harley who fed Priskin who finished neatly. Game over: Priskin's last minute solo effort was a garnish the home side didn't deserve. The consensus after the game was that Alexander was missed in his defensive midfield role, the absence of which fully exposed the limitations of Carlisle. That's five straight League defeats now, and down to 9th. (Courtesy of Phil Whalley *London Clarets* magazine)

Glorious in the Cups but woeful in the League was another apt summary; the team clearly in need of a break with several players running on empty but with a squad too small to allow them respite. Coyle let rip:

> They know exactly my feelings on it. When all's said and done, if they are not going to do it, then it might have to be a kid (a threat already made but not carried out). It might have to be something as drastic as that. I'm not going to stand back and watch that defending week in and week out. At 42, I can probably defend better than that. It's just not on. We lost a goal within a minute when Chris McCann slipped, but having said that, the defending for it was really bad. You could have driven a double-decker bus

through the middle of the defence when the lad played the pass. There's no getting away from how poorly we defended as a team, it was abysmal and it was there for everybody to see where the problems we've been having lie. People have to be really clued in to what they're doing. We're not going to hide behind anything. The bottom line is we did not defend well enough and we paid a heavy price.

At this point it would be fair to think that Coyle saw all the previous good work going up in smoke. Plus, the local Press had printed an interview in which the manager had hinted that he felt that money for new players that might have been made available following the Cup runs had been withheld. In the light of Brendan Flood's business problems and consequent lack of ability to invest further in the club, plus some directors being allegedly reticent about giving further financial support and feeling somewhat disgruntled anyway at lack of decision-making involvement, Owen Coyle might well have been forgiven for thinking 'why am I bothering', being somewhat dissatisfied with his lot.

His frustration was clear:

> We can't stand still. We have to keep on striving to improve and that's the difficulty we've got just now with the way the credit crunch is everywhere. Everyone's been hard hit by that, but we probably have more than most clubs because everything I'd put in place in terms of the development of the whole football club, had had to be put on hold. I've identified three or four (players), which I hope nobody else has. I can't do anything on it just now but maybe come the summer when things change financially I might be able to make inroads. We're not in a position to purchase anyone in terms of a fee. We've asked about a few of them on loan and been priced out of them. We're still talking to different clubs about various players, but if someone's demanding X amount of pounds and we've not got that then we can't give it.

With the Brendan Flood investments and loans at a standstill, Coyle was now experiencing the constraints that had so badly affected Steve Cotterill in his first two years and Stan Ternent during his final season. He continued:

> This team will improve. I've said it before that there are a number of things I'd love to add to it. Obviously I can't do it at this present time but I know in my mind what I want to be doing at the football club. I know how to take it on and I know what I need to take it on. It's just being able to get the finance. It's come at the worst possible time for us because when you see what we did and the position we'd put ourselves in, that was the time I believe, for you to improve things while you were in a very good position. But if the finance isn't there, sometimes there have got to be sacrifices made and we just need to get on with it.

Exactly what Coyle meant by sacrifices was never made clear but he was certainly mindful of the money generated by the Carling Cup. Flood responded in the Press announcing that he was still looking to be involved long-term and nothing had changed. He was quite forthright: 'Anybody who has got their head screwed on will be more cautious, so I would be more cautious than before.'

The only action Coyle was able to generate was the emergency loan signing of full back Rhys Williams from Middlesbrough. Forgotten man Gabor Kiraly was sent out on loan to Germany thereby freeing up some money saved in wages.

Five League defeats on the trot, some dreadful performances, the club cash-strapped, no money for serious reinforcements other than one loan, supporters resigned to the inevitable slump, a major credit crunch; and money-man Brendan Flood's Modus business in serious decline. Another defeat was simply unthinkable. Next to come was bottom-of-the-table Charlton. January 31st and this was already the 40th game of the season for the creaking squad.

Perhaps it was at this game that the football Gods came to Burnley's rescue, or the silver angel returned to Coyle's shoulder. Burnley 2 Charlton 1 had 14,404 supporters, players, management and directors all breathing a sigh of relief. Charlton led 1–0 until the 76th minute. Defeat number six was looming but Coyle's substitutions and shuffle once more changed the game. On came big Kev McDonald and Steve Thompson. The latter equalised in the 76th minute, the celebrations joyous. With Coyle urging them for the win the referee added **six** minutes of extra-time. Charlton boss Phil Parkinson was incensed, and even more so when Thompson struck again in the fifth minute of injury time. Is there anything that causes more celebration than a winner so late? If there are goals that change or turn a season round, was this the one? People would point to the win away at Blackpool later in the season as a key game, but this win over Charlton was up there in the list of pivotal games. Even better, from this point on until the end of the season there would only be two more defeats.

Coyle was understandably delighted:

> The courage and bravery the players showed was tremendous. There was real bravery in their performance. We have the courage of our convictions and it was important to win today. We have played 40 games and are just two points away from the play-offs. It would have been easy to hide at 1–0 down but my players don't know when they are beaten. We have a great spirit at this football club.

After the next game and a Cup replay against West Brom with a 3–1 victory the manager waxed lyrical about striker Steve Thompson who had scored four times in two games, and then in general about what was in prospect.

> Sometimes as a striker you get little spells when everything goes in for you. In some of the games before he's been outstanding and he's hit the post or the keeper's made great saves. It's a just reward for all his hard work.

Regardless of whether they're young or inexperienced I think it's important to speak to them all on a daily basis so that they know the role they've got to play at the club . . . We're probably two thirds of the way through and you've not realised it because it's gone really quickly. We're three points behind the play-offs with a game in hand and we want to be in the mix and run that hand in hand with the FA Cup campaign. So we have to really look upon this as the season starting now. Let's kick on and make a real go of it. It counts for nothing if they don't keep on delivering those results. The next two games are massive. We're probably underdogs in both of them but that's something you relish, and we'll have to get to our best.

They certainly gave of their best at Birmingham and the first 45 minutes saw a superb performance of skill, and pass and move that totally dominated the half. Ahead in three minutes there were no more goals although Burnley could have been four or five ahead by the break. But a Caldwell clanger gifted Birmingham an undeserved equaliser.

Coyle returned to his theme of times being hard and more bodies being needed. All managers make these noises and all directors usually switch off their hearing aids. But, one wonders whether the tolerance of Brendan Flood is starting to be stretched a little. Fighting as he will be to keep his property business healthy in the current climate, Flood could presumably be forgiven for pointing out to the manager that he was given a clear budget with no guarantee of any extra, and he's spent it. The club has lost so much money for so long now that a run to every Cup Final going still wouldn't balance the budget. (Phil Whalley *London Clarets* magazine)

At the end of February a defeat at Turf Moor inflicted by a strong, bustling Sheffield Wednesday was a major upset. Burnley dropped to 9th. Coyle had another grumble about lack of finances curtailing any possibility of loan signings. With the next game away at Blackpool, he talked of having shot themselves in the foot, the need to re-focus, show character and belief, score a few goals and keep it tight at the back. And then: 'Ideally we'd like to try to get a couple in but finances dictate we're not able to do it, so we just have to get on with it.'

At this point there was a degree of speculation about his future at Turf Moor. Bolton was a name that cropped up and what followed was an interview and statements that would be hurled back at him within months. Of course what he said were in no way promises, but nevertheless they were clear and unequivocal. Football fans have long memories and above anything else it was these statements that would result in him eventually being branded Judas.

There's been all sorts of speculation but I've no intention of going anywhere. We're not anywhere near where I want to be in terms of taking the club on, and I've said that to the lads. But our focus is on staying together. I didn't bring players into this football club to be up and leaving at the first opportunity. That's never going to be the case. I'm not upping and leaving at the drop of a hat. I'm here for as long as the club want me, and they know that, so much so that Brendan, the chairman and I have had a chat about it, about making it [my contract] a bit longer, and we'll deal with that at the right time. I'm very on board for that, because we have ambitious plans to take the club on. I want to be here, I don't want anybody to be distracted, there's a job to be done here; that's what we're concentrating on. We want to develop a team that will serve the club well in years to come.

As announcements go, it was emphatic and unmistakable. 'I'm here for as long as the club want me.' It was upon these words that the shock and condemnation would be founded when he left just nine months later. People listened to him eagerly and believed that here was a man who meant what he said and would not desert them. They were avid followers of a man who talked about journeys and adventures. 'We've come on in leaps and bounds from when we first came through the doors, and it's still very much a work in progress.'

Some games have defining moments. One was the home game against Charlton and Thompson's last minute goal. The next was away at Blackpool. This was a night when the skies raged with winds so strong that it was almost impossible to play any kind of proper football; when everything was a lottery against the wind, and when the ball would not stay still for the goalkicks. Coyle shuffled his small squad, the sacrificial lambs being Jordan and Duff. They were probably well pleased to be warm and sheltered instead of being out on the pitch exposed to the full fury of the savage wind coming in off the Irish Sea. It was, in truth, a night so foul you would hesitate to put your dog in the back yard. The pitch was bumpy, the exposed fans freezing cold in the Heath Robinson makeshift stand, and in the second half down came the rain as well, slanting straight into players' faces. It was a game that could well have been abandoned had captains and managers agreed; the referee seemed close to doing this in the first half but played on. Chairman Barry Kilby recalled that when the referee asked the managers what they wanted to do, it was Coyle who wanted it calling off. But Tony Parkes of Blackpool said play on. How fortunate that he did. Players, fans and Coyle were rewarded five minutes from time. Another late goal, this one scored by full back Kalvenes, won the game and three precious points.

An injury time goal against Charlton and a decision by an opposition manager had effectively turned the season. The Clarets moved up to seventh. The bedraggled fans went home exultant. It was the game that Kilby pinpointed, as did many fans, that kickstarted the final run-in. Coyle was able to get on his favourite theme—character and desire.

The goal was a fantastic footballing move and a cool finish,' he beamed. 'But the biggest thing that summed us up was character. The desire to come back from Saturday was immense and to come and get the shut-out after how poorly we defended on Saturday was pleasing. Blackpool put us under pressure, but if there was any football played, with all respects to them, it was us that played it. I believe that was game that we would have lost when I came into the club last season. But the lads rolled up their sleeves and showed desire. It really was a must-win for us.

A routine FA Cup defeat, 0–3, away at Arsenal, surprised no-one. But League results that day favoured Burnley leaving them just one point behind 6th place Preston with a game in hand. Ten games remained. Robbie Blake spoke:

> You have to aspire to play teams like Arsenal every week and with the results going for us on Saturday we're in a good position to go on and push now. We've certainly got the players and the ability. We have two massive home games now and we know we've got to take maximum points. There are that many teams around us, we can't afford any slip-ups. We've got ten big games to come and we're up for the fight, we're in the mix and there's all to play for. We want to be involved in big games and we have ten Cup Finals now. We're in a great position to go on and do something special this season.

As soundbites go Blake had strung enough together to as good as forecast the remainder of the season. The next two home games resulted in six points and nine goals. In the first against Crystal Palace Burnley trailed 2–1 until the 83rd minute. The Gods looked down kindly and a penalty levelled the scores. Manager Warnock fumed. In the final two minutes Burnley slammed in two more. Warnock was incandescent. In the next game the 5–0 win over Nottingham Forest was more straightforward. Burnley moved into fifth place with 61 points. It was one of those games when the chances were tucked away by five different scorers and it all ended with Burnley coasting home in style.

Purred Coyle:

> Some of the finishes were exquisite and fit to grace any game. A few of them would probably deserve to win a match in their own right but the fact they all came together we're delighted with. It certainly helps the goal difference as well. I don't think there were ever five goals in the game but the bottom line is we were clinical.

Some games are scraps, and the phrase that managers use is 'winning ugly'. Burnley did just that away at Plymouth. It was a real banana skin game, Plymouth down near the bottom fighting to stay in the Division. At the furthest ground away from Burnley, the Burnley support was quite outstanding just about filling the away end. There cannot be a better supported club away from home relative to the size of the town and average home gates. So many people have left the town in the past that they are settled in numbers all over the country, especially the south. A London game draws hundreds of exiles. It was no game for the purists and as the final ten minutes approached it looked like an untidy draw would be the result following a typical Burnley defensive calamity. But, up stepped Robbie Blake and rifled home a 25-yard shot that had the away end in raptures, the Burnley team exultant and the Plymouth fans stunned into a distraught silence. Other results were in Burnley's favour and Burnley moved into fourth spot, the play-offs well and truly in prospect.

Coyle was ecstatic:

For me it's the biggest three points of the season bar none because it's the business end of the season. It's now when you have to get those points and gain a bit of momentum and look to push on at the right time. To get to the places we want to be, you have to come to places like Plymouth, and we knew we were going to have to be up for it because they're fighting for their Championship status. You're never going to get an easy game here, but we did all the dirty work and came away with a fabulous three points. On days like this it's sometimes going to be about grinding it out. Blakey's popped up and as soon as he's controlled it on his chest we all felt it was hitting the back of the net. People will say we've played too many games, we've used the fewest amount of players in the Championship, we've got the smallest squad—those things are true, but the players we've got are giving everything they can to win games for this football club.

Six games remained. Nothing was certain. There was one more defeat on the cards and a disappointing draw to come at Southampton. It was tight but the way was open, the reward enormous; with fans and directors alike on tenterhooks.

9

DARE TO DREAM

At the time of the Southampton game on 25th April, few people knew just how close to real financial difficulty the club was. The true state of the finances was kept in-house. A move to involve American investors got as close as one potential investor attending a game and the sum of £15million was mentioned. It came to nothing. Towards the end of April the transfer embargo was still in place and the club would have struggled to pay the wages without yet another injection of Directors' money. Four of them stepped forward; Barry Kilby, Ray Griffiths, John Sullivan and Mike Garlick. Alan Mahon and Ade Akinbiyi left the club but there was still no scope to strengthen.

Six games remained: Derby away 1–1, QPR home won 1–0, Cardiff away lost 1–3, Sheffield United home won 1–0, Southampton away drew 2–2; and finally Bristol City home won 4–0.

With four games remaining there was a seven point gap between Burnley in sixth place and Preston below. It looked healthily secure. But then Burnley went to Cardiff. When it ended with a 3–1 win for Cardiff it left things in the balance and nervous tension amongst followers. For three-quarters of the game it was even; a tight, competitive game in front of a passionate crowd. Cardiff too were in the mix. Cardiff took the lead but then Blake equalised with just five minutes to go. The away fans were sure a point had been earned but when Cardiff scored twice in the last five minutes there was a feeling of huge disappointment. Sloppy defending had again been the undoing of Burnley and Coyle was well aware of it:

> You cannot switch off for a second in this League and I am disappointed in the manner of the goals we lost. We controlled the game for large periods and looked very comfortable. We restricted them to very few opportunities but the first one was basic defending from a throw-in, even though their lad has put in a top quality finish. We got back in with an equaliser but straight from the kick-off we have switched off again from a long ball put through. It was naïve at best and I have let the players know that. I don't know if it was two games in two days, but the concentration levels have to be at the maximum at this level. I am disappointed by the goals to be honest but we will dust ourselves down and look to bounce back quickly. If somebody had said to me at the start of the season we would be four points clear, then we would have taken that.

110

To everyone's horror, the four point lead was then whittled down to just one when both Swansea and Preston won to reduce the gap. It seemed unthinkable that this could have happened and suddenly doubts emerged about Burnley's ability to sustain the play-off place. Next to come was the burly, no nonsense Sheffield United side, themselves in the top six. It was a Monday night televised game and this had given the teams below the chance to catch up. The anxiety was palpable. It was an utterly must-win game; and this against a team with a formidable away record. It was a situation when everyone saw each remaining game as the biggest game of the season. It was the start of the period when in hindsight one can see how the football Gods looked down on Burnley and gave them a clear helping hand. The Sheffield game was the first of four clean sheets out of the final five games including the play-offs. And this, a defence that had given away daft goals all season.

Coyle spelled it out:

> Monday night is our Cup Final, there's no doubt about that. And we'll give everything to try and get three points. It's a massive game. We've given ourselves a terrific chance this season to be involved in the play-offs. Television dictates a lot of things these days so when it comes about we'll be ready. All we can do is concentrate on our own performance, looking to get every point that's available to us and that will be the focus. Sheffield United are a good side, carrying all before them. They're obviously striving for automatic promotion so they'll come here and be positive. I'd imagine they'd fill the away end so the atmosphere is going to be conducive to a really good footballing environment, which we really love at Turf Moor. I think there's something special about Turf Moor, the atmosphere for me, being old-fashioned, it's just a real footballing environment and the place will be rocking.

Four days before the game there were only 12 players fit for training. Things were so bad that Coyle himself turned out for the reserves at Accrington. Supporters wondered if this was now the point where it would all implode and the lack of cash and strengthening have its long awaited consequences. At Accrington Coyle scored a delightful goal that was shown on Sky over and again—a neat flick over the head of the defender and then meeting the ball on the other side and lobbing the 'keeper. The grinning Coyle was even more delighted when the first-team beat Sheffield 1–0 in this must-win game.

> What a vile, nasty, ugly, horrible side Sheffield United are. If this is the way to the Premiership then God help them. The word dire is not good enough. Three players could have been booked early on. Halford stamped on Blake, Jensen was elbowed on the head by Morgan and Kalvanes is lucky to be walking after a vicious tackle on the sideline.
> Sheffield: I watched them on Sky against Reading and knew what to expect. It was hoofball, all long throws, elbows, muscle, pushes, shouldering; get the ball at all costs. 'The land of the giants,' Clarke Carlisle described them. The win for Burnley was a triumph for attempted football

and skill over brawn and power, but according to Carlisle, Burnley's industrial defending was a key.

It could have been more than 1–0. Kenny was in the right position to stop a number of superb attempts. One run along the by line from Blake and pull back to McCann who met it with a superb strike, was in itself worthy of the entrance money. It was a throw-back to the great Jimmy McIlroy who did this half a dozen times during a game. Blake is enjoying a superb season.

At the back Carlisle and Caldwell were utterly immense repelling every long ball that was hurled at them. Eagles, on song, had one of his best games. The cameras were there. His value will have doubled. McCann drove forward at every opportunity in possibly his best ever game. And Paterson, surprisingly back after injury scored the single winning goal with a deft header from a diagonal cross.

Sheffield fans on their messageboards were less than charitable towards their team, the manager and style of play. They were in agreement about two things, firstly that their hoofball was inadequate, and secondly that Carlisle was the Burnley rock on which it foundered. (Personal Diary April 20th 2009)

Two games remained. Win at Southampton and Burnley would be in the play-offs. Coyle made a point of explaining that he wanted the top six position decided at Southampton so that his grey hairs would not increase, adding:

It's the biggest game of the season, it's as simple as that. We've had big, big games all season and we've loved every minute of it but the bottom line is we can't affect what's behind us, but we can go and try and get three points at Southampton that would ultimately push us into those play-offs. That's got to be the focus and I'll be stressing that to the players. We have to see the job through now, and to do that, we have to be at our best.

My personal diary charts the game against Southampton as follows:

They were not at their best; in fact for the first 45 minutes Burnley were dreadful. The away end was again packed. The final 2–2 result was very fortunate. And when Preston amazingly won away at Birmingham once again it was all in the melting pot. What had once been a healthy seven point cushion was now a situation where only a last day win would suffice. Nobody would have imagined that Preston would put six past Cardiff and then beat Birmingham.

How one rues that last minute equaliser at Derby that lost us two points. How one thinks back to the two ridiculous penalties Preston were awarded in the Burnley game that gave them the points. And down at Southampton how we may come to regret the wasted chance of a win when Rodriguez, clean through, elected to shoot when a simple pass to Paterson on his left would surely have resulted in a goal.

Burnley were terrible in the first half and but for Jensen could have been well out of it. Southampton way down at the bottom end, with serious financial problems, facing administration and points deductions, were by far the better side and were the team looking desperate for the points. They took a deserved lead but then Alexander scored a penalty equaliser well against the run of play. The football Gods smiled again. Coyle shuffled the pack and Elliott back on the right wing caused havoc so that for a 20-minute spell chances were made and the football was back to some normality. But with Southampton fighting for survival there was almost an 'Orient' feel to the game and again they went ahead; adrenalin, emotion and energy powering them forward against a Burnley side that clearly thought the points were a formality. Again Southampton took the lead and were then awarded a penalty that would have made it 3–1 and put the game well out of reach. Jensen saved the tame penalty and when Carlisle scored an equaliser there was total jubilation (and relief) at the Burnley end. Superb against Sheffield United; awful against Southampton; one can only hope the real Burnley turns up for the final game of the season. (Personal Diary April 25th 2009)

Coyle fumed:

I was annoyed and made that clear at half-time. We are not good enough to just hit a switch and think we can just turn up and play when it suits us. We're not anywhere near that level. We have to be so focused and concentrated from the outset. I felt there was nervousness about the younger element in the side. They certainly weren't themselves and we missed that pace and dynamic. We were very fortunate to come in at 2–1 down, but the second half was a lot better, and we could have won the game. I thought we started the second half well and then we gave away a soft penalty. Brian made a couple of big saves in the first half and then the penalty save was a big turning point. We picked up again and scored the equaliser and had a gilt-edged chance to win the game then. Over the balance of the 90 minutes it would have been a travesty on Southampton had we won, but we showed even when we're not playing well that we hang in there. I wanted the job done and put to bed to save me a few grey hairs next week.

The week leading up to the game against Bristol was a worrying one for Burnley fans as my diary suggested:

Football fans would be a happy lot if they knew the results of key games in advance and a game would be won. It would solve a lot of angst and no end of worries. If everyone had known that the final game would be a walkover (unlike the heartbreaking Coventry game during Stan Ternent's time) they would have enjoyed the week leading up to it. And had they known that the Bristol game would be the first of four consecutive clean sheets, something quite unheard of at Burnley, they would have been ecstatic (and not a little surprised).

All week since the Southampton game and the unexpected Preston win at Birmingham there must have been more than just a few of us natural born pessimists who thought that we would be pipped at the post. I left Southampton in high spirits. They were replaced by doubts and fears when that final Preston result of the day was known. All week I pondered on the starting line-up. Williams had been looking more and more suspect. Was it not time to bring back Duff? Exactly what do you do with Eagles and how best do you play him? Was Elliott not better at wide right than in midfield? Would Thompson be back in contention after injury? He had been missed.

Would Carlisle continue his incredible run of form and scoring at vital moments? Were we not more potent with two up front? At some point in the game should we not unleash the power and muscle of McDonald?

Many of us can remember the last Sunday game of the season (was it 2002) when we were denied a top six place by just one goal as Coventry's Hedman made those two stunning saves from Gazza's free kicks in the dying moments. After that game was over I sat in my seat for 15 minutes or so, just numbed with disappointment. Were we about to see something similar? Today then was not about entertainment, it was about winning. Nothing but a win would preserve the place in the top six. Preston will not slip up against QPR I kept telling myself, they are the in-form team.

Three teams were in the mix for the sixth place, Burnley, Preston and Cardiff. My gut feeling was that Preston would win, Cardiff would lose and Burnley would draw. It's what we fans do isn't it, ponder on the permutations, try and figure out the end results, worry and fret about the outcomes; try and work out what the final table will be? Only Wolves fans could have slept easy. What would it be at the final whistle—joy or disappointment, elation or dejection, head in hands, or high in the air in exultation and celebration?

Sunday and another display like the one against Sheffield United was desperately needed; plus a little bit of luck, good refereeing decisions and big performances.

And win they did.

But no-one could have envisaged such a comfortable 4–0 win. Nerves, anxieties, tensions, apprehension all evaporated when Alexander's first penalty went in. From the kick-off we knew they were up for it. Two undisputed penalties and each coming at a point in the game that gave us back the initiative. When was the last time we were awarded two penalties? There were those football Gods again smiling down on us.

From the first minute Burnley came out like an express train. For several minutes we ripped Bristol apart, made chances, had shots and eventually a fizzing move ended with an Eagles shot, when he hit a screamer that hit the woodwork with such ferocity it's a wonder he didn't shatter the crossbar. For a while Bristol came back into the game but then Elliott was clobbered in the back of the neck as he burst into the area. Blatant foul though it was, some refs would have waved play on but this one gave the penalty. Alexander didn't miss. Minutes later a corner was headed out to Elliott who sent a superb cross-shot through a dozen bodies into the net. It would have graced any Barcelona game. The ground erupted. Surely this was game over. Unless we did anything stupid the game was won, the play-off place safely gathered. We looked at the scoreboard and pinched ourselves.

Bristol had a good spell in the second half but then the second penalty came for a glaring handball. Alexander smashed the ball home this time into the other side of the net. From then on it was party time despite the bitter cold. Blake came into the game more and more. This season he has added a willingness to work and track back into his game. Now he set off on a mesmerising Jimmy McIlroy run and beat man after man. It was worth the entrance money on its own. Eagles then created the icing on the cake. The goalkeeper saved his stunning shot, but Gudjonnson lashed it home for the fourth. Eagles had a superb game for the whole 90 minutes. But there were huge performances from them all.

How blessed we are with rich attacking talent on days like this. Not only did we win, but we won with style and flair, panache and entertainment. Coyle's creation and philosophy was on display for all to see. When Elliott runs at defences he creates panic amongst anyone marking him. The non-stop Paterson must be a nightmare to mark. Blake's close control at times is simply bewitching. Chris Eagles on form is unstoppable, unless you flatten him which happened several times today. And it's good to see the burly Thompson back again. At the back were the two rocks, Carlisle and Caldwell. (Personal Diary Sunday May 3rd 2009)

With the play-off place secured, it meant that Burnley's two games would be against Reading. The other two teams playing each other would be Preston and Sheffield United. At least Burnley would be spared Morgan's elbows again—unless both teams got to Wembley.

Coyle's after-match analysis was as ever, calm and measured:

I thought the way we started we probably should have been 2–0 up in the first ten minutes. We hit the bar and had a couple of missed chances by the post, and you think it's never going to go in. There have been enough superlatives used about Graham Alexander, but the level of composure he shows in that environment is why he's been a top player all his days. He's put us in front, and we've got the second one just before half-time, and it put us in a relatively comfortable position. I don't think we started the second half particularly well; we were protecting what we had when I asked them not to. I asked us to go and replicate the first half and really be on the front foot trying to get the third goal. As it was, I think the third goal settled everybody's nerves because we knew it was going to be a wee bit tense.

He then moved onto the subject of the play-offs:

We have a chance, the same as anybody else. We're good enough to take it if we stay focused and tuned in. I'm led to believe it's the club's highest position for 33 years, but we don't stop there. The work ethic we've got and the desire and hunger to do the best we can, it's so evident, and we've got an opportunity now to really push ourselves to where everybody wants to be. Everybody aspires to play at the very highest level. As a player I wanted to be the best I could be and as a manager I want to be the best I can be. I sampled it at Bolton in the Premier League, and I want to sample it again.

We now have two tough games against quality opposition. And I think to be fair, Reading will be saying the same about us because they've come here and know we can play a bit. I think it's two very good footballing sides. We've been in terrific form, I believe, and all credit to Preston who have got a bit of momentum as well. But we've only had two defeats in 17 or 18 games; and our level of performance has been outstanding. They've given everything they've got and considering it was such a tense occasion, some of the football I thought was all the things we're good at—passing with precision and moving with pace. If we can carry that momentum and replicate it in the two games, we've got as good a chance as anybody.

My diary suggests that win or lose against Reading, Burnley supporters were still pleased with the club's outcome that season:

No Burnley supporter thought it would be a disgrace to lose over the two legs to Reading. There were probably more than a few who thought this is as good as it gets; for us this has been a success and the extra money will be very nice. To get to Wembley, surely that was just a fairy tale, too much to hope for, just a dream. 'Dare to dream', said the slogan coming out of the club. But, supporters recalled that earlier in the season Burnley had been very fortunate to beat Reading 1–0 at Turf Moor. Then they had been thumped emphatically at Reading. Could they dream of a Burnley versus Preston North End Final—surely not? As it turned out Preston lost to Sheffield over their two games, neither of them distinguished or graced by good football.

Nearly 19,000 turned up for the televised first-leg with Burnley the home team. Unable to attend the game I watched on TV.

Here in Hornsea watching on TV there is a strange sense of detachment and non involvement until the game starts. Then—as poor a 45 minutes from Burnley as we have seen for ages. No Elliott, and how it shows, no running and no penetration. Eagles is having a poor and ineffective game. Long goalkicks continually give the ball to Reading and the closest chances go to them. Burnley have just two off target shots. Gudjonsson is disgracefully taken out of the game by the carthorse Duberry. Little Paterson against the giant Bikey is a non contest. No football at all from Burnley, almost hoofball as they give the ball away time and time again. The long high goalkicks up to the diminutive Paterson are embarrassing. So far, a total non-event; Reading are by far the better side and the lack of any fluent football from Burnley very disappointing.

Second half: more of the same, flat, listless and almost aimless. The hapless Eagles is replaced by the more robust Thompson who can now take the weight off Paterson. Coyle's substitutions have worked all season. Will this? Reading still dominant and have the majority of possession. They must surely score and win this game.

And then out of nothing, suddenly Thompson is clear and through into the area only to be hauled down by Bikey, dragged by the shirt for all to see. **Penalty**: will this be the one that at last Alexander misses? No it damned well is not. The man is a robot, he never misses and incredibly the score is 1–0, this is quite unbelievable.

And still the drama is not over. With just minutes remaining Bikey stamps on Blake. The referee sees it and gives the red card to the defender, whereupon he storms and rants around wailing with temper and resentment. The word 'mental' would not go amiss. At last he leaves, ripping off his shirt. Burnley then coast home and supporters leave shaking their heads at this improbable win. I can't think when we last played so badly, so ineffectively, with so many players off form or even invisible. From feelings of being distant and detached I now feel quite drained especially as this tie is now in our own hands and Wembley is so close. Can we do it? (Personal Diary May 9th 2009)

Coyle confessed that the Clarets had been poor:

> This game wasn't really what I anticipated in terms of two good footballing teams getting the ball down and playing. I think Reading came with a game plan to stifle the threat we have, and all credit to them, I thought they were successful in doing it, if truth be told. It was a game of very few clear-cut chances. Brian had an outstanding save in the first half, and Martin Paterson popped up to clear one off at the goalpost, but that's what he's there to do. It's finely balanced. There's still an awful lot to play for, there's no doubt about that. We have to go, and to be honest, play better. I can't ask any more as a manager from the players. We keep placing high demands on them, but as much as we weren't fluent in our passing, the courage and desire and hunger to win football games is so evident. It wasn't pleasing on the eye in terms of a footballing show, but anyone watching knows the heart and bravery these players have.

The day before the return game the Wembley word appeared, and he vowed to go for the win:

> We try to win every game, home or away, and that will be the same again. It would be naïve to sit back and allow Reading to get on top of you. There will be times when that happens because of the quality they have, so we have to make sure we stand up to that. But what we have to do is be positive when we have the ball, look to move it quickly, get our flair players and match-winners on it and create opportunities. Wembley is a magnificent stadium and a real opportunity. As a player I always said you wanted to play in the best stadiums against the best players, and the game at Reading provides that opportunity. They know if they do their job right and go and get that positive result, they'll get a real crack at it. We have to earn the right to that Wembley slot. I think with regards to the play-offs there's no doubt that people are sounding each other out in the first leg; they're not wanting to give too much away, so it's been tense, not just our tie, but everybody's I think. But when all's said and done, with the second leg, that's it. It's closure after that game. I think in all the second legs you'll see more. Not that they're gung-ho, but teams are more aggressive in going for it. So we have to be ready for that and make sure we get to our maximum in terms of performance levels.

Reading at this point were going through a spell when they couldn't win at home for toffee. Coppell left out Hunt and Kitson and offered a debut to a 20 year old rookie striker, Simon Church. The home seats were sparsely filled; Reading had the better first half, but then when Burnley scored through Martin Paterson all hell broke loose in the Burnley end.

We were still in Hornsea when the game was played. This time there was no sense of detachment but pure nerves and apprehension with the Wembley prize so close. In the afternoon we walked on the beach, had an early meal, and then fidgeting and anxious, watched the game. My notes afterwards were scribbled and almost illegible:

> **WE'VE DONE IT**. We bloody did it. Got to Wembley, won the game, done it and it still hasn't sunk in. In hindsight (such a luxury) it was a comfortable

win, 2–0. There was an early storm to weather and then a difficult nervy first half with Jensen making a couple of good saves. Reading were up for it, they moved forward relentlessly. The second half began in the same way with Burnley playing just a little more football than in the first leg. Coyle allegedly was not happy at half-time. Whatever he said may or may not have been the key to the game's result. But what certainly turned it came in the 50th minute when an astonishing world-class strike from Paterson won us the game (though we weren't to know it at the time). Out came the ball from defence. Thompson (my man of the match) found Paterson on the right round the halfway line. He set off diagonally, defenders retreated, space opened up in front of him like a prairie. And then **WHAM** a superb and wonderful strike from surely 35 yards arrowed its way into the left side of the goal top corner, and then there it was nestling in the back of the net. There was a stunned silence at the sheer audacity of it; the utter splendour and magnificence of this once in a lifetime perfect strike. This was a wonder goal, a candidate for goal of the season at any ground in the country, a goal that would have graced the Nou Camp, the Emirates, a quite mind-boggling shot that summed up the modern game; that you can be under the cosh for long spells and then in seconds the game is turned on its head. The light ball that bends and curves, the speed of the game, the accuracy of the passing, the speed of the shot, this was a goal that you would never have seen in the 50s or 60s. I watch it still and every time I feel sure that the goalkeeper must save it, it seems to happen in such nail-biting slow motion.

And still there was more to come and if we thought Pato's goal was fabulous, then Thompson's almost rivalled it. A long goalkick, Thompson gathered it, controlled it, turned and hit a wonderful dipping shot that arced over the goalkeeper, hit the underside of the bar and ended up in the net. Cue delirium and a wall of noise and joy at one end of the ground, and dejected silence and crestfallen faces at the other. It was game over for Reading and they knew it. Burnley coasted home for the remainder of the game. Proper Burnley football emerged, possession, skilled passing, ball to feet, little passing moves and intelligent movement. In the Burnley end it was party time.

The morning after, I bought six newspapers. You do this sort of thing on occasions like this. When Thompson's goal went in, our non-football friends had been amazed to see me dive full length off the settee and beat the carpet with my fists in utter elation. Normally I'm quite sane.

Is this a fairy tale? Can it continue for one more game? Can a small town of just 80,000 people get as far as this and into the Premiership? The opponents will be Sheffield United and it seems that unless you are from Sheffield everyone wants Burnley to succeed. They admire our football and flair. They admire, as we do, the manager. He took a bunch of under-performers and made it happen. To do this after such a poor start to the season and then five defeats over Christmas is astonishing. The man has charisma and the people of Burnley would eat out of his hands. (Personal Diary May 13th 2009)

It was a cliché but Burnley were the 'People's Club', admired for the Herculean efforts on a shoestring and such slender resources, one of the smallest squads, the smallest budgets, the little club against the city clubs with their parachute payments and unfair advantages. The manager was clean-cut, media-friendly, articulate, and always available for a quote, everybody's darling, a Sky man's dream. The town identified with him. He identified with the town. It was the shattering of this feel-good factor some months later that would affect people so deeply and turn their venom on their hero when he turned his back on them.

'Little Burnley,' we kept saying. The pundits, Ian Wright, Stan Collymore and Alex Ferguson all wanted us to succeed. They, and we, remembered the heartbreak of the Tottenham Carling night and two minutes more that would have seen Burnley in a Cup Final. That was a night when the Burnley players realised that there was another route to Wembley and this gave them an impetus and a desire. From dejection came resolve; from heartache came determination and the man Coyle was there to focus them, cajole them, nurse them and persuade them to believe.

After the Reading second leg he emphasised that the job was not yet done:

> I haven't been back to Wembley since the play-off Final and it's something we'll look forward to, there's no getting away from it. I'm not trying to underplay how good the result was, and the opportunity that awaits us, but that's what it is, and we have to try and grasp it. The prize which awaits the winners is the Premier League, where every coach and every player aspires to be. Everybody wants to be involved at the highest possible level. I wanted that as a player, and I want that as a coach and manager, but you have to earn the right to do that. We went over to thank the fans for their support because they were magnificent, so vocal, even though they were outnumbered ten to one. They sang their hearts out and gave the players their backing particularly in the first half when we were under siege at times. So we acknowledge their support but we also recognise that we haven't achieved our goal. We're delighted to have come through, but that's all we've done and we'll have to make sure we're at our very best because Sheffield United are a quality side.

There was a long interval between the second leg game and the Final on May 25th. Supporters faced frantic efforts to get tickets from an office at the club that could barely cope. Around 36,000 were sold and more could have been if Wembley Stadium had made all seats available, instead of leaving swathes of them unoccupied. Coyle spoke at length about the task ahead:

> I said when I came to Burnley that I would try to embrace the history and tradition of the club, and I think that's evident. Certainly in the style of play, the youth we're trying to bring through, Burnley were always known for that. I think we've re-energised the supporters, not to blame what went on before, but we're playing a brand of football everyone seems to find enjoyable. It doesn't go to plan every game, but we set out to try to entertain and try to win games in a certain style. The goodwill and backing of the town has been there for everyone to see, everyone is behind the

club, and there's a feel-good factor. It's important we continue that. I don't want to contemplate losing; my focus is only on winning. It will be nice at the end of the season when you look back on things and there are pivotal moments within the season. The energy and desire the players have shown to play 60 games, at the level they have, they deserve every plaudit. But we have to deliver in the final game, because, for all those games it boils down to this one. We have to be at our very best. We produced two of our best performances of the season against Sheffield United and we'll need to do that again. They are a terrific club and they are set up for the Premier League. They feel aggrieved to be out of the Premier League, we all know what happened. It's the League everyone wants to play in and we both have the opportunity to try and get the prize. I don't think any other motivation is needed. At the end of the day, accolades and things people say about you are nice but that's all it is. Ultimately you have to go and deliver on it. I knew coming into the club how difficult it would be financially and as much as Brendan and the chairman were interviewing me, I was interviewing them as well, seeing what I would have at my disposal. They were very upfront and open, in that we might have to sell from time to time. That's proved to be the case, but I knew we could still build a team and we've shown we can compete, and not only compete, but blossom and flourish at this level. We want to take that a stage further, and that's an exciting prospect for us all.

The game itself was a nail biting affair that produced a variety of emotion at its end as my diary describes:

The game itself: as ever in hindsight what a comfortable win it was. After the game Jensen said he had little to do. A couple of routine saves, a block, a few catches, rarely troubled. Sheffield had a decent first ten minutes and there was some inevitable pressure in the final ten. But in between, Burnley controlled the game. Might there have been two penalty decisions against Burnley? Who knows, Mike Dean said no. Another referee might have said yes. But when the gods are on your side these decisions go in your favour. And today the gods were truly on Burnley's side, as they have been for the last few games. We made all the best chances and only heroic last-ditch Sheffield defending on at least three occasions kept the score down. Paterson might have replicated his wonder strike at Reading with a similar shot that went just wide. Thompson shaved the post with a looping header. Gudjonsson missed a golden close range chance when the ball fell for him. A Sheffield leg was in the way but it was a chance that should have been taken and would have made the game safe.

Every Burnley player played his part and rose to the occasion. Man of the match Carlisle yet again, but they were all on top form. Blake worked tirelessly, tracking back, and twisted and turned till we all went dizzy. Caldwell was not far behind Carlisle. Paterson ran and ran. Eagles in his cameo caused mayhem on a couple of occasions.

And the goal that won the game: one man, one moment, one strike, one moment of destiny as if it was all pre-planned up above somewhere. A stunning, weaving run from deep by Elliott; he slips the ball to McCann, the tackle on McCann sends the ball back to Elliott way outside the box. He looks; he carefully weighs things up, strikes the ball, and places it beautifully into the top left corner of the net. Not many minutes have gone and had we known that this was the winning goal how much easier we would have felt. Instead we bit nails, counted the minutes, watched the clock, agonised. The minutes in the second half dragged by; five minutes of extra-time but for once they went quickly as Burnley were then rarely troubled.

The spectacle of the Burnley end is simply stunning, a sea and riot of claret and blue, of banners and flags and painted faces. The clock winds down, the Burnley end screams for the final whistle. Mike Dean blows and the tears flow. The noise is deafening as we celebrate and dance and hug with strangers who are now our best friends. Exultation, exhilaration, exhaustion and joy tinged with disbelief.

The Sheffield end quickly and quietly empties. They are as emotionally drained as we are, but for different reasons. Football, bloody hell, it wrecks your head and health.

The players receive the salutes but it is Owen Coyle's triumph. It was he who took over the bits of the jigsaw and figured out how best to fit them together. It was he who took over a jaded bunch of disenchanted players and reshaped them, added his own men into the mix and brought a new style of football, and all in a matter of months. At Burnley Football Club he has had the magic touch.

Home at two in the morning; the flags and scarves are still flying outside the house. It will be several days before I take them down. And at 7 I'll be up to buy every single paper I can lay my hands on. (Personal Diary May 26th 2009)

Elliott fires Burnley back into big time wrote Henry Winter:

A party 33 years in the planning began in style last night, with Wembley awash with Claret and Blue champagne corks flying up towards the famous arch. The party will be loud and long, sweeping Burnley and their wonderful supporters through the summer months and into the new Premier League season. And for those graceless bookmakers who immediately installed Owen Coyle's play-off winners as favourites for relegation, think again.

Burnley boast a savvy manager, intelligent and hard-working players and a track record of troubling celebrated opponents. Just ask Chelsea, Spurs, Arsenal and Fulham, who all suffered against Burnley this term. Just ask Burnley's Board, who have £60million coming their way. Coyle's squad undeniably needs strengthening, particularly in attack, but Burnley will lack nothing in belief, organisation or backing from the Boardroom and stands. Half the town's 70,000 population must have been at Wembley, relishing the opportunity to end so many years of hurt.

And how long had they waited. To place Burnley's absence in perspective: the last time they were upstairs among the aristocrats, 1976, the Eagles (the American ones not Crystal Palace) were releasing 'Hotel California' while the UK even managed to win Eurovision with Brotherhood of Man's 'Save all Your Kisses for Me'.

For all ages of Burnley fans, yesterday was so special. For the young ones dancing in their 'Dare to Dream' T-shirts, victory means a chance to see modern-day footballing icons like Cristiano Ronaldo and Wayne Rooney on a weekly basis. For every Burnley kid who had left Turf Moor, hearts broken when Roman Pavlyuchenko and Jermain Defoe denied them a place in the Carling Cup Final, yesterday made amends. Smiles replaced tears. For middle-aged men, holding up their mobile phones at the final whistle to record the celebratory sights and sounds for all time, this was reward for all those years of following Burnley through lean decades, hoping against hope for nirvana like this. For the older supporters, it was all about the restoration of the natural order, a return to a time when Burnley were an established force in the land and, adding to the historic occasion, club legends like Jimmy McIlroy were present to witness it.

And, in their moment of triumph, Burnley fans sportingly spared a thought for the vanquished, applauding all the Sheffield United players lying disconsolate on the pitch and the fans from Yorkshire holding their heads in disbelief. Lancashire had won this War of the Roses but there was no gloating.

Burnley were deserved winners. Sheffield United can legitimately complain about Mike Dean's refereeing frustrating them again, this time he refused two clear penalties yet he was not alone in the sub-standard display costing the Blades dear. Too many of Kevin Blackwell's men failed to rise to the occasion. Stephen Quinn disappointed. Jamie Ward came on and was dismissed for two foolish and very obvious deliberate handballs while Lee Hendrie, often a combustible mix, even managed to get himself sent off for foul and abusive language in the tunnel afterwards. The only real stars in red and white stripes were the two Kyles, Naughton and Walker. Naughton attracts interest from Manchester United while Walker arguably had the better game, making a couple of magnificent last-ditch tackles. With wealthy predators circling this pair Blackwell hardly picked the most opportune moment to cast doubts over his future as manager. Sheffield United need stability, to build for another promotion push.

The painful truth for Blackwell and his players is that they were out-thought and outplayed. Both managers used versions of 4–5–1 formations but Coyle's tactics were the more fluid and effective. Coyle deployed Steven Thompson as the spearhead, rightly deciding that his more physical presence would work better against Chris Morgan and Matt Kilgallon. The smaller, pacier Martin Paterson, who often plays through the middle, moved to the right and had a storming game, creating constant problems for Sheffield United. Coyle's tactical nous was also seen in midfield where Graham Alexander anchored with his usual diligence, the 37-year old defying Old Father Time and opposing midfielders. Most significantly, Alexander allowed Wade Elliott to raid midfield.

Within 13 minutes, Elliott made the game's defining move, bursting through the midfield, shrugging off the attentions of Quinn and Nick Montgomery before laying the ball off to Chris McCann. Kilgallon blocked but the ball rebounded out to Elliott who swept an unstoppable 25-yarder past Paddy Kenny. Burnley had the lead and were rarely troubled.

Blackwell's men screamed for penalties; Alexander clearly brought down Brian Howard and Christian Kalvenes wrestled Walker to the ground. All appeals were waved away by Dean. The Cheshire referee then expelled Ward for first impersonating the Hand of God, and then controlling the ball with his arm. Burnley threatened more. Paterson bent a shot wide. Michael

Duff failed from close range. Joey Gudjonsson's poacher's touch was somehow blocked by Montgomery.

Barring the occasional break from Naughton, Sheffield United's attacks lacked sophistication. Long balls rained down but Clarke Carlisle and Stephen Caldwell stood firm. Behind them, Brian Jensen formed a large impregnable barrier. At the final whistle, Paterson sank to his knees, knowing that all his endeavour had been worthwhile. Fittingly, the ball was in the control of Elliott, the man of the match for his composure, energy and magnificent goal.

And so the party began. Duff launched into a dance that one of Beyonce's bodyguards would have been proud of. Coyle cradled the play-off trophy gently, as if emerging from a maternity ward, kissed it, and then lifted it to the heavens as Burnley fans went crazy chanting, 'We are Premier League'. Wembley's excellent new pitch received the ultimate test of its durability when Jensen, Burnley's burly keeper, leapt high in the air and landed with a thud on the grass. It survived. Robbie Blake then ran in front of the jubilant players spraying them with champagne. No more Coca Cola, Burnley are tasting headier stuff now. (Courtesy of Henry Winter)

Not only did Blake spray everyone with champagne but he danced and skipped along the goalline with his shorts dropped to his knees and boots discarded, revealing the bright red Bad Beat Bob underpants first seen at Coventry, to the Claret thousands. Kamara and the pundits in the studio were hysterical. It was a magic moment, the sort, just like Elliott's stunning goal, that lives long in the memory. Alastair Campbell was there of course:

Well that was up there with the birth of my children, winning a general election with Labour after years in the wilderness, even better than playing football in a charity match with Diego Maradona in front of 72,000 people. There is nothing quite like football for delivering the anxiety of anticipation, the stress of the 90 minutes itself—not to mention the five minutes of injury time, and the unadulterated joy that accompanies the moment of victory. The joy last night was all the more special because of the agonies Burnley fans have endured following the team from top to bottom of the football tree. We are now the smallest town ever to have had a club in the Premiership. Home games next season will house the equivalent of one in four of the local population. Today, expect the town to turn out in their thousands to welcome the players home. It will be another great day in a fantastic year for the club. (Courtesy of Alastair Campbell)

With Coyle having been at the club just 18 months, the triumph was all the more remarkable and he was assured of his place in Burnley folklore. But after the game he was almost muted in his celebrations, keeping his emotions in check, simply turning to shake hands with the backroom staff. There was certainly no unrestrained, wild galloping onto the pitch. Even on the balcony when the presentations were made he was relatively undemonstrative. The general consensus was that this remarkable achievement could not have happened without him. As one pundit put it, he was the adhesive that bound the players together and made them strong. Another described him as 'the heartbeat of the club'. At Liverpool on the Shankly gates there is the message, 'He made the people happy'. The same thing could be said of Coyle at Burnley on Wembley day. Maybe Flood's comparison was apt after all. But that feeling would be tarnished within months.

Wembley cameras homed in on the banners that proclaimed 'Owen Coyle is God'. 'I took it as banter and not a statement of fact,' he said dryly. No man, at that point, could have enjoyed so much hero-worship. No man would fall from grace so horribly just seven months later.

Coyle had earlier told his players to wake up as Championship players and go to bed as Premiership players. He said afterwards:

> I'm delighted, obviously. In terms of the game, we were worthy winners. I thought from start to finish we got the ball down and played. We knew at times we would come under pressure when Sheffield United put the ball in the box but we stood up to that, limited them I have to say to very few goal scoring opportunities, and if truth be told we merited certainly more than one goal.
>
> I think it has been well documented that we have used the fewest amount of players and don't have quantity, we know that, but I believe we have real quality and again I think the goal itself was fit to win any game and I would hope typify the way Burnley play in passing and moving culminating with a great finish. I felt we did that in the most part; we looked dangerous on the counter attack.
>
> We'll certainly enjoy tonight and take whatever comes after that. What I will say is that each and every one will be given their opportunity. I think we had around seven ties with Premier League teams and we showed that on our day we can stand up with the best, although it's easier to play in one-off competitions than it is to play weekly in the Premier League. There's no doubt we'll need to add to the squad that we have, but we do have a terrific team spirit and that will never go away. We'll do everything we can. It's a challenge we're relishing. I mean, we'll not be naïve, but again that's not a problem for tonight. We can look at that tomorrow.
>
> The fans have been magnificent from day one during my tenure here, there's no doubt about it. I mean we had 36,000 here today didn't we? Each and every person at the football club is in this together and we've shown that. You would need to be around on a daily basis to see how they go about it because there is a real sense of community and that will see us through and certainly help next year, there's no doubt about that. When things go against you that's when you see the spirit.
>
> We had a terrific pre-season but you wouldn't have thought so three minutes into the game at Sheffield Wednesday. It's easy for people to criticise and be negative but we knew within the dressing room that we could turn it on its head and we did that through hard work. After losing five games in the League over Christmas it would have been easy to think it's never going our way, but we knew we could turn a corner and we got that head of steam running.
>
> It's easy when you're winning to come in and talk about team spirit and camaraderie but I said this at the start of the season when we went to

Sheffield Wednesday and we were one down after about 12 seconds and we lost the game 4–1. And then we lost the next week to Ipswich 3–0. We didn't play too badly, just everything went against us, but I still saw the same togetherness on that training ground and that's how we were able to turn that around and that's going to be important to us next season.

We are under no illusions about how difficult it will be when it comes about. How will we fare? Well, I know we'll give it everything we've got. We'll do everything we can. And again, we're not being delusional here but if we were to finish fourth bottom (and survive) then it will be a better achievement to where we are now. It's terrific to have brought ourselves back to the top flight but when it comes about there's no doubt it's going to be difficult. But it's a challenge we'll relish and I think we've shown this season we've always been the underdogs and every game we enter next season we'll be the underdogs for it, home or away.

Just before the Plymouth game some weeks earlier, Coyle had outlined how and why Burnley were finding success. Though the Clarets played with a holding midfielder it was not seen as a platform for just keeping things tight and nicking a goal and a 1–0 win. Was there any kind of secret to Burnley's progress? 16 players had scored for Burnley during the season and it was that factor plus the willingness to risk losing that Coyle explained were two of the keys:

We have players from all areas of the park who can score goals. We're not one-dimensional; we have different facets to our play, which is so important at this level. If people nullify your threat in one area, then we can pop up in another area. We've been able to change things in terms of substitutions and we can alter systems—we're flexible in that. The performance level has been great as well, when sometimes at this stage of the season that can be sacrificed. I believe the way we play; we can win by being positive. You won't win every game but you have to risk losing it to win. It would be easy to be negative and keep things tight but we are expressive, we have so many offensive players within the team that we have to get forward.

They've shown the character to be brave enough to get on the ball and not change their style. I don't want them banging the ball from back to front. I want them to get it down and pass it, and then when the opportunity presents itself, and when they're in one v one situations, I want them positive. Mistakes will be made but we accept that because we're trying to win a game.

Throughout the season he had been delighted by the quality of the goals:

We've shown we can score goals and the quality of goals has been there. I can't think of many scrappy goals we've scored. I would love to get some of those as well but it's the most exciting feeling in football seeing the ball hit the back of the net. A couple of managers were on to me during the week saying we've got goals in us from different players, which is nice to hear but we need to keep bringing that to games. We've also shown that when we're at the top of our game defensively we can go and keep the best at bay. It's all about going out and trying to win each and every game.

His players joined in the praise. 'He's so relaxed around the players,' said Robbie Blake, 'And makes the place so relaxed, you'd think you were just going round in the car park for a kick-about.'

First-team coach Steve Davis felt that it all stemmed from the top believing that Coyle had instilled a sense of freedom in the players which then blossomed:

> Owen's just very relaxed, he fills everyone with confidence, gives the players licence to go out and express themselves and play with no fear, which I think is vital. You need to go on the pitch and know if you make a mistake, as long as it's an honest one, that you're not going to get slaughtered for it. They're allowed to make honest mistakes which any human being should be allowed to do, and as long as you put the graft in, which is what supporters expect and the manager, Sandy and myself, the staff and the players who set their own standards, expect—you'll be fine. The manager's been great from the point of view of just letting everyone play and relax. The squad is all set up to play attractive football.

It was hard to see some of these comments being said about Coyle's predecessor Steve Cotterill, a manager who the longer he was at Burnley, seemed to be filled with foreboding and never ever seemed relaxed. Yet again, supporters looked at the players, the same players who had seemed so restricted and had so little confidence during the long winless run, now so bright and attractive under Coyle.

* * * * *

It isn't too often that *The Spectator* waxes lyrical about Burnley Football Club or one of its players but in May 2009 there was an exception to this rule.

> Thank heaven for Burnley who played their hearts out to win the Premier play-offs. Afterwards their heroic defender Clarke Carlisle picked up the man of the match award and in a short and graceful interview he gave every sign of being one of the most impressive human beings on earth. Moved to tears, he spoke with wisdom, articulacy and passion about the game, players, supporters and his own personal journey through a host of injuries as well as alcoholism. If anyone should carry a torch for all that is great and good in the beautiful game—it is Clarke Carlisle.

Nor is it very often that *The Guardian* picks out Burnley as being one of the shining lights of football. But it did on May 30th, 2009, when David Lacey bracketed Burnley's football ethos with that of Barcelona:

> In football it has been a good week for fundamentalists, those who believe that amid the hustle and haste of the modern game the basics of good passing and movement plus the ability to make space and not give the ball away are too often taken for granted. To which might be added the willingness of players to run with the ball when the opportunity is there, a habit in danger of being coached out of teams fearful of losing possession

and being caught on the break.

On Monday Burnley displayed many of these qualities in beating one United, Sheffield, to win promotion to the Premier League. On Wednesday Barcelona did as much, and a bit more besides, when they outplayed another United, Manchester, to win the Champions League Final in Rome. In each case the match was run and won by medium-sized men with the brains and technique to outwit the athletes whose power and pace are beginning to dominate football at the expense of the subtler arts . . .

Forty-nine years ago Burnley set standards which were embodied in the Tottenham double side the following season. So it is good to see Turf Moor back in the big time and the Lancashire heartland is promised a rare pantomime now that Burnley's Cinderellas have joined the Ugly Sisters—Sam Allardyce's Blackburn and Gary Megson's Bolton—with Wigan playing Buttons . . .

There are those who would say that the game against the powerful athletes of Sheffield United was no classic. But try telling that to the 36,000 Burnley supporters who were there. It was the match of their lives.

Lacey was right in his assessment. No-one could call Burnley's Wembley team that day a team reliant on nothing but muscular, powerful, physical athletes, good at running and pressing, but lacking in flair and deftness. This was a team, and it was a team in the proper sense of the word, where the sum of the parts is greater than the individuals. In this respect it continued in the tradition of the McIlroy–Adamson Championship team of 1959–60 and then Adamson's golden team that flowered so briefly from 1973 to 1975. What the team of 2008–09 had was a blend of strength at the back, creativity in midfield and pace and skill up front. Above all there was flair and, as Lacey says, it was the small men who ran the show; Wade Elliott, Robbie Blake, Graham Alexander, Joey Gudjonsson and Martin Paterson, not one of them a giant. In their victory Burnley demonstrated to the nation that passing skills and ball control can prevail and succeed over might and muscle.

Ironically the only physical giant in the Burnley outfield was Carlisle, at 6"3' a powerful colossus who, on the day, was unbeatable in the air and impassable on the ground.

In an interview after another game, ironically against Sheffield United again in a League game only a few weeks earlier, Carlisle described the experience as like playing in the Land of the Giants. Again it had been a game where Burnley's smaller men had won although Carlisle was honest enough to describe some of his defending as 'industrial', a case of needs must. This is an articulate man indeed, and in that single word, he conjured up the image of his approach and method. He is not a man to weave his way out of defence with elegance and sophistication. He is not a man to make pinpoint 40 and 50 yard passes to the feet of a colleague on the other side of the pitch. He is direct, simple and uncomplicated. He wins it, he makes the simple pass. His job is simple—to defend. 'It is up to the likes of Chris McCann, Robbie Blake, and Martin Paterson to produce the pretty, eye-catching stuff, but the defensive unit to keep clean sheets.' At corners in the opposition half it is his job to move up into the penalty area, steam in and attack the ball. Burnley's progress to Wembley in the final weeks was marked by a string of games in which there were clean sheets and he received the man of the match award.

Club programme notes outlined the key role he played in 2008–09. They referred to his never-say-die attitude, the way he was able to dip into his own well of strength after a dip in form briefly cost him his place.

> I have got to a stage in my career where I can't be dipping below a seven out of ten. I've played 300-plus games and I am approaching 40 games this season and I haven't done that for a while. I should be experienced enough to know what is expected of me and produce it every week. It's about having a mindset and knowing that when you cross the line you are not going to take any chances or risks and just focus on your job. I get paid to defend and sometimes it may not be aesthetically pleasing as some might want and it might be quite industrious at times, but as long as the ball is not in the back of our net my job is done. I am feeling great, probably the fittest I have ever felt at this stage of the season, having played more games than in the last six or seven years.

Wembley on May 25th, 2009 was certainly the match of a lifetime for this dignified centre back in which yet again he received the best player award. It was clear from the on-pitch interview that this was a day he will never forget. The story of his journey to get there is that of a fall from grace and then a lesson in self-appraisal, determination to recover, rehabilitation, and then ultimate triumph. This is a man who faced his demons and found his renaissance.

Born in Preston in October 1979, his first club was Blackpool. There he made 100 appearances between 1997 and 2000. His form was such that QPR paid £250,000 for him in the summer of 2000. He made appearances for England at U21 level and really was seen as an emerging star. However, the injuries began and a cruciate ligament tear kept him out of the game for a year. Doctors thought he was finished. In his first game back, a reserve fixture at Bristol City, there were fears he had repeated the injury when he was forced to limp off. Fortunately it was not as bad as feared, and he was back within a month.

Carlisle spent four years with QPR, helping them win promotion to the Championship and in January 2002 he won the title of Britain's Brainiest Footballer in a TV Quiz. In a close Final he beat Alan Brazil 6–5. It was QPR's first major trophy since 1967 one newspaper pointed out not without humour.

But, by the 2003–04 season there were problems and he was admitted to the Sporting Chance Clinic for treatment for alcohol problems. The trigger came when he was axed from manager Ian Holloway's squad after going AWOL on the eve of a game.

With the knowledge I have now, I realise it had been affecting my

Stan Ternent brought promotion to the Championship

Courtesy of Burnley Football Club

Steve Cotterill followed Stan Ternent

Picture courtesy of Burnley Football Club

Matchday emotions

Pictures courtesy of Burnley Football Club

Owen Coyle, the intensity of a matchday

Picture courtesy of Burnley Football Club

**Sandy Stewart, Owen Coyle, Steve Davis
and Phil Hughes. All went to Bolton**

Picture courtesy of Burnley Football Club

**The return of Owen Coyle with
Bolton for the Carling Cup tie**

Picture courtesy of Burnley Football Club

Happy days and unbridled joy

Picture courtesy of *Burnley Express*

A triumphant team after Wembley

Picture courtesy of Paul Sandiford

Town Hall celebrations

Picture Courtesy of Paul Sandiford

A Grand Day Out

All pictures courtesy of Richard Moore

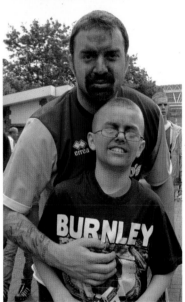

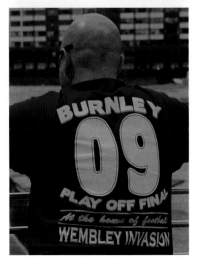

All pictures courtesy of Richard Moore

Clarke Carlisle, hero in action

Picture courtesy of Burnley Football Club

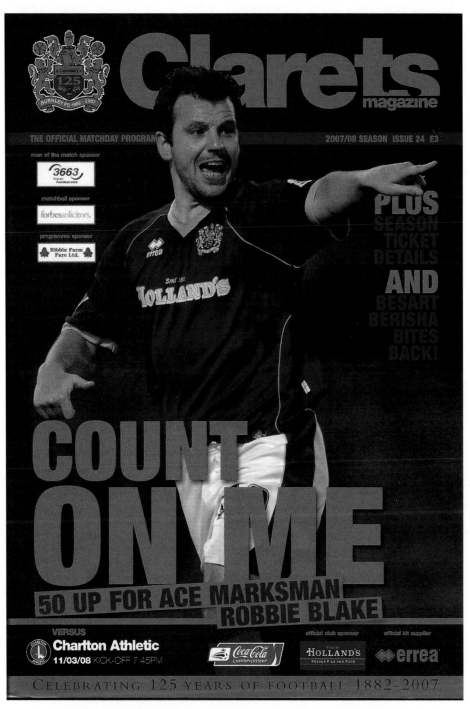

**Robbie Blake, man of the match in the Carling
Cup game against Spurs at Turf Moor**

Courtesy of Burnley Football Club

Happy days for Chairman Barry Kilby greeting Martin Paterson

Picture courtesy of Burnley Football Club

Matchday action

Picture courtesy of Burnley Football Club

Matchday moods—the faces of management

All pictures courtesy of Burnley Football Club

The new man Eddie Howe

Picture courtesy of Burnley Football Club

Carling Cup Burnley 1 Bolton 0

Picture courtesy of Burnley Football Club

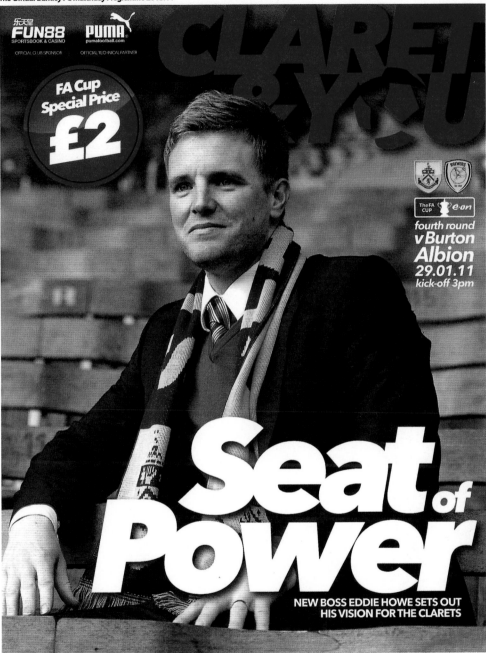

First home game for Eddie Howe

Courtesy of Burnley Football Club

Jack Cork and Chris Eagles after a Burnley win

Picture courtesy of Burnley Football Club

performance for a long time. I had been playing at nowhere near 100%. At one stage I found I wasn't actually that bothered. Then, suddenly, I had a moment of clarity and thought: Clarke what the hell are you doing? It was when clarity set in I felt at my lowest. To be honest I was scared.

Tony Adams' Sporting Chance Clinic nestles in the tranquil Hampshire countryside. There are several football stars who have attended the centre but wish to remain anonymous. Clarke Carlisle has never wished to do that. There is no pampering to ego or salary, the kitchen is a place where beans on toast are on offer. There are facilities for retaining fitness but definitely no facials. Instead of pampering there is a regime of individual and group counselling sessions. TV is allowed only in the evenings. It was at QPR that he turned to drink.

'After training I'd go to my local and have a few pints and then when I was bloated I'd shift onto cocktails or shooters and then when my friends had finished work we'd crack on into town.' His turning point was when he arrived for a match looking the worse for wear and was sent home. He was days away from getting the sack. It was then that the realisation hit him that his career was going rapidly downhill. Once there he found it mentally and physically draining going through all the emotions that came to the surface. 'There are reasons for behaviour and getting to the roots of the problems was liberating.'

He acknowledges now that what the clinic and its staff did for him was lifesaving. He acknowledged them again in his interview on the pitch immediately after the Burnley Wembley Final. The effect they had on him was not only to combat the drinking but also to help him realise that it was his reaction to certain situations that triggered the drinking. 'It was an intense and emotional 28 days.'

'Clarke's shown bravery and was man enough to face up to his problems,' said manager Holloway. 'I can only applaud him for what he has done. Nobody has seen the best of him yet and my message is to watch out for him. He can go on to play in the top flight with the new tools he's been given to deal with the rest of his life.'

Carlisle's prophetic comment was: 'I do believe I can do a lot more than almost anything I've shown in football so far.' His contract at QPR ended in 2004 after 212 appearances and six goals. Kevin Blackwell took him to Leeds United on a free transfer. There he spent just one year, playing 38 games and scoring four goals. Here too there were injury problems, torn ankle ligaments during a game at gloomy Rotherham, when there was a 0–1 defeat, keeping him out for six weeks.

Leeds accepted £100,000 for him from Watford (Stoke City too would have signed him) and he signed a three-year deal. His potential remained clear and manager Aidy Boothroyd tipped him to become one of the best defenders in the Championship. It would be five years later that Boothroyd's prediction was proved correct. Boothroyd identified that he had enormous strengths and was certain that he would become an even better player. Watford finished third in the table in 2004–05 and gained promotion to the Premiership. But by the time of the play-offs Carlisle had been injured again, this time a thigh injury, and he took no part in the final games or the Final. Nor did he take much part in the Premiership season. He missed eight months of the season finding it hard to cope with and by the time he was able to play again Watford had been relegated. He regarded the small number of games he played when he returned as a taster of Premier football. He could not have known that in 2009 he would be instrumental in another club's promotion to the Promised Land.

In the summer of 2007 Burnley manager Steve Cotterill was the next man to recognise his abilities signing him for a reported £200,000. He replaced Wayne Thomas who was sold to Southampton for over £1m. These two moves were amongst the smartest of Cotterill's deals and once he arrived at Burnley Carlisle was an almost ever-present.

The move back north was not in Carlisle's script. He had just forced his way back into the Watford side after injury and presumed he would figure in Aidy Boothroyd's plans for the season. Cotterill's phone call changed all that:

> I was all set for Watford's season and this phone call came out of the blue—apparently not so for the gaffer—he said he'd been after me for a few months, but I was completely unaware of it,' said Carlisle. 'It all just fell into place. It was excellent. I don't just want to tag along in the background, I don't believe that's a stage of my career I'm at. I believe I'm definitely a first-choice centre half and that's what I'm here to prove.

If constant injuries had been a problem for him until joining Burnley, he avoided them at Turf Moor. But tragedy might have struck if he had not had a miraculous escape from a car crash in October of 2007 when his car spun into a ditch on the way to training ahead of a game against Crystal Palace. The car was a write-off yet he emerged unscathed. In fact his wife collected him and they continued the journey to training. The following weekend he played against Crystal Palace.

'Anybody else doing another job might have had a week off work in a neck brace and a doctor's note signing him off,' commented manager Cotterill. 'Clarke did remarkably well even to play on Saturday.'

It could certainly be argued that the arrival of Owen Coyle as manager at Burnley took Carlisle's game to another higher level. Carlisle said about Coyle:

> The manager, Owen Coyle tells us week in, week out, it doesn't matter what other teams are going to do or who they've got in their side. It's all about what we do and how we can perform, because he believes—and it filtered all through the club and the squad—that if we play to the best of our ability we're more than a match for anyone . . . There's a lot of pressure . . . but when we cross that white line, a freedom to go and express ourselves and play the game in the right manner has been instilled into us, with a knowledge that the manager supports you in that—and that if we,

as a team, play to our strengths and abilities, we can win the game.

The two semi-final games against Reading were won, 1–0 at Burnley and 2–0 at Reading. Yet again Clarke Carlisle was immense in both games. To reach Wembley within the context of all the background problems, limitations and pressures was a miraculous achievement. To have actually won it was quite simply an astonishing fairy tale and with a £60m jackpot at the end of it, how those directors celebrated, although one of them, Ray Griffiths, lay in a hospital bed unable to attend this most marvellous of days.

They came from all over the world, from Bermuda, Philadelphia, Sydney, Adelaide, Melbourne, Wellington, Mexico, Bulgaria, California, Vancouver, Seattle, Yemen, Kazakhstan, Florida, Belgium, Malta, France, Norway, France and Cyprus. They came from all points of the UK compass, Ireland, Dublin, Belfast, from the tips of Scotland to the ends of Cornwall. There is a family of Burnley expatriates for whom the umbilical cord will never be stronger. And Burnley itself was half empty.

How many miles did people travel during the season to watch them, how many thousands and thousands of pounds did they spend? Which of them during the opening month of the season did not think that disaster lay ahead? Which of them did not live on their nerves towards the season's end when the prospect of success was close? Which of them did not feel despair when Burnley could only draw at Southampton, or Derby scored their last minute equaliser with just a handful of games remaining?

'Little Burnley,' the football world kept saying and little Burnley became the 'people's club' as the feeling grew in the outside world that here was a hard-up, modest club from a small town battling against the odds. The pundits and the great and good wanted them to succeed. They remembered that horrible night against Tottenham in the Carling Cup when Burnley were just two minutes away from the Final.

None of us dared contemplate with certainty a win over Sheffield when the actual day came. To be there was a bonus we consoled ourselves but for Graham Alexander it was his seventh experience of play-offs, the previous six all failed. Surely this time he would be lucky.

As it turned out, the football gods were on Burnley's side. Every Burnley player played his part none more so than Carlisle who gave a masterclass in the art of defending. But they were all on top form. Blake twisted and turned until he sent us all dizzy. Caldwell was not far behind Carlisle. Paterson ran and ran and did the work of two players, in attack one minute, defending the next. Elliott was all guile and darting runs, Duff and Kalvenes solid at the back. Thompson up front was more than a match for the physical Morgan. And the Beast, the player of the season, had a quiet day, rarely troubled by Sheffield, but was there on the rare occasions he was needed.

This was little Burnley, a founder member of the Football League and no-one could say that they had not earned their place in the Premiership. On that warm sunny afternoon the members of that team had they lost would have been heroes still. But in winning they, and Clarke Carlisle, became legends forever.

Carlisle afterwards described his feelings on the day.

Words will not describe how it felt at the final whistle to stand in that centre circle. I didn't know what to do, whether to laugh or cry. It was unbelievable—such a magnificent achievement.

It was awesome. I cried like a little girl on the pitch. It was an unbelievable time and a moment to savour. What an achievement, 61 games, 23 players. It was such a compressed workload but we did it.

Every single one of us, from the gaffer and Sandy Stewart and Steve Davis and Phil Hughes all the way through the playing staff, what I'm so proud of is from a town of 80,000 there were 36,000 out there, more wanted to come, and we performed and we gave them something to sing about. We respect their support and we're Premier League now. It's awesome.

I'm just trying to say to the lads who have always been on the fringes of success, and young lads like Alex Macdonald, Adam Kay, Jay Rodriguez, savour the moment. Moments like this don't happen ten a penny in your life. Just enjoy it and make sure you experience the 36,000 out there and all the trappings that come with it. It's an awesome day.

It had to be a normal 90 minutes, and that's why we stayed at the Bull where we stayed before the Cup games against Chelsea and Arsenal, and we made it as normal and down to earth as possible because when you step into the arena, the last thing you want is to have been daunted already.

The lads went out, did what they had to, and I was just blessed and privileged to have been a member of this.

There is no doubt that the media and the experts widely welcomed Burnley's return to the bigtime, and just about everyone who saw Carlisle's after-match interview could not fail to have been deeply moved. The press were enthusiastic in their praise for the team:

Neutrals sighed with relief at not seeing Sheffield United playing Stoke in the Premier League next season . . . instead Burnley will grace the top division, 33 years after they left it and 22 after they nearly slipped into the Conference. It gladdens the heart and makes you feel good about the old game . . . *Daily Express*

It was settled by a goal that deserved to win any game. If Burnley's tale, on a club level, is a romantic one for having been away from the top division for so long, then the goalscorer encapsulated the fairy tale nature of their ascent. Wade Elliott, 30, who settled the outcome after only 13 minutes, was a free transfer from Bournemouth having previously played in non-league football at Bashley . . . *The Independent*

Grown men cried, strangers embraced, and under a shower of ticker tape

Wembley saw an emotional outpouring that brought an end to 33 years of hurt . . . it was hard to avoid being consumed by the euphoria that greeted the minor miracle overseen by Owen Coyle . . . among the Claret and Blue hordes few ever imagined they would see this day come to pass . . . nobody can say they do not deserve it . . . *The Times*

For all ages of Burnley fans, yesterday was special . . . for the older supporters it was all about the restoration of the natural order, a return to the time when Burnley were an established force in the land . . . *The Telegraph*

All over the pitch there were Burnley heroes . . . Carlisle didn't put a foot wrong. Then there was Elliott who can dine out for life on his winner... make no mistake the better side won . . . *The Telegraph*

Burnley are back in the bigtime and ready to bring a touch of much-needed romance to the billionaire world of top-flight football. They are the smallest town ever to boast a Premier league club and their entire population could fit inside Old Trafford. What Owen Coyle and his players have achieved this season is little short of a miracle . . . and no-one could begrudge brilliant Burnley their long-awaited return to the bigtime . . . *The Sun*

It will be 50 years next season since Burnley won the title and the anniversary will be celebrated among the elite. A Lancashire town has burst into the limelight, their elevation back among the elite constituting a staggering achievement by one of the Championship's thinnest squads . . . *The Guardian*

Burnley has had its well-documented problems in the past, both social and political. But this was a match and victory that brought a town together. It was a glorious triumph, in particular for Clarke Carlisle.

10

OWEN COYLE IS GOD

It was a placard that first appeared in a vast sports stadium thousands of miles away in the USA at a Wrestlemania event. There it was; being held up in front of thousands of spectators and televised to millions more around the globe. The folks who saw it there must have wondered what on earth it was all about and who on earth was Owen Coyle. But there it was, in huge letters—**OWEN COYLE IS GOD**.

In Burnley it went down well. Here was the revered man who had achieved the impossible dream and brought Premiership football to the town. He could do no wrong and Burnley supporters would have followed him through the wilderness if necessary. When he spoke, they listened and believed. As yet, they had no reason to do otherwise. They pinched themselves regularly, and weeks after Wembley still asked was this really happening? Coyle himself shrugged off the banner and saw it simply as good natured banter. But, it would only be a matter of months before the appellation changed to something abusive, and if you had forecast that to any Burnley supporter at the beginning of the new season they would have looked at you askance. Coyle's stock was sky high and still rising. The BFC Supporters Club wrote to him:

> On behalf of Burnley Football Supporters Club, and I'm sure every true Claret, we would like to thank you, your backroom staff and players, for such a memorable season, such as Burnley supporters have not seen for many a long year. There have been many high points, with few lows, too few to mention, and it has swept us through the season and now suddenly we are at the end, dizzy, giddy, and for many still not believing that we are back in the top tier of English football for the first time for over thirty three years.
>
> We started the season with our tour of Scotland and Ireland which we enjoyed, with some excellent football and meeting a few friends. We thought we were going to be going places and a top half finish was not out of reach. The first few games were a shock and we were at the wrong end of the League table which we didn't expect. Don't know why—as the bookies had placed us there and realistically that is where we should be, based on the size of our support in comparison to other Championship sides; but that's football supporters for you. Doom and gloom were being sounded all over. However you kept the faith with what you had and the results started coming in.
>
> The Carling Cup runs, Bury, Oldham, then Fulham followed by the magical night at Chelsea, when we all went down to enjoy what we believed to be our Cup Final. But no, it was Chelsea's, but it didn't end there. Next up, the football

gods were determined to end our run and gave us Arsenal. They were also sent away with their tails between their legs. Spurs next, oh the gods were toying with us and this time after starting so well, it was a lesson that you cannot give these teams a sniff of a chance otherwise they will take it, and they did, in fine style, 4–1. The return was a formality, all we wanted to see was that we didn't disgrace ourselves, but we saw so much more. The flair and spirit was there. That night we won many friends and in the rules of any other competition we would have been through. Nobody can say that it was not our Charge of the Light Brigade, and glory in defeat. We had taken on the pride of the London clubs and given them, as so aptly put at the time, 'Capital Punishment'.

Riding high in the League, a play-off place virtually from September to the middle of December, then we had our usual winter decline, no matter which team or which manager; this is our fate. It was said that we had exhausted ourselves in the Carling Cup and now with a new run in the FA Cup we found ourselves by the end of January down to ninth, without a League win since December 20th. You again stuck by your guns and as promised always gave us good attacking football. The results again started to come good. Another good run in the Cup was obtained which fittingly ended in London where again you showed that even against the best we could play football.

You took us to the play-offs and finished with that wonderful day at Wembley. All this was done with little money and one of the smallest squads, if not the smallest in the top divisions. It was done by playing attacking, attractive football.

Mr Coyle, your name will go down in the history of Burnley Football Club and we at BFSC were privileged in being able to say we were there in the 2008–09 season to watch our team PLAY FOOTBALL under one of the greatest managers we have had. We look forward to our time in the top tier of English football which is regarded as the best of the best. In all your time you have conducted yourself as the perfect ambassador with your modesty and decorum. We again say thank you for the memories of such a fantastic season. (Courtesy of Barrie Oliver Chairman BFSC)

The memories of the fantastic season will indeed never be taken away and the thanks will remain for that wonderful period. But when Coyle's unforeseen and totally unexpected decision to leave took place just months later, parts of the letter would be re-appraised.

After Wembley, indeed even during it, there had been the Celtic scare. On the day of the game, Celtic parted company with manager Gordon Strachan. The job was Coyle's if he had wanted it. For several days when asked his intentions he was guarded with his answers. Celtic were his boyhood team. On the Town Hall balcony after the victory parade through Burnley, Alastair Campbell asked him in front of thousands would he be staying at Burnley? But the emphatic one-word answer that supporters wanted to hear was unforthcoming. What they heard was seeming avoidance of a clear unambiguous statement and what came was broad and non-committal.

Alastair Campbell for this book explained the feeling he had at the time.

I felt there was something odd about Owen Coyle on the night of the promotion itself. I joined Barry and Sonya at the team hotel for a drink; lots of players there, also some of the Celtic boys, and a great atmosphere. Owen seemed a bit distant and non-celebratory. On the balcony I sensed the same thing, only even more so. His answer was a politician's answer. I said to my son that night—he won't be with us that long.

It is arguable, although conjecture, that Coyle's thoughts were on Celtic, that he was undecided at that moment about what to do, and might well have looked wistfully once or twice at those Celtic boys and thought, those could be my players next season.

Although Chairman Kilby and Director Flood publicly insisted he would stay, one director privately revealed that some directors were unsure as to his intentions, to such an extent that possible replacements were mentioned informally, one of them being Roberto Martinez, then carving out a good reputation at Swansea.

Brendan Flood, in his book, glossed over the whole issue, maintaining that he always knew that Coyle would not leave:

> There were probably about 80 people back at the Stafford (Hotel), comprising the directors and their families and guests and lots of different people associated with the club. Owen's mate Alan Nixon turned up and Tony Livesey joined us for a few drinks. But one or two of the directors had barely shared the enjoyment before they started worrying about the rumour of Celtic being after Owen. A group of us were determined to enjoy ourselves because I knew that wouldn't be the first thing on Owen's mind. I spoke to Owen a couple of times. He was at the Grosvenor with his family and the players and we agreed to meet the day after for the bus tour around the town. But then at half twelve that night while the Clarets revellers were singing a chorus of 'Que Sera', I had a phone call from Owen and I said:
>
> 'How are we Owen?'
>
> 'Wonderful Brendan, but I want to let you know that you might get a call from up the road.'
>
> 'Up the road,' I said, but I knew what he meant. Celtic really did want him. (Courtesy of Brendan Flood)

The *Lancashire Telegraph* as early as the 26th, the day after Wembley, announced that Coyle had pledged his future to Burnley and that he had distanced himself from speculation linking him to the Celtic job.

His response to early questions was:

> First and foremost I didn't know there was a vacancy at Celtic. Someone asked me last week and I've said before, my only focus is on doing the job I'm doing. It's flattering, of course it is when people mention your name and I think it will be similar with some of my players the way they have played. That's all well and good but we're concentrating on the job we're doing here; and long may that continue.

Chris Boden on May 29th in the *Burnley Express* put the saga to bed in his article: 'Panic Over Owen's Not Going':

> Panic over, Owen Coyle has pledged his future to Burnley. Reports suggested Coyle was being lined up to take over at Celtic before the final whistle was blown in the Clarets' Championship Play-Off Final win on Monday. And the

speculation has continued all week, reaching a crescendo on Wednesday with speculation that the boyhood Bhoys fan had requested permission to speak to Celtic, and that he was about to be unveiled at Parkhead before he takes a well-deserved family holiday today. One newspaper north of the border suggested that Coyle had even met Celtic chief executive Peter Lawwell at a hotel in London's Mayfair—which Turf Moor sources struggled to believe, as he celebrated promotion with the staff. And it was even claimed he was at Celtic Park for talks on Wednesday afternoon, when he was at Turf Moor, planning ahead for an assault on the Premier League.

Coyle has been irked by the speculation, and was yesterday finalising his retained list, while holding discussions over his budget for next season with Chairman Barry Kilby. And he put to bed any doubts in continuing his 'work in progress' at Burnley.

'The bottom line is it is always flattering to be linked with other jobs. That tells you that you are doing well. But this was pure speculation. There was never any approach, and so there was no job to turn down. It is simply people putting two and two together and making five. I am going on holiday with my family this weekend and I can assure you I will be doing so as Burnley manager. All I would say is the same I have said from day one. I am fully committed to the job in hand at Burnley Football Club. We have an unbelievable adventure ahead of us, and we want to make sure that when the season kicks off, we do our best to stay in the best division in the world. It is the 50th anniversary of being champions, so what a fitting season to be back in the Premier League.'

Coyle who is contracted until the summer of 2011, and has been in discussions over an extension to his contract, was linked with the job at former club Bolton back in March before Wanderers boss Garry Megson agreed a new rolling contract. (Courtesy of Chris Boden)

It later transpired that he had spoken to Celtic two days after Wembley to see what they had to say.

On May 30th Brendan Flood in the *News of the World* claimed that he knew that the move for Coyle was doomed a month earlier even if there was a move from Parkhead.

I am 100% certain that Owen will be the manager of Burnley when the Premiership starts. There were a few rumours at the time about Strachan maybe moving on from Celtic. But Owen said to me that he would be staying at Burnley regardless of what other jobs became vacant. I genuinely believe that even if we'd lost to Sheffield United in the play-off final, Owen would still have stayed with us.

On May 31st, Alan Nixon in a *People* article wrote that Coyle was happy to take on the challenge of keeping Burnley in the Premiership after 'turning down the chance to quadruple his wages with Celtic after Strachan's departure'. Yet, in Chris Boden's piece Coyle had said there had never been any approach and therefore no job to turn down. Now, here was Nixon saying that he could have quadrupled his wages but had turned it down.

On June 1st the Chairman spoke:

I heard in the post-match conference last Monday that Strachan had gone and Owen was mentioned. It has been a big distraction and we've lost valuable time that we should have been putting into other matters, that's for sure. The Glasgow Press have been stoking this up and both of us have been a little annoyed by it all. But Owen is adamant that he's happy here. We've never had any other communication with any other club; it's all been Press speculation as far as I'm concerned. Owen is contracted to Burnley Football Club for another two years.

The Chairman's statement again begged the question: if there had been no communication with any other club; upon what was Alan Nixon basing the information that Coyle had turned down the chance to quadruple his wages? It also illustrated the whole meaninglessness of contracts in the football world. Was Coyle sounded out behind the scenes even before Wembley? Did the Wembley win put him in a real quandary? To stay or not to stay, was that his question? It was certainly something that Alastair Campbell sensed at the hotel celebrations and on the balcony steps of Burnley Town Hall.

There is no doubt that the uncertainty, to a certain degree, spoiled the victory and the occasion for many people. As it turned out, the lure of managing a team in the Premiership swayed the day. But fans (if not Flood) wondered what would have happened had Burnley lost. What would his answer have been then? It was more than reasonable to suppose that under those circumstances he might have accepted an offer. And in truth it is doubtful that anyone would have blamed him. He would have been seen as the man who took the club to Wembley, gave it his best shot, rejuvenated an ailing assortment of jaded players, and departed a hero still. No-one would have begrudged him the chance to manage the team he had grown up with and supported.

But, stay he did. The Premiership lay ahead; and its money would solve Burnley's financial problems at a stroke, securing its future for years. It would not, however, be enough to keep Coyle at the club when Bolton and Gartside eventually came sniffing.

It was around early June that the far-reaching news emerged that Brendan Flood's Modus Ventures business had been placed into administration. It was the finances behind this business that had so far allowed Brendan Flood to make significant investment in the club, thereby allowing him to take the lead in much of the decision and policy making. Flood described it as a spiteful move. 'Good news is never allowed to go unchecked and I think the connection between me and Burnley where I own 60% of the club by value, and where the Premiership is likely to mean a financial lift, hasn't gone unnoticed. It was a spiteful move.'

Flood and Modus had been badly affected by the worldwide recession, and all the associated banking and credit problems. The liquidity necessary for implementing his large scale shopping-arcades projects was no longer there.

Spiteful or not, the administration process would cost the club dear later in the year, when the administrators clawed back £5.5million from Burnley

Football Club. Flood's loans to the club had been repayable if and when promotion to the Premiership was achieved. The administrators KPMG called back the loan of £3.7million; the interest added was another £1.8million. It was paid to KPMG on January 13th, 2010. Coming at the same time as Coyle's defection to Bolton, it is arguable that had that money been available for player purchases and team investment, then he might have been persuaded to stay. Flood himself would not have recalled the loan and possibly would have increased it for Coyle's use.

His business problems, and his curtailed voting position on the Board, did not stop Flood from continuing his high-profile position at the club and Press appearances. In fact he would be referred to as the 'club-owner' more than once in the Press, when in fact he was not. It was Flood who outlined the club's forthcoming policy and what Coyle would be looking for, now they were in the Premier League.

Chris Boden wrote in the *Burnley Express* on June 5th:

Burnley are set to buy British as they prepare for life in the Premier League. As the Clarets look to build on one of the secrets of their success—the strong bond between players—Owen Coyle is likely to maintain his focus within these shores. But don't be surprised to see a couple of foreign players adding to the flavour at Turf Moor. With players flooding in from the continent since the advent of the Premier League in 1992, with agents trying to secure moves for clients left, right and centre, there is a tendency to look abroad to strengthen. But Coyle is always careful to ensure any signings are of the right character, however, and will be loathe to taking any gambles.

Operational Director Brendan Flood said: 'We think we can be successful with British players and perhaps some of the Scandinavian lads like Jensen, Gudjonnson and Kalvanes. They seem to settle better in England, so I think we'll go for more of the same, people who are settled foreigners in the UK, or more of a British theme.'

It is a policy partly operated by Manchester United who have added to their conveyor belt of young talent from their academy with the likes of Rio Ferdinand and Michael Carrick while signing players such as Edwin van der Saar, Carlos Tevez and Dimitar Bernatov, who had all played in England prior to moving to Old Trafford. Speaking of Tevez, Flood mused:

'It's a dangerous game. The best thing we've got is that team and club spirit, and if we break it, it would be breaking the hidden secret. We've got to keep everyone nice and grounded but believing in themselves. That's the message. We're not going to sign anyone who's demanding £30,000 a week. If they're chasing the money then it turns Owen off. If they want to play football, but obviously get paid a fair rate, then that's more in his mind. I think we'll try to get the right type of people for the club and try to add to what we've got.'

Burnley have a squad of 26 professionals including five apprentices who have been given their first deals. Coyle is expected to bolster that number significantly, although, as Flood added: 'There's no-one in the squad that we're instantly thinking "he's going to have to go" because the ones who have got us there are a tight squad and they've all played their part. I think he's very much focused on giving them a chance. There'll be six or seven players tops. Not all bought—I think there'll be a mix of bought and loaned. We know we've got three or four who we'd like to get now and we're working on, but with holidays nothing will happen for a few weeks. But the identity of the players we're after is younger, probably the 20 to 24 years old bracket.' (Courtesy of Chris Boden)

Hopes were high behind the scenes that Burnley could emulate clubs like Stoke City, a club that had struggled to cope at first, made mistakes after promotion, but learned from them, then bought shrewdly and played to their strengths. But it was also a desire 'to do a Stoke with style'. Coyle above all wanted pace at the back and the two young Sheffield full backs that had such impressive games at Wembley certainly came under the spotlight, until it became clear they were out of the Burnley budget bracket, one of them in fact going very quickly to Spurs. Hopes were high that a good relationship with Manchester United would lead to loan deals for a couple of their emerging stars.

The stage was thus set for another influx of players, several more magical moments in the club's story, full houses, pride and passion, and one night in particular when a Robbie Blake goal would cause celebrations of such a magnitude that the very walls and foundations of Turf Moor shook to the core.

The fixtures were released. There were gasps at games two, three, four and five, and disappointment that game one would be away at Stoke—the land of the giants where it was compulsory to be 6"2' or more. But it was the next four games that made people think that Burnley would end the month on nil points—Manchester United, Everton, Chelsea and Liverpool.

If fans were apprehensive, and battling through long queues to get season tickets, Coyle simply got on with the job of signing players. Never short of a soundbite, he provided the next one having worked out a new contract deal with the club:

Everyone knows my feelings for the football club and how much I've enjoyed it from day one. I said, with some of the players I brought in, I wasn't bringing them for the sake of a short fix. It was for the longevity of the club. There were overtures in terms of one or two of our players and I said that I wanted them to stay, so it would have been remiss of me thinking that I want them to stay . . . but if something comes up for me in terms of a wage . . . it was never an issue.

The signings rumours began, first Jason Scotland from Wigan, and then Danny Welbeck from Manchester United. A wage ceiling story of £15,000 a week was unconfirmed. Coyle commented:

We have all seen some clubs spend beyond their resources and finish up in peril. I have my budget and will respect and work within that budget and buy the best players I can. I want players here who are willing to represent this club. The motivation has to be about football. If your motivation is about money, then you are not for me. There will be some players who are happy to sit around as squad players, but there is also a group of players who want to play and that is the type I need to bring in. In terms of Premier League salaries, we will be the lowest payers, but equally, they will still be good salaries in life, so players have to be aware of that. We are looking to strengthen every area and I am clear about what is required.

Tyrone Mears, a pacy specialist full back, was the first signing from Derby County. From there he had gone AWOL to have a trial for Marseille where he was eventually allowed to go on loan. There were comments about his professionalism, but at Burnley Coyle indeed brought out the best in him so that his pace and ability to get forward became key assets once the season began. His progress and displays were such that at one stage he would be seen as worthy of an England call-up. Mears commented that he signed because Coyle had told him he could bring out the best in him and he 'wanted to work with this manager'. Coyle's persuasiveness was in full flow again. Mears commented that Burnley were 'a little bit behind other clubs in terms of facilities'. In truth he must have looked askance at the lack of modern and comfortable facilities at the Gawthorpe training ground and at the antiquated dressing rooms and shared baths at Turf Moor that had changed little since the last time Burney were in the top-flight, 33 years earlier.

The next rumour involved Adam Johnson from Middlesbrough. The names came thick and fast, Steven Fletcher from Scotland, Marcus Tudgay from Sheffield Wednesday. Next up were James McCarthy from Hamilton and Matt Mills from Doncaster. Of these five, Fletcher from Hibernian was the one who signed. The name 'Coyle' was clearly useful. Fletcher said, 'As soon as I heard that Burnley were after me, and knowing Owen Coyle from my time in Scotland, I thought this was the right place to come'.

The next speculation involved Andrew Driver from Hearts. But it was David Edgar, a tall centre back, who was next in from Newcastle. However, he, along with two other young signings, Richard Eckersley from Manchester United, and Brian Easton from Hamilton, would feature little during the coming season. These were young players that Coyle saw as being lads to develop for the future, 'the longevity of the club', as he put it and an expression that once again had people thinking this was not a man who would be leaving very soon. If these players were made aware of this when they signed, then it says much for Coyle's powers of persuasion that they agreed to sign. Eckersley said that he 'was desperate to play first-team games'. He did not get his wish.

There were a few comments that Coyle was signing boys to do men's work. His response was emphatic:

> The easiest thing, from a selfish point of view, would be to go out and sign four or five players and cost the club big salaries, but it would be remiss of me to do that in my duties as manager of the football club; and I won't. It means that if we put a team out that have to learn quickly then that's what we'll do. But I've got no doubts these players can evolve. We haven't got the finished article and many haven't played at this level, but what I know is that we have the desire and ability to cope. We want to hit the ground running—every team will want to do that and we're no different—but it's

not about today or tomorrow. It's making sure we can put in place a team that can get better year by year. We're trying to make sure that anything we put in place is part of a long-term plan for the longevity of the football club. That's the only way forward. Otherwise you put yourself into the realms of financial ruin, really.

It was spin such as this that made Burnley supporters believe that, if he wouldn't be Burnley manager forever, at least he would not leave too quickly. Here was a man who talked about 'longevity . . . a long term plan . . . it's not about today or tomorrow . . . plans that will serve us well for years to come.' These were the words, people believed, of a man who, if not at Burnley permanently, would be around for at least the coming season.

Alan Nixon wrote of the financial restraints Coyle would experience:

Burnley is just 25 miles from Manchester, but boss Owen Coyle is living in another world to Mark Hughes and his City money. Coyle is reeling from the realities of the Premier League—after coming to terms with the mind-boggling figures he is up against in the big time. As it was revealed that Manchester City's wage bill alone this season will top £100million, Coyle admits his entire budget for salaries and buying players is just £16million. City spent that much alone on Kolo Toure. It is a good job Coyle has a sense of humour as he looks forward to the new season.

And, he confirmed that Burnley were so skint last season they were banned from signing players. He said: 'I did have to smile when the LMA sent out the figures for the budgets from the 2007–08 season. Derby were bottom of the table and still had twice as much then to spend as we do. There's no doubt we have the smallest budget by a country mile. People talk about winning promotion in the £60million game, but it's not like that. You don't get that amount the next day. I soon realised what we have to work with. But this club doesn't want to put itself in a position like Southampton and Charlton and be over-stretched. We have put in place a plan that will serve us well for years to come.'

Coyle knows every game will be a financial mis-match but is used to that. He said: 'I had a good upbringing as a manager in Scotland where finances were tight. I know the hardship involved at a smaller club and that stands you in good stead. You have to deal with it, if you don't it affects the whole club, you shield people from that.'

Coyle kept Burnley's plight from anyone outside the club last season. They had two embargoes from signing new players because they were late with payments to Scunthorpe and Manchester United for Martin Paterson and Chris Eagles. He said: 'Those weren't ideal circumstances, but nobody knew. It was just cash-flow problems but this is an honourable club and the money was paid in the end. It shows what a remarkable achievement it was to get promoted. I couldn't sign anyone, but in the end it was the making of us. I had such a tight group of players that pulled us through.'

Coyle has made some signings, Steven Fletcher from Hibs joined Richard Eckersley, Tyrone Mears, David Edgar and Brian Easton. He said: 'We could not afford to bring in experienced Premier League players because of the salaries. Our lads are on roughly the same, so we didn't want to disrupt that. The guys who got us here deserve their crack, some want to show what they can do and others have something to prove. It will be daunting, we will be massive underdogs, but we are not scared.' (Courtesy of Alan Nixon)

The results of pre-season training friendly games were mixed. There were games in the USA. One was lost. Straight off the plane and back home there was an unconvincing draw with Accrington Stanley. There was a defeat away at Bradford City. And in the final pre-season game at home to Leeds United there was a 1–2 defeat and more than a few worried supporters although others claimed that pre-season games weren't about results, but only fitness.

We all make forecasts before the start of the new season. Supporter Pauline Pratley was at the game and got her predictions spot on, though one thing she did not foresee, was the manager's untimely defection. You could see where the game was heading. She wrote:

> Downhill faster than a ferret on a waterslide.
>
> I always think that one's immediate reaction to an event is the most meaningful. As time passes, even the worst experiences can be rationalised into something better, possibly even (in a quasi religious 'suffering is good for you' kind of way) into something beneficial. Time does indeed heal all wounds. At the moment though, I'm thinking that if last season was a dream, the coming one could well be a nightmare. I tend to agree with the triumphant Leeds fans that they will indeed see us in the Championship in 2010–11 (yes I think Leeds will go up). I say this not because the Clarets are the bookies' favourites for relegation, but because today they seemed to lack both commitment and cohesion. I'm going to do my best to enjoy the coming season, but I'm so pessimistic that I'm going to predict a bottom-three finish. It gives me no pleasure to say this, but you heard it here first. (Courtesy of Pauline Pratley)

Coyle himself admitted that although results weren't important, nevertheless it was a pre-season that hadn't gone quite to plan. Of the Accrington and Leeds United results he said:

> I can't say I was pleased with that. That wasn't about progress and development. That was a bit of courage at the end and a bit of bravery. We know the reasons for it because the flights back were gruelling, but we felt it was important we took the game to help Accrington financially. Our fans turned out in numbers so it's nice they have been rewarded with a couple of goals late on, but it's certainly not the result I would have envisaged before the game. We looked very fatigued and we lost soft, soft goals. Accrington acquitted themselves very well, but we were well short of our standards.
>
> We've done the longer fitness stuff; we'll look to add that sharpness, to progress the speed and movement of the ball, which we didn't move quickly enough against Leeds. It seemed very one-paced. We're known for our sharpness and movement, so that's what we'll look to increase now. Results in pre-season aren't important, but it's always nice when you do get them

along with performances. We got neither on Saturday. There's plenty to work on, but that's what we like doing. We've got a tremendous work ethic and we'll make sure we get on the training ground and work our socks off to rectify those things. Nobody ever handed us anything, we earned the right to be here by working hard and showing quality, and that's what we'll have to do again. There's a tremendous anticipation and sense of excitement, and when it comes about we have to make sure we're ready for it. You only have to look at the opening fixtures to tell you you're in the best League in the world, and that's why the players will look to drive themselves on and increase that sharpness so that come Stoke we're ready to progress.

With just days to go another new arrival was announced. Though he had featured in the American tour it was early August before South American Fernando Guerrero put pen to paper in a loan deal. Supporters were intrigued by this one. He was a young winger, could dribble at pace and had once been a starlet at Real Madrid. He would be another one who rarely featured although he quickly became a fans' favourite.

Through July and August the media homed in on Burnley and Coyle. Alastair Campbell had a lengthy piece in the *Observer* Sunday Supplement. Not often do you see a big football piece in there. In all the dailies, including the *Telegraph*, *The Times*, *Guardian* and *Independent*, there were almost regular full page features. Several featured Wade Elliott, scorer of the Wembley goal. Alan Nixon in the *Mirror* appeared to have a hotline direct to Owen Coyle. *The Times* feature stoked up the old Flood reference to Coyle being the new Bill Shankly and described how he still loved playing, be it in reserve games, Friday morning training sessions or the old pros Masters Team. A *Telegraph* piece drew parallels with Harry Potts. Another article spotlighted Burnley's quiet-man chairman, Barry Kilby. Features on Wade Elliott in two other newspapers both included references to Turf Moor, 'the old turnstiles, it's wooden, it's rickety, a little bit boisterous and the crowd are right on top of you. It's old school, a bit of a departure from what you're used to in the Premier League'. Oliver Brown wrote about 'dank concourses, pervaded by the aroma of fish and chips [although he must be the only person who has seen anyone inside the ground eating fish and chips] and the evocatively English panorama of slate-roofed terraces meandering up to the cloud-crested Pennines.'

But it was the changing rooms that featured in more than one piece, one of them in the *Independent*. If not exactly a secret weapon, the players at Burnley quietly chuckled at thoughts of the big stars arriving to find the almost Dickensian conditions.

When the football fixtures were announced in June, Burnley's Chief Executive Paul Fletcher was quick to point out that opposition teams could like the Turf Moor set-up or lump it. Not for Fletcher the subservient outlook of a small town club that snuck its way into the world's most demanding top flight via the play-offs. Yes Turf Moor would get a lick of paint and probably a few new light bulbs, but change does not come fast in these parts, and that includes dressing rooms which Fletcher pointed out have not been improved since he played for Burnley 35 years ago.

Robbie Blake commented:

> To be fair they've spruced the dressing rooms up a bit. I don't think the away dressing room here was up to standard for the Premier League, now they've put a couple more showers in. I've heard it's not much more than a lick of paint and a new light bulb though. But we can't make it too hospitable for them. We can't go putting sofas in and things like that. It's not the best place to come, but we like that. We want to make Turf Moor as difficult as we can for teams to come here. It might be an advantage for us if teams are walking down the cold tunnel thinking this looks a bit dodgy.

Graham Alexander agreed: 'It's a bit dark down there in the depths of Turf Moor. If you haven't experienced it before, it's definitely different from the big new grounds that you get in the Premier League, and even at Championship level.'

Fletcher laughed it off thinking of the stars who expected saunas, individual baths; private showers, and heated floor tiles, rather than the 35-year old communal plunge bath where in the old days 11 players all piled in and turned the water muddy and black within minutes: 'They've got pegs, coat hangers and the bath. It isn't palatial but they're here to play football, not stay in a hotel.'

First up ironically, of the big boys to visit the bath, were the glam boys, Manchester United. Supporters couldn't wait for this mouth-watering first home fixture under the floodlights. Unfortunately the computer had not provided Coyle with an easy first game. Stoke City awaited. And along with it, the pundits waited too, pens and pencils sharpened so that they could report their predictions, that with the arrival of reality, the fairy tale was about to end.

11

A RESPONSIBILITY TO DO THE RIGHT THING

The emotion was palpable. The sense of pride was huge. The ranks of Burnley supporters massed behind the goal in the away end at Stoke to a person were still shaking their heads at what they were about to witness and its improbability. Burnley in the Premiership, the first game, the first kick-off; it was wonderful. Dream, fairy tale, call it what you like, the band of brothers and the inspirational manager had brought something that few people, if any, thought possible. Alas, Stoke soon handed Burnley a couple of salutary lessons in the Britannia Wind Tunnel Stadium after an immaculately observed tribute to Sir Bobby Robson.

Burnley were neat, tidy, industrious and employed the brand of football that had impressed so many the season before. 'Caressing the ball with a natural grace,' said one report. But whilst Burnley were lightweight, Stoke were Stoke; big, physical, powerful and stronger. There were shouts for penalties twice that might have gone Burnley's way, once when McCann nearly had his shirt removed and the second for a clear handball.

But, if the fairy tale was destined to continue, Burnley would have contained the usual Stoke tactics of long ball and long throws. But they did not. A free kick from just outside the box floated onto the head of the unmarked Shawcross, 1–0. Fifteen minutes later the famed Delap long throw was hurled over and Jordan headed into his own net. Stoke must have thought Christmas had come early.

But losing at the Britannia was no disgrace. Stoke had won there ten times in the previous season and were well used to the wiles of the Premiership. However, the worry was, if Burnley had succumbed so easily to an average side like Stoke, what fate awaited them at the hands of the superclubs. Overcoming Premier teams in one-off Carling games was all well and good, but over a full relentless season was far different. Clarke Carlisle was still confident. 'We're not scared. This is where we want to be. Results on your own patch are integral to any team's success from the top of the League to the bottom. We'll be looking to make Turf Moor a fortress. It'll be a culture shock for a lot of teams going there and we've got to capitalise on that.' Nor was he worried by the approach of

Manchester United. 'That's why we're here, bring it on.'

'We've seen today that the margins for error in this League are minimal,' said Coyle. 'People often get too caught up in, "Did West Brom go down last season because they played flowing football?" No, they went down because they created a lot of self-inflicted mistakes. That's what happened to us here. We shot ourselves in the foot.'

The bigger news, however, was that Coyle was trying to sign Andre Bikey from Reading, but too late to figure in the Stoke game. It raised everyone's eyebrows, not just because he was just the sort of powerful, physically strong player with a real presence that Burnley lacked, but because of the memories of his astonishing behaviour during the Burnley versus Reading play-off game.

'Burnley on their Bikeys', headlined Alan Nixon:

> Burnley are trying to rush through a £2.8million deal for Andrey Bikey to give him a dream debut against Manchester United tomorrow. Bikey headed north from Reading to talk personal terms and have a medical ahead of joining Owen Coyle's men in time to face Sir Alex Ferguson's men at Turf Moor. Coyle and his money men have pushed the boat out for Bikey who should go straight into the back-line after an opening day defeat at Stoke City exposed their defensive weaknesses. The Cameroon defender will be clear to play as he serves a four-match ban as a Reading player—even though he should join Burnley hours before that match. Bikey was suspended after being sent off against Burnley in the play-offs. He then tore his shirt off and threw it to the ground in protest. But because of a technicality Bikey's ban will be completed when the Royals visit Swansea—a loophole Spurs exploited as they fielded Sebastien Bassong on Sunday. Coyle will have spent his entire budget with the powerful African his second-most expensive capture after striker Steven Fletcher. (Courtesy of Alan Nixon)

Burnley fans welcomed the signing of this excellent player seen by many as the best centre half in the Championship. It was seen as a real acquisition by Coyle. The Burnley players welcomed him in the well-worn manner of typical footballers' schoolboy pranks. When he joined them for training for the first time—they all greeted him by ripping off their shirts. Wednesday August 19th and it was a date in the calendar that had supporters drooling in both exhilaration and trepidation.

Coyle set the scene:

> The atmosphere will be brilliant and we will have to replicate the form we showed against the elite teams in the Cup last year. If we do that, we have a chance but we will have to be at our maximum, anything less and we will be undone. If we get to that standard and consistency, I've no doubt we will get points. We'll do everything we can to try to get about the champions and show we can play a bit.

There could not have been a better first home fixture. Nobody confidently predicted a win, fans might have hoped, dreamed, but there was no expectation. And yet, the unexpected happened. I recorded the amazing evening in my diary:

It was just a wonderful night and on the drive over I began to think this might just be the kind of night that we had against Tottenham with a huge upset on the cards maybe. And so it was, with Robbie Blake scoring a wonderful volleyed goal, and Jensen saving a penalty . . . A warm, summer evening, blue sky and shirt sleeves, the ground a packed mass of claret and blue . . . Expectation and the hum of excitement . . . anticipation rising all day . . . the ground immaculate . . . the pitch perfect . . . everywhere shoulder to shoulder, the noise deafening . . . United skilful, finding spaces, wonderful movement, silky smooth, first touch passing, until the edge of the box and then so weak . . . their approach play foundered against Burnley's resolute defence now including the awesome Bikey with his shirt kept on tonight . . .

And then around 20 minutes gone . . . out of nothing Blake sees the ball coming to him somewhere on the edge of the corner of the box, headed out by a defender . . . he doesn't think but simply lashes it on the volley and it's in the back of the net before anyone can realise . . . for a second there is astonished, disbelieving silence . . . then all hell breaks loose . . . the noise is volcanic . . . the effect bedlam . . . three sides of the ground on their feet, exultant, wild . . . utter unrestrained madness.

Probably no-one in the ground thought Burnley could hold out especially when Blake gives away a penalty . . . since when has he ever been a box to box player . . . but now he is . . . heads droop, hearts stop . . . but Beast saves miraculously and we wonder is the impossible about to happen . . .

The second half . . . nerves . . . time dragging the longer it goes on . . . grim faces . . . chewed nails . . . on and on it goes . . . vocal support incessant . . . next shot of the game from Elliott from 25 yards . . . why isn't Rooney sent off for a savage tackle on Mears? Four minutes extra-time . . . come on, hold on, hold out . . . and then final whistle . . . disbelief . . . incredulity . . . astonishment . . . speechless . . . a result that will travel round the world, this is huge news . . . from New York Times to Shanghai South China Press. Blake's goal fabulous and will be played over and again on Sky . . . this was a night of nights, an occasion to cherish and remember for years . . . a shining, glorious result that knocked us all for six . . . (Personal Diary August 19th 2009)

The Press were ecstatic in their praise:

What an incredible evening, what an incredible goal . . . The James Hargreaves Stand shook so violently it was unnerving . . . They just do not build stadiums like this these days . . . A brilliant night, one that re-affirms your faith in everything that is good about the Premier League . . . when form, logic and just about everything else were turned on their heads . . . where the impressive Owen Coyle out-thought Sir Alex Ferguson . . . This was as good as it gets . . . One of the greatest upsets in Premier League history . . . a stunning strike from veteran Robbie Blake . . . As collectors' items go, Blake's goal will take some beating, it was a peach of a strike . . . Chants at Rooney, 'You're not Robbie Blake, you're not Robbie Blake' . . . A

33-year wait but boy did it taste sweet . . . No-one could argue the Clarets did not deserve it for their energy, enterprise and resilience . . . Fireworks lit up the sky more than an hour after the final whistle and the town was still vibrant with the sound of car horns . . . A night to remember that served as a warning to every other Premier League club that this fantastic little ground could prove a difficult place to visit.

Coyle beamed:

I'm absolutely thrilled with the three points. If anyone looked at our first five fixtures, people probably thought Burnley would be sat with zero points. Each and every one of the players played their part and I would hope that we'll take that belief and confidence into another massive game against Everton. It's nice to prove one or two wrong and what we have to do is disprove more over the course of the season. If you look at the financial side and everything else, Burnley in the Premier League is a total mismatch, but we have belief and quality and an unbelievable work ethic. We're going to have to produce that each and every game. At times Turf Moor gets a bad reputation. They want to call it ramshackle and there are two old stands. But for me, I'm from the old school that loves that atmosphere and that type of stadium. We had that atmosphere last season against Tottenham Hotspur in the semi-final, and when this place is at capacity and the fans are on song, the place is absolutely rocking. At times it was hard to hear the whistle. The fans have a part to play and they did that.

The result changed a few opinions. The certainty that Burnley would be relegated was now tempered. The pundits looked and wondered. Brendan Flood was sure they would stay up in football heaven because they had manager Coyle and his flock of players:

We have got 'God' and you don't get higher than that. It's that simple, Owen took us up. He saw what the players here had and that if it isn't broke, don't fix it. He knows his men and how to keep them happy. He looks after them individually and they all feel wanted and part of the team. His biggest talent is man-management and he will find a large part of this year will be dealing with the lads who are not featuring, but he has the skills to cope with that. Owen wears his heart on his sleeve but he is also measured at the same time. I've known lots of people in life and I know when you've got a winner—and I've got one with him. His team around him are winners too. It's a great combination and a good staff led by a very committed manager.

He was sure that the passing style would flourish:

When you have the United guys up your backsides it's a fair test of how much control you have got. You could see that we were comfortable on the ball; our midfield gave as good as they got. I also saw us against Stoke; they put five passes together at best and we regularly managed nine or ten in our movements. I just wish there was more time between games, there are too many highs all at once at the moment.

Flood's confidence and ebullience was the result of the euphoria following the United night but much of what he pointed to, was appropriate. His forecast of a tenth place was tongue in cheek, but a lower half-place was not beyond the bounds of possibility—as long as Coyle remained. How was Flood to know that Coyle would leave?

Henry Winter spotlighted Coyle and Burnley in the build-up to game three against Everton again at Turf Moor. He pointed to a local saying— 'if you kick a person in Burnley the whole town limps'. Togetherness was a major factor. The kicking analogy would never be more appropriate in January when Coyle left. After the win over Manchester United Coyle told his boys to go out and enjoy the night knowing that he could trust them to down a beer or two sensibly. Coyle had 65 texts after the game and answered every one. 'Coyle stirs loyalty,' wrote Winter. It was a loyalty he developed in the supporters as well as the players.

'So the directors worship him. As the players do; as the fans do.' However, they would all feel their devotion and loyalty had been betrayed when he departed.

After the game, Coyle was eager to be hospitable towards his illustrious visitor. Ferguson had a well-known penchant for good wine. A staff member was despatched to acquire a couple of bottles of the finest Red for the occasion with Coyle hardly expecting to entertain Ferguson after a 1–0 win. He memorised the tasting notes of the two expensive bottles. But then, as a non-drinker himself ordered that the wine should be put in the fridge little knowing that this is not exactly what you do with a fine Red.

'Worth his Wade in Goals' headlined Alan Nixon when Burnley then beat Everton 1–0 at Turf Moor, another result that had pundits wide-eyed.

'One Ell of a start, one Ell of a bunch of players, definitely one Ell of a manager and certainly one Ell of a story', the piece opened, Ell being Elliott who scored the single winning goal.

> Burnley were meant to be the Claret at the bottom of the Premier League barrel. Instead they are playing the champagne football that could see them in the top half at this rate. Wembley promotion hero Wade Elliott scored the worthy winner to prove he and his unsung pals can cut it at the highest level, and how, in a thrilling performance packed with passion and skill. This was no fluke, even though Everton missed a dodgy penalty. And that let Owen Coyle celebrate a double dream.
>
> In the space of five unforgettable days Coyle has become the new managerial king of Glasgow, seeing off Sir Alex Ferguson and now David Moyes to confirm he is the rising star of the game. The amazing thing is that Burnley looked every inch a Premier League side from the first explosive minute when Martin Paterson headed against the bar and Steven Fletcher hit the rebound at Tim Howard. Paterson missed a point-blank header from Elliott's delightful cross as Everton were blown away by their invention. The touches of Robbie Blake, Chris McCann and Elliott were

definitely top-drawer. Blake and McCann set up Fletcher for a volley on the same spot where the famous Manchester United winner was struck, but he dragged his effort wide as the Goodison men hung on.

Everton could not impose themselves on the Clarets because Coyle's crew matched them for effort and stood strong against their physical players. Clarke Carlisle and new boy Bikey were immense. And Burnley made them pay after a concerted attack, started by Blake's trickery and finished when Elliott curled a shot past Howard with a slight deflection off Phil Neville's despairing tackle. It was Elliott's first goal in top-flight football, with the under-rated star proving he can hit them with his left foot as well as the legendary right that won the play-off final.

The quality of both sides dipped as the game went on, their midweek exertions taking their toll, but still Burnley had the maturity to play at their own pace and in their own way. Blake and Elliott enjoyed the time and space on the ball that ironically they were never given in the lower levels and some of their combination work was a joy to watch. McCann almost scored from a glorious Blake ball, but they needed a second goal as Everton are resolute even on their bad days.

Tim Cahill put one shot wide and was denied a close-range header by the impressive Bikey. Burnley were stung into a reply and McCann's overhead kick was just kept out by Howard. Moyes threw on Jo and put two strikers up front, a positive move that almost brought reward. Tony Hibbert won a dubious penalty when he dived dramatically over McCann's challenge. But, there was some justice when Louis Saha capped a sloppy performance by missing the target completely—the second game running where Burnley have survived a spot-kick scare.

Elliott was the hero again at the death when he blocked Jack Rodwell's shot after Brian Jensen had been caught out of his goal. But, overall few could complain about the result. (Courtesy of Alan Nixon)

Coyle was careful to keep his feet on the ground after the game:

> I believe we were the better team, but the big moment of the game was the penalty. The players are adamant that there wasn't any contact but it was a gilt-edged chance to equalise that went by. We started at a terrific pace and with quality football. The players did everything we asked of them. We were 1–0 up and still put three strikers on, that's the way we're going to play. We have had a great week, but that's all it is. We will still be favourites for relegation. But the good thing is we have points on the board. It's Chelsea next and we will be respectful but we will look to go and play our game by committing men forward.

The six points on the board were six points that few people expected. Fans had looked at the fixture list thinking okay our season starts in September. The comment about still having three forwards on the pitch when 1–0 up in the latter stages of the game, was telling. It encapsulated the Coyle philosophy. It was fine when it worked, and so far it had, but it didn't in the next three away games and the goals flowed in—at the wrong end. At Chelsea Burnley were given a football lesson, the Carling victory, simply a blip in the great scheme of things as far as Chelsea fans were concerned. At Liverpool, although Burnley competed well, four more goals were shipped making seven in just the two games. The experts nodded their heads; was this not what they had forecast? And then at Tottenham another five went in provoking the joke that Burnley would surely ship six in the fourth away game.

At Chelsea it might have been so different had Paterson made more of a golden chance that came his way with the score at 0–0. And even right up until the stroke of half-time it was still 0–0. But then, once Anelka scored it was game over, and two more came from Ballack and Cole. Coyle took a lot of positives from the game however:

> We certainly tried to contribute to the game; we obviously came with a plan, as you do when you come to places like Chelsea. We were well in the game there's no doubt about that. We had one or two opportunities in the first half. We are not deluding ourselves, Chelsea had a host of chances and Brian had some big saves. You think you're going to get into half-time at 0–0, and with everything to play for, and the first goal I thought there might have been a suspicion of offside but there's no doubt over the piece that Chelsea were deserving winners. There's no argument about that, we are just a little disappointed as a group that we have come here and lost 3–0 and that's a measure of how far we have come in such a short space of time. We'll take that disappointment on, but I've thanked the lads in there for the start of the season and everything they have given me. Everyone has seen the effort and commitment we have in the team and we have to continue to do that. We'll take our medicine, it was a lesson at times, the way Chelsea pass and move the ball, but that's why they're world-class players. The disappointment was losing the goal on the stroke of half-time and then five minutes after the break. You have to focus and be so concentrated and we should have cleared the ball for the second goal. Ashley Cole popped up with a wonder finish and at 3–0 the game's beyond you. Pato is so honest he's in the dressing room apologising to the lads. I've said to him, 'I've no problem with people missing chances. I had a career full of them, I can assure you'. The problem comes when you are not getting opportunities, so there are positives to take. What we do recognise is that we are not going to be playing Chelsea every week. What we have to focus on is the teams that will be in and around our group and make sure we get the points in those games.'

With goals starting to pour in through the leaky defence, Alan Nixon, before the Liverpool game, cast the spotlight on defender Clarke Carlisle, man of the match at Wembley.

> Clarke Carlisle has found out that the Premier League's superstars are not as big as he thought they were—in size anyway. Burnley defender Clarke Carlisle has waited a playing lifetime to take on the best in the game and admitted he was intimidated by them until he actually stood next to them. The far-travelled centre half stands at 6"3' and confessed that he thought he would be looking up at the top-flight elite before he came face-to-face with them. Carlisle laughed:
> 'I had only really seen those guys on TV and I was shocked when I played

against the likes of Wayne Rooney and Michael Owen. They're only little. These players are just not as big as I imagined. It's only when you see them that you realise I'm bigger than you. It's all very psychological until you come up against them. You think they have an aura about them. I was shocked when I realised, but you soon find out that their football 'presence' is still vast all the same. I only watched these guys on *Match of the Day* before, just to see the goals. The other surprise is that the game is not that fast all the time. It can be slow, slow a lot of the time and then in a few seconds they go from left back to right-wing to the back of your net in the blink of an eye. Your concentration levels have to be so high. The top five sides keep the ball for fun.'

Carlisle goes to Liverpool today for the very first time. And that comes on the back of facing Manchester United, Everton and Chelsea in a crash course of learning. (Courtesy of Alan Nixon)

At Liverpool the talking point was not so much the final scoreline, but how quiet and uninspiring Anfield was. This was not the awesome, fear-inducing, passionate temple of football that supporters had been led to believe was the norm. But, in went four goals. Coyle was hurt but remained upbeat:

We certainly take no points from it, and I'm disappointed we lost 4–0. I felt we started well, and at 0–0 there was nothing in it. Liverpool had a couple of long range shots and we looked comfortable, but as I said to the lads in the dressing room, what we do take from it is knowing that if you switch off at any given moment, the quality Torres, Benayoun and Gerrard have will punish you. The first goal, albeit it was a very good finish, came after we backed off into our own box. To do that against the Liverpools of this world, you're going to be punished. The second goal looked offside on the rebound, and that gave us a mountain to climb. We still kept trying to come forward, created a few opportunities, and over the piece I can't argue with the result. Liverpool certainly merited three points. There are positives to take, but equally, there's work to be done in terms of stopping gifting soft goals. Collectively when we're at the top of our game, then we can win points in the Premier League, and that's what we'll look to do. The start was the pleasing aspect, and we lost the second goal when it was our best period of the game. At 1–0 down we were controlling the game, but that's what Chelsea, Liverpool Manchester United and Arsenal all have at their disposal. They suck you in, you pass and move the ball, look tidy around their box and, all of a sudden, there's a misplaced pass and they're down your throat in two or three seconds. That's why their players play at the very top level on the world stage. My group of players have been magnificent from day one of my tenure. They'll continue to give us that quality and work-rate. That's all I can ask for as a manager.

In perhaps only the Chelsea game so far had Burnley looked totally outclassed. The Liverpool defeat owed much to the display of one man who had an individually outstanding display for Liverpool—Benayoun. At Spurs it was Robbie Keane who stole the show when he scored four of the five Spurs goals, in a scoreline that in truth flattered Tottenham. So far

Burnley had yet to score away from home, had suffered four defeats, and leaked 14 goals. Whilst Coyle insisted he would solve the problems, supporters did begin to wonder for the first time if this was where the limitations of his football philosophy were being exposed. It was all very well being devoted to attacking play, but now that Burnley were being regularly cut open in the Premiership, did this reveal a tactical naivety and inability to adapt to different needs at this new higher level? It was another game, however, where a good Burney goal by Fletcher was disallowed at a time in the game that would have made a real difference.

The nine points so far that Coyle referred to were the six from Manchester United and Everton, plus another home win against Sunderland. Coyle vowed that he would never resort to parking the bus in front of the opposition goal and commented again about the five goals Tottenham scored.

> The easiest thing in the world when you've lost 5–0 is to say we were wide open, but we could have stuck ten men behind the ball and lost 3–0. I believe that I have an obligation and a duty to try and win matches. The fans work all week, and then come here; they don't pay good money to see ten men behind the ball.

In the meantime, Robbie Blake was continuing to wear his lucky underpants, although the ones that had danced along the pitch at Wembley after the final whistle, had been redesigned and were now white in honour of the Premiership. Blake said:

> I think they will re-appear. But scoring the goal against Manchester United wasn't the right time. There was still plenty of time left in the game and I didn't want to pull them down knowing it might upset Manchester United. It's part of me, more a superstition than anything, but I continue to wear them. They've served me and the club well, brought us a bit of luck so I continue using them. They were red last season but I thought this season it's a new League so I'll change them and they're white with some blue writing on the back. If I do score an important goal to leave us comfortable in the game, then you'll see them. And if we stay up, oh God, you'll probably find me walking round town with them on. The celebrations will be so big, everyone will have them on.

Superstition apart he went on to praise Coyle:

> The manager does not have many weaknesses, just strengths. His man-management skills are fantastic. Last year when I was out of the team I'd go into his office ready to knock his door in, and come out half agreeing with him. He's down to earth and won't get too above himself. He can go all the way. He's shown that here and he's done it on a shoestring. He can go right to the top.

Despite hammerings away from home, including a defeat in the Carling Cup at Barnsley, the home wins continued and Burnley remained the media darlings with features as far away as the *New York Times*. The

Barnsley defeat was unexpected, after all Burnley was the club that had reached the semi-finals in the previous season. But the loss of Peterson during the game was crucial and the biggest blow. He would be out for months and would not return to the side until near the season's end. Crucial too was the loss of McCann earlier in the season. His comeback later in the season was brief and he was effectively out for the season. The loss of these two players was critical and to come later was the loss of centre half Caldwell for just about the rest of the season. Three key players lost from the small squad. It had a huge effect and was one of the major contributory factors to the eventual relegation.

But, one player who came in was David Nugent, rescued by Coyle from his personal hell at debt-ridden Portsmouth. Nugent whilst at Preston had been awarded one England Cap but following his £6million move to Portsmouth he found himself played out of position and then cast aside by Harry Redknapp. Just a month after joining, Redknapp was making it clear he could leave. 'After a few weeks he didn't fancy me as a player,' said Nugent. Nugent hated being far away from his family, describing it as horrible with everything going downhill. It was the lowest point of his career so that he was delighted to return north to Burnley. Signed on loan just before the August transfer window closed he scored twice in his debut game against Sunderland, the same game that saw McCann injured. Nugent's first was a classic centre forward's header when he leapt like a salmon and nearly broke the net. The smiles came back to his face.

It was at this time in a *Telegraph* feature by Jim White that Coyle made some fascinating comments about working at Burnley. The theme of the article was the close bond that Coyle was developing with the town as well as the club, and the growing rapport. If ever people need to see why the people of Burnley took this man to their hearts the clues are in this article within Coyle's own words. By the same token it is easy to see, Coyle having said all these things, why people turned on him in their thousands when he so abruptly left.

'I'll never tell my players a lie and they know it', White began. It continued:

> Coyle is forging a special relationship between town and team in Burnley. No wonder he did not want to join Celtic:
>
> During the summer, Owen Coyle received an extraordinary offer of employment: after just six years in management, he was contacted by Celtic and asked if he would become their manager. Almost surprising himself, Coyle, who as a boy used to dream in green and white, rejected the overture. The thing was, he reckons, despite his personal history, despite the possibility of returning in triumph to his home town, there was no need to move on, because he was already in possession of the best job around: manager of Burnley.
>
> 'If someone had said to me two years ago that I'd be turning down Celtic I'd have said: 'away you to the asylum',' he explains in his rapid-fire, Gorbals delivery. 'But there were good reasons for staying. We live in a lovely place

and my wife and children are very settled. Also, people say Owen Coyle has been good for Burnley Football Club, but Burnley Football Club have been very good to me too. They gave me a platform. I came here from St Johnstone; they gave me a chance when not everybody would have rated someone from the Scottish First Division. They believed in me and I think I needed to repay that loyalty. Besides, we haven't nearly finished what we started.'

From a distance, it might be thought that Coyle made a bit of a blunder when he decided not to head back home. He sits, for instance, in his modest little office at Burnley, a facility that would easily fit into the manager's hospitality cabinet at Celtic. Above him are the creaking wooden boards of Turf Moor's main stand, which holds a fifth as many paying customers as its equivalent at Celtic Park. And, sure, he might have been responsible for guiding the club back to the top flight for the first time in a generation, but he hardly has the resources to keep them there. He has on his desk a file detailing his annual budget, a sum roughly equivalent to the Celtic players' annual bill for car valeting. Yet, he says it is partly because of the parsimony of his surrounds that he stayed on.

'When Derby were relegated two seasons ago it was with the smallest budget in Premier League history at £27million,' he says. 'Ours is about half of that. All but four teams in the Championship have bigger budgets than ours. If, touch wood, we are still in this Division next season, it will be ten times the achievement it was to get here.'

Although he touches the side of his desk a lot, an hour in Coyle's company does not leave you with the feeling that he is trusting solely to luck as he sets about his seemingly impossible job. In the manner of his fellow Scottish managers plying their trade in the north-west, David Moyes and Alan Irvine, Coyle is busy, organised, energetic, a meticulous planner. No matter what the heightened claims on his time that have come with elevation to the Premier League, he is for instance, out on the training ground every day. His purpose is to create a team dynamic that will overcome the budgetary shortfall.

'Footballers thrive on confidence,' he says. 'If you tell them, "you know what, you're a great player", they love that. But it's no good just saying "that was brilliant". You have to explain why it was brilliant and tell them if they do it again, it will be brilliant again.'

It sounds simple, but the team spirit at Burnley is something to observe. It is there in the raucous laughter that emanates from the manager's office as he concludes a meeting with his staff. It was there in the sweat-soaked shirts when the team hung on to beat Manchester United and Everton at home. It will be there again this afternoon when they try to gain their first away point of the season at high-flying Tottenham. According to midfielder Wade Elliott, it is there in the certainty that the players would run through a brick wall for Coyle. So where did he learn to foster such loyalty?

'Some of my experiences as a player were not great,' he says. 'Now I've got the chance to be a manager, I hope I might go about it in a different way. I'll never, ever tell them a lie and they know that. I always do things openly. It was a bugbear of mine when you expected to play and you were out of the team and no-one told you why. I had managers who pinned the team sheet to the dressing room wall and you had 15 or 16 players crowding round to see if they were in. I prefer to deal with it one on one, man to man. They might not agree with my decision, but at least they know why I have made it. The most important thing is they know if they are doing well they will stay in the team. Ultimately I don't put them out of the team, their performances do. So they know it's a fair fight. If they feel they are treated fairly, footballers will give you everything. And I owe it to this club, to this town, to make sure that they continue to do so.'

Coyle mentions the town a lot. He believes he has a responsibility to a much wider constituency than that contained within the Turf Moor dressing room. 'Here's a statistic for you. There will be more people at a match at Old Trafford than are living in this town. [The 2001 census put Burnley's population at 73,021]. We get 18,000 watching us; that is by far the biggest proportion of any of the clubs in the Premier League. The police tell us when we are playing the crime rate drops to non-existent. When we win absenteeism disappears, people want to go to work on a Monday morning.

'We are the public face of this town. And if we mean so much to the people, and we do, then we have a responsibility to do the right thing. We have a duty to entertain them. The way we behave towards referees, towards opponents, is how they will behave on a Sunday when they play the game. I firmly believe that. So yes, we have a moral duty. And I couldn't walk from that. I love it here too much to do that.'

Indeed, it may not be Celtic, but right now, six games and nine points into his career as a Premier League manager, Owen Coyle appears to be living in his football paradise. (Courtesy of Jim White)

Words such as: 'Burnley Football Club have been very good to me . . . They gave me a chance . . . I think I needed to repay that loyalty . . . We haven't nearly finished what we started . . . We have a responsibility to do the right thing . . . We have a moral duty . . . I love it too much here . . .' All these things would be hurled back at him in just a few months time and seen simply as shallow soundbites, spoken by a 'silver-tongued charmer', as one furious fan described him on a radio phone-in.

A win against Birmingham City at Turf Moor brought three more points to make the total 12 and it was still only the beginning of October. During this game you would never have thought that it would be Birmingham who went on to have an excellent season and Burnley would be the relegated team.

And then, next up on Sunday October 18th, was the small matter of Blackburn away. The media build-up was huge. A meeting in the Premiership: a fixture that no Burnley supporter had ever envisaged just two or three seasons earlier. For any Burnley fan it was the game of the season, the one they had looked for when the fixtures were first published. If there was just one game that they wanted to win, this was it. The years of Blackburn success, based on Jack Walker's millions and a title win that was bought, wrankled and irritated Burnley supporters. There hadn't been a Burnley victory for years. This time, hopes were high.

The newspapers were filled with background articles and build-ups, one of them by Frank Keating:

Fabled duels are never run-of-the-mill: On Sunday is renewed one of organised sport's most ancient rivalries when Burnley make the short journey to Blackburn Rovers' Ewood Park. It will be the first of the fabled 'cotton mill derbies' to be played in the 17 years of the Premier League and local boasts and tensions have been nicely bubbling since Burnley's dramatic promotion was sealed at Wembley in the Spring.

Blackburn and Burnley were two of the 12 auspicious trailblazers, who formed the Football League (annual subscription two guineas) at Manchester Royal Hotel on 17 April, 1888. Only three clubs of that debutant dozen are still based at their original home, these two and Preston North End. In 1888 of course, Blackburn and Burnley were at the very throbbing hub of the world's intense cotton industry and although both the stadiums and the manufacturing landscape have changed beyond all recognition, at lunchtime on Sunday any romantic historian will be able to half-close his eyes and picture the terraced hillsides of flat caps jam-packed under the foggy fug and pall of tobacco smoke and, if he cocks his ear, imagine he hears again the urgent hiss of railway steam, the clink-clunk-clang of the trams, the clack of clogs on the cobbled streets and even, faint and fond in the distance, the warmly earnest rhythms of a brass band at rehearsal.

Certainly I did when, entranced, I first squeezed into a packed-out midwinter Blackburn Sunday 40 years ago in the 1960s, and that was even before Hovis bread chose Ewood Park for its soppy, sentiment-ridden, sepia-washed television advert.

After the momentous Manchester meeting in the Spring of 1888, the neighbour's first derby was at Burnley's Turf Moor that early November when, on 'a day of wind and driving rain', the Rooney of his day, Blackburn's England international Jack Southworth inspired Rovers' 7–1 victory, the ferocity of his opening goal apparently bursting the ball. When not footballing, Jack was a leading violinist for Manchester's Halle Orchestra and later, for another 30 years, was a popular member of the Pier Pavilion Orchestra at Llandudno.

Cotton-mill derbies continued to be passionately charged. For the match at Burnley in 1891, the FA's domineering martinet and president-to-be Sir Charles Clegg came over from Sheffield personally to referee, and in no time the Blackburn team had walked from the field and refused to surrender the ball in protest at a disallowed goal.

Blackburn probably had fable's grander cast. At the beginning of the last century there was the illustrious Bob Crompton, in the middle of it the cultured Ron Clayton and the wizard dribbler Bryan Douglas, and at the end of it the swank and oomph of Alan Shearer. For Burnley's 121 topsy turvy years of League membership a single maestro takes utter precedence in the roll of honour, designer-architect of the claret and blue side of the late 1950s and 1960s. Now 78, Jimmy McIlroy is a Freeman of the Borough, has a Turf Moor grandstand named after him, and he remains as articulate and poetic as his football ever was. To mark the half century of Burnley's League Championship, McIlroy and his author friend Dave Thomas have produced an appealing and welcome biog, *Jimmy Mac Prince of Inside Forwards*

(Hudson and Pearson) which will be launched at Turf Moor on Friday week. And before Christmas, for connoisseurs of the claret, they publish a bumper A3 sized doorstop, *The Jimmy Mac Scrapbook*.

The author and subject fondly revisited derby days for me this week. Ah, remember the day in the sixties when 'baby' Ralph Coates simply sat on the ball at Blackburn as his way of inviting Rovers' players to try to clog him again? Or the afternoon in the eighties when they seemed entrenched and unhappy in the old Fourth Division and Blackburn fans hired a plane to fly incessantly over Turf Moor, trailing a banner: STAY DOWN FOREVER, LOVE ROVERS, HA-HA-HA.

Recalling the half-century anniversary, Jimmy Mac grins and sighs at how near his Burnley had been to beating Tottenham Hotspur to the 'double' by a year. Until, damnit, it was Blackburn who did for them. 'It was the 1960's sixth round of the Cup, we are leading 3–0 and strolling, less than 20 minutes left, when the ball hits a divot and clips dear old Alex Elder on the arm. The ref gives a penalty out of sympathy for Blackburn. A joke—but it inspires them to level to 3–3 and, in the end, go on to Wembley. All Burnley was stunned and Alex Elder didn't leave his house for a week. (Courtesy of Frank Keating)

Burnley's long 43-year wait for a win was in vain. Robbie Blake gave them the lead as early as the 4th minutes with a wonder strike following a swift move out of defence. But it ended 3–2 to Blackburn courtesy of Burnley's dodgy defending rather than Rovers' efforts, Burnley's second coming almost on the whistle. Burnley had plenty of chances, Fletcher missing a couple either side of the break. Caldwell and Alexander had efforts blocked. Blackburn fans crowed: 'Can we play you every week?' But a Burnley banner prepared in advance was unfurled. 'Beaten but still above you lot.'

Coyle by now was well used to the Press questions after yet another away defeat:

There's a lot to brush up on, but there are a lot of positives to take and what we have shown is that anyone who writes us off does so at their peril because there is no doubt we will pick up points in this League. I am disappointed to lose a derby especially the local one with all the rivalry that goes with it. But here we are with 12 points that nobody envisaged us having and with probably the lowest budget the Premier League has ever seen. So there is a lot to be positive about Burnley Football Club. I think there was a ten minute period in the first half when we conceded soft goals after a great start. The equaliser—we feel we have good possession in the last third and after being dispossessed it's a great finish in the end by Dunn. The second we all saw and after we lost a poor third goal we found ourselves with a mountain to climb. I suppose you always pick the bones out of any goal and for the second I was convinced Di Santo leaned into Stephen Jordan and did enough to put Brian Jensen off. It was my initial reaction and nothing will convince me otherwise. It was a comfortable ball for Brian to deal with and the only way he couldn't is if he was knocked off. I know people will say it was only a nudge but when you are off balance it affects you. I am not going to sit here and blame referees though. I spoke to the referee Chris Foy at the end of the game and I know it's a difficult task. I just felt a large percentage of those marginal decisions all went against us. They say things balance themselves out and if that's the case then I'm due a few at the back end of this season.

As the next home game approached against Wigan Athletic, a game that on home form Burnley might have been expected to win, Coyle spoke again:

When all's said and done it was disappointing to lose, as it is with any game. But you always know in football you get another bite of the cherry and when it comes about in March that game will take care of itself. It was important we came in and got lifted and got going again. I said to them that as disappointing as it was, you have to get up in a morning and realise where this football club is from, where it all started for us altogether as a group, how far we've come and how far we want to go. And we're the only people who can decide on that. Nobody is going to decide our fate bar ourselves and we have to make sure every time we cross that line we're ready to give everything we can. We have to remember the season's not over in one game. In my time here there have been many ups and downs but the bottom line is you do one of two things, you either feel sorry for yourself or you get up in the morning prepared to do something about it and that's the way I've always approached it.

But who motivates the motivator? My family pick me up. That's why it's important you have such a good support system in place. As a player you pick yourself up from your own experiences. I've never had any doubt in terms of mental strength and how to deal with things. I'm not saying you don't have lows along the way, but we're in the best game in the world and if you can't get up in a morning, look to enjoy it and bounce back and really get to your maximum then there's something sadly wrong.

Wigan are a good side who like to pass and move the ball. That's a trademark of Roberto Martinez teams and they've been in terrific form. Having beaten Chelsea at home, the performance last week against Manchester City proves this is a good Wigan side. They have terrific footballers, they have match-winners and they look to pass and move similar to ourselves in many ways. We have to make sure we come out on top.

Alas Burnley did not come out on top and the home record crashed when Wigan arrived with their assortment of South Americans and won 3–1. They were an inconsistent side, brilliant one day, beatable the next. At Turf Moor it was a good day and they looked like world-beaters with a midfield that dominated much of the game, their long-legged, mobile and athletic players totally outshining Burnley. Burnley took the lead very early but the equaliser came when Jensen slipped, fell and gifted Wigan the goal. From thereon it was all downhill. 'We went down without a whimper,' said Skipper Caldwell.

For a second consecutive game Burnley were at home again, this time to Hull City, a team out of form with manager Phil Brown in a very precarious position jobwise. By this time too, Coyle had switched Andre

Bikey, the club's best centre back, to a midfield role to fill McCann's absence. He had played in this position before at Reading on occasions. It was a move that never really suited him, but he was preferred to both Kevin McDonald and Joey Gudjonsson. Guerrero occasionally came on as a sub. Two Alexander goals, in his 900th game, one a penalty, won the game and three more points. In truth, nothing went right for Hull City. They never do when a team is heading towards relegation, and Burnley too would succumb after Christmas to that basic law of football—that when your card is marked with the word relegation—if there is something that can go wrong; it will.

For Hull it was infuriating. They had a player sent off and a perfectly good goal disallowed. Brown was on borrowed time. 'You're getting sacked in the morning,' the Burnley crowd sang in that characteristically, endearing, heartless way that football crowds latch on to a member of the opposition's misfortunes.

If Brown was incandescent with rage at the referee's decisions, Coyle felt he could have no complaints over the result:

> When the game's on we're all going hammer and tongs to win our respective points. We did that and thought we were fully deserving of it over the game. My players lost a home game last week for the first time in nine months and all of a sudden it was open season on them. But I felt they were due my loyalty and I picked the same team as last week. We had to show people what we're made of and I think we did. My focus was on winning because if it wasn't I know somewhere along the line then Owen Coyle will be in the same bracket as Phil Brown. So we have to make sure we get enough points to do ourselves justice for this football club.

Coyle's comment about being in the same bracket as Phil Brown was an interesting one and a reference to the fact that as soon as results go wrong in a results-oriented business, it is so often goodbye to the manager. Ironically Burnley is a club where this does not happen; the Chairman Barry Kilby showing loyalty to his managers even at the worst of times. There is no history of instant dismissals at Turf Moor. Perhaps it was simply a throwaway remark from a very loquacious talker. But within it there is perhaps a clue to his decision to leave the club just months later. 'Leaving while your stock is high,' was a Coyle mantra. In other words leave before you are asked to leave and the results start to conspire against you. And, was it already possible, behind the confident and ebullient Press conferences that he was beginning to wonder if survival in the Premiership was really possible. Over and again in the Press he referred to the size of the Burnley budget.

No-one was to know it at the time, but this was Coyle's last win for the club. At the end of October it took them to a respectable 15 points and a position well out of the bottom three. It was a good time to take stock at the end of the first three months in the Premiership. Another five points per month would have seen Burnley comfortably safe at the end of the season. But despite the signs that it was all a huge struggle with poor away form, individual mistakes, collective errors, and a limited budget, there was no mention at this stage of the possibility of relegation. There was confidence in the home record and the firm belief that the elusive away win was still attainable.

The Press homed in on Alexander after his astonishing landmark game. The influence of Steve Cotterill remained. It was he who moved Alexander to the midfield holding role and Alexander was taken aback initially. When Cotterill brought him to the club, Chairman Kilby raised his eyebrows at the idea that Cotterill wanted to pay money for someone at the end of his career struggling to get out of the Preston reserve side. One hundred games later here he was playing and scoring goals in the Premiership, still fit as a fiddle, lean and hungry for more games, with a routine of proper diet, good sleep, spotless boots and ice-cold baths.

'I'm not alarmed picking a 36-year old,' commented Coyle. 'I see what he is capable of and Graham can play in the top flight as long as he has the fire in his belly and that shows no signs of abating.'

Coyle's second anniversary at the club was approaching. He had achieved so much. There was still utter and total belief in him. The players believed in him, the supporters worshipped him; the town embraced him. Despite the away defeats, the first three months had seen unexpected and joyful success. But, by the end of the next three months supporters would see the club turned upside down, the players would see their inspiration vanish; the heart would be ripped out of the club, and the town reduced to a state of disbelief.

12

I THOUGHT THIS IS THE GUY

November 2009, and Owen Coyle's second anniversary at Burnley; it had been a wonderful two years, with floodlit nights to rival those of the 1960s European games, and occasions to match those at Maine Road in 1960, Preston in 1973 and Scunthorpe in 2000. Wembley 2008 was arguably the best of them all.

Coyle was pleased enough, commenting in his programme notes for the Aston Villa game that he had just attended the North West Football Writers' Awards dinner in Manchester and had:

> . . . proudly picked up an award on behalf of everyone following our promotion. To sit on the top table alongside Sir Alex Ferguson is a measure of how far we have all come in the past two years. When I was told it was the second anniversary as Burnley Football Club manager, I couldn't quite believe it. Time certainly flies when you are having fun. There have been so many highlights and I suppose I speak for all of us when I say Wembley is right up there. But my mantra is never to look back. You can only influence what is in front of you.

At around this time various newspapers asked him about his time at Burnley:

> Well it's absolutely flown. It's been a whirlwind, but I have to say that I have loved every minute of it. In terms of my expectation, you always have ambitions and aspirations and when I first spoke with Barry Kilby and Brendan Flood, I said I wanted to take Burnley into the Premier League. I never said that I would do it in 18 months but that's what we've done. I have to say though; we've worked collectively, including the fans, to bring that to fruition.

His responses also outlined what it was like to be a manager and gave an account of the loneliness of the job:

> On the whole I don't think it is. By nature I'm a people person and that's how I go about my business. I'm surrounded by great staff. It's not a one-man crusade, and all the backroom staff have played a massive part in that. Obviously when you lose games, and we all hate losing games, it's a horrible feeling, so yes, at that point it can be lonely because as much as we are unified, you are the manager and the responsibility rests with you. It's not a nice feeling.

He gave his thoughts on playing football in general to one newspaper:

> For me, there's no substitute for playing. Your playing days are the best days of your life. If you're playing well the manager will pick you. Coaching and managing is the next best thing, there's no doubt about that. But as a manager you're responsible for not only picking the squad, but also a football club and an entire town. Because of the support we have, this football club plays a huge part in the life of Burnley, and our results affect people. That is a massive responsibility and it's not one I take lightly.

More specifically he provided his thoughts about playing for so many clubs:

> There's no doubt that personal experiences mould your character and if you channel them in the right way, they can only benefit you. I've had a fair few kicks in the teeth, but they help to form the person you are. I was very fortunate to play to a very good age and I've been a player-coach since my early 30s. Then I progressed to be a co-manager and a player assistant manager. So I was able to learn a lot of the coaching tools while I was still playing.

His views on the Coyle brand of football were also discussed in the Press:

> With a small club coming into the Premier League there is the temptation to try and win ugly. Plus, we have the smallest budget in the division by a country mile. If there was a financial league, we would fall off the bottom of the page. It's a total mis-match but we have the belief that by passing the ball and showing quality on it, that we can win points. And, to an extent, we've done that. There will still be trials and tribulations along the way but we're up for the battle and we're desperate to remain in the world's best League. I always felt that when the time came for me to be a manager, I would always encourage my players to play entertaining and attacking football. And yes, I think that comes from some of my playing experiences being a striker against some of the bigger clubs when I was asked to double up as left back! Now, I would carry those instructions out to the letter, out of respect for the manager, but I can't say it was enjoyable playing defensively. I wanted to score goals and show I was good enough to play against the best players and best teams. So, I now encourage my players to be positive, albeit in the framework of a good shape and desire to work hard when they don't have the ball. But I also wanted them, when they had a chance to play, to go and express themselves and try and win. You have to be respectful of the fact that your fans have worked ever so hard all week, and they've earned the money they've used to pay for the ticket. In the current climate, they've probably also made sacrifices to come to the game. So with that in mind, I believe they've come to watch a team who is trying to go out and win. I don't think they'd get a lot of enjoyment from me putting 11 men behind the ball and trying to hold on to a point from the first whistle to the last. For me, that's not football. It's not for Burnley Football Club and it's not for Owen Coyle. And that's why I've always, and I always will, try and win football matches.

He was also thoughtful about what he and the club had learned since Wembley:

> We've learned that if you switch off for a single minute, you're liable to be punished. That's happened to us, particularly in our away games against Chelsea and Liverpool. I'm confident that with more Premier League experience behind us, we'll cope a lot better. It's a learning curve for us all. The players don't have all the answers, I don't have all the answers, but I'm prepared to listen and learn on a daily basis and I'm trying to get my players to do the same.

His feelings about the forthcoming Manchester City game were decidedly optimistic:

> You can't be thinking about how much a team has cost before you've played them; when all's said and done, it's 11 against 11. I have a belief in my squad that they will perform to their maximum, physically and mentally, each and every day for us to achieve points in the Premier League. If we do that we can, because we have quality. We are good to watch, we have players who can hurt the opposition, but we have to do that as a team. The thing about our football club is that, as good as the individuals we have, our strength is our unity, belief and hunger as well as our organisation. We work hard when we're in possession and we work hard when we're not in possession. I think those factors give you a chance against anybody, regardless of finances.

Coyle provided an insight into his biggest achievement:

> Reaching the Premier League was an unbelievable achievement for us given that we'd played 61 games in the season, we'd used the fewest number of players in the Championship and our turnover and revenue was in the League's bottom four. To stay in the Premier League would totally surpass the achievement of getting here. There are very good players in the Championship. But what each and every Premier League team has is quality players with pace and power, so at any given moment they can hurt you. It is the best League in the world because of the world-class standard of players which are present in every team.

Finally the Chairman, Barry Kilby paid tribute to Coyle and his achievements:

> At first Owen was just a name among others. But I had booked for a weekend with Gleneagles which is just down the road from Perth so I said 'I'll meet this guy' and I met him on the Saturday morning. His integrity came through. I thought this is the guy. We could have gone safer but I just felt it was right at the time. I realised he knew how to handle a smaller club. He has understood right from the start how Burnley has to work its budgets. I don't think anyone will ever forget last season and we are certainly not trying to kick our way to stay in this League. I don't want to decry other managers. Both Stan Ternent and Steve Cotterill did good jobs in their own way to give us the platform and Owen certainly grabbed it. You have to give him credit for the way he has welded this team together.

The next game filled supporters with trepidation—Manchester City away—the club that had spent £200million on players and wages in the last 12 months. Alan Nixon previewed the game but the headline was an eye-opener. 'Burnley boss Owen Coyle wants £30million to push club forward next season'. This was the first time that any mention had been made publicly about money and budget needs. £30million was a massive amount for Burnley, and these things were usually kept in-house.

Seconds out: it's the biggest mis-match in Premier League history. Manchester City versus Burnley, the battle of the megabucks and the down-on-their-knees. Burnley's weedy budget for the whole of their squad this year would barely cover the wages of heavyweight earners Emmanuel Adebayor and Carlos Tevez alone in their debut season at Manchester City. Evergreen Graham Alexander would have to play till he was almost 50 to make what rival midfield general Gareth Barry will pick up in his first 12 months at Middle Eastlands. The Clarets' own Robhino, Robbie Blake, is on around a twentieth of the Brazilian. And that's only talking wages never mind the transfer fees.

Yet for 90 minutes today, Owen Coyle and his men can rip up the balance sheets and prove they are worth their place in the elite and the young Burnley boss does not mind counting the pennies while Mark Hughes counts the millions of pounds. Coyle said with a trademark smile: 'If the table was based on finances we would have fallen off the bottom and be off the page. It's a total financial mismatch. But, on the football field it's not. I think two of their best players would cover the whole of our budget. But there are always disparities in football. Manchester City are just doing their best to make the top four and I think they might do it. Our target is just to stay in the League.'

Coyle has had a crash course in football finance since he arrived at Burnley two years ago. He walked the financial tightrope successfully outside the big time only to find that the Premier League is not a land of milk and honey. In Burnley's case someone had swiped the cream and had a go at the honey too. The club's backers Brendan Flood and Barry Kilby were due some of their cash back and there were bills to pay to bring Turf Moor out of the 1970s. All of that left Coyle with around £15million to spend in his first season, a figure laughably low but the hard fact of life that the Lancashire club took on. Coyle said:

'I knew it would be a challenge when I saw the figures, there was a lot going on at the time. But I sat down and knew the players I wanted with me and that we had to work together. I fully understand what was happening. If Brendan and the Chairman had been putting £3million in, with no guarantee they would ever see it again, it's only fair that they get it back when things looked up. I have no complaints about that. If it wasn't for them the club would have been in real financial trouble. It is to their credit that they kept it going so long. They needed to be applauded for that. We have also spent a lot of money on the ground. I know we got caned for the dressing rooms, but the Chief Executive worked his socks off to get the facilities up to scratch. It was 33 years since we were in the big time so it's only natural we needed improvements and that takes money. There was a lot of finance on that sector, but rightly so.'

Coyle's canny ways, including making an unheard of profit at his first club St Johnstone in his first season as boss, will make him a Boardroom darling as long as football tightens its belt. But he does not want to be the penny-wise chancellor all of his days. Coyle would love Hughes' money, but first he wants to get some more money at Burnley next season.

Coyle's money men have assured him he will get a crack at the full £30million-plus, if they stay up. He said: 'Brendan and the Chairman know my thoughts on that. It's a long way away, but if we survive we would have a platform to push the club on. If we don't then it will be a battle every season up against the odds. Of course I am as ambitious as the next man, if not more so, and I would like the cash and be on a level playing field. But I am not getting down about it. I want to be the very best I can be as a manager. I want to win things. But I also want to move this club on.'

Burnley will probably be the only club making a profit in the Premier League this season because of their budget and Coyle knows that will give him some consolation if they fail. He said: 'If, God forbid, we went down we would not go the way of clubs like Southampton or Charlton. The way the contracts are set up would even make us one of the lower payers in the Championship. I am quite happy to work within these restraints. We spent less than we brought in when I arrived and we came up, playing 61 games and with an embargo on us for two or three months.'

No matter how tight things are now, Coyle knows nothing will match the shock of finding out he could not sign a player at the start of the year because of the ban. He revealed: 'In the January window I spoke to Mick McCarthy about a player at a time when we were decimated by injuries. I had put five out on loan to raise the money and that had left us short. We had more or less agreed the deal, but two hours later I found out we were under an embargo. I had to call Mick and he was brilliant about it. He never asked why.'

Now, a few months on, Burnley should never have that financial embarrassment again. So, being bottom of the table for spending power does not feel as bad for Coyle in that light. And if the budget is a fraction of City's then so is the heat on the manager. Hughes will have to deliver the top four. Coyle will be more of a legend if he finishes fourth bottom.

'It's a different kind of pressure for the two of us. Mark has brought in undoubted world-class quality, the onus is to win honours. Ours is just to stay in the League.' (Courtesy of Alan Nixon)

Both Chief Executive Paul Fletcher and Chairman Barry Kilby responded to this and other items in the Press about Burnley's transfer policy. Fletcher was quite blunt: 'Burnley Football Club isn't going to win matches by throwing a fat chequebook at it . . . Anyone can speculate on what is needed but it won't be through getting the chequebook out, it'll only be by encouraging players to give their ultimate skill and effort.'

Chairman Kilby was a little more diplomatic when talking about the forthcoming January transfer window but it was a statement that applied equally to calls for £30million:

We've got quite a few decisions to make, but we're sitting down and discussing how we need strengthening. Let's be steady, let's only afford what we can afford. Things can turn very quickly in this game so we've got to be careful. One of the problems you've got is being balanced on cash flow; if you buy a player, that's capital investment. But it still takes cash and you've got to find it out of your general trading. As for David Nugent, we have until the third week in January. We like him, and I think he likes us, so we will be looking to negotiate with Portsmouth.

When the stadium announcer went through the Manchester City team list at Eastlands on November 7th, Burnley fans could only laugh at the absurdity of the star names that were read out, one after the other. It was a who's who of the best marquee names . . . Given . . . Toure . . . Lescott . . . Wright-Philips . . . Barry . . . Tevez . . . Adebayor . . . Bellamy . . . On the subs bench there were even more of them.

And then, it seemed the impossible was going to happen as Burnley swept into a 2–0 lead in front of their disbelieving, joyous supporters. Was this the game that would break the away duck? Sadly no, as a Wright-Philips shot spun off Jordan and was deflected into the net. Deflections would play a huge part in the season's story. After half-time City then took a 3–2 lead but the resolute Clarets came back to force the equaliser with just minutes remaining. So near, so close to an improbable win as Nugent then burst clear but found himself without support. Mark Hughes cut a forlorn figure on the touchline at the final whistle. The Burnley hordes sang and danced all the way home. Surely this was a team that could survive in the Premiership. Surely that elusive away win would come. City jetted off to Abu Dhabi to meet the owners. Burnley returned to the windswept steppes of Gawthorpe, the training ground that couldn't even boast warm, dry changing rooms.

After the game, Coyle spoke with mixed feelings.

> If you'd offered me a point beforehand we'd have gladly taken it. It's a monkey off our back. So much has been made of this away form, although I'm loathe to use the word 'form'. I can accept people are being critical because of the away results, but bear in mind we're coming up for two years since I took charge when we were languishing 15th in the Championship. Now we're in the Premier League and are trying to get better. It's always nice when you get what is perceived, I believe, as a bonus point, coming to one of the top clubs. But we believe, home and away, that we can earn points. There's still work to be done though, because we conceded three goals which I'm not entirely happy about. I felt very comfortable at 2–0. We'd have loved to get to half-time but Wright-Philips came up with a great strike that deflected off Steven Jordan.

What Coyle did not mention was, once again, his uncanny knack of making the right substitutions; on came young McDonald and Nugent later in the game, and it was the former who scored the equaliser.

There are some games, which in hindsight, can be reviewed, and a defining moment or a turning point within that game can be identified. When Aston Villa arrived at Turf Moor Burnley were still playing superb football. For much of the game Villa were battered, and it seemed that it would take a miracle for them to secure a draw and a point. In the first half Burnley were outstanding and as early as the ninth minute Caldwell headed home from a Blake free kick. In the rain and wind that swept across the ground it looked like Burnley would surely add to that single goal but one way or another they contrived not to.

The time was ebbing away and with Burnley fans already beginning, a little prematurely, to whistle for the end of the game, Emile Heskey scored an improbable and ill-deserved equaliser. Three sides of Turf Moor fell silent and stunned. Heskey had lumbered on for the final ten minutes, his goal scoring reputation hardly glistening. In fact after his goal, it was suggested T-shirts should be rushed out with the message 'I saw Heskey score'. As an 86th minute goal it was a heartbreaker. Goalkeeper Jensen punched the ball out from a corner, it fell to Milner who lobbed it back in, and there was Heskey to head home.

There is more than one Burnley fan who will point to that goal as being the moment when the tide began to turn against Burnley in their valiant attempt to win enough points to survive. Not only was it so late in the game, it was scored by the one player who just 'never' scores, but on he came to score against Burnley and take two points off them. Who can say what might have happened had Burnley hung on to all three points. There are so many 'ifs' in a season, and this, was a huge one.

Coyle was publicly disappointed, but no doubt privately shaking his head in annoyance at the ball punched out to Milner.

> We were well placed to get the three points. We were outstanding in the first half. We scored a good goal and Friedel made one or two exceptional saves. But we have paid a price for not clearing a corner properly and not dealing with it when it's come back in. We have to learn at this level, evolve and make sure we retain our Premier League status.

Unfortunately, it was not just defensive aberrations that were costing games but a lack of clinical efficiency in front of goal. Chances that were made were not taken and at Premier League level no team can afford to do that. Centre forward Fletcher was particularly culpable in some games and also unlucky in others when good goals were disallowed for offside. The learning curve applied at both ends of the pitch but football being football it is usually defensive and goalkeeper mistakes that are remembered longer than forwards' misses.

With games coming up against teams below Burnley in the table, games that had to be won to ensure survival, nobody was prepared for the craziness of the game at West Ham. Mistake after mistake cost Burnley this game and if ever a game demonstrated that Burnley had no real idea how to play defensively, or tailor their strategies differently for away games; then this was it. At 5–0 down after an hour there were real fears that this was going to be a scoreline of embarrassing proportions;

and, at a club placed below Burnley. Great with the ball, Burnley were far too casual without it, marking poorly, allowing chance after chance, and actually presenting them with goals. Not only that, but Jensen was lucky to stay on the pitch after bringing down Jiminez in the box, a challenge that gifted West Ham the second of their penalties. In a game that cried out for half-time Burnley changes, none came till later.

And then came the fight-back. If the game had lasted another ten minutes it's a reasonable bet that the score would have ended 5–5 or even as a Burnley win. For 20 minutes Burnley carved West Ham open time and again and scored three times. This surely can be the only time a team has won a game 5–3 and still been booed off the pitch. But that's how it was as West Ham supporters chewed their nails and hid their eyes as West Ham collapsed; and all this with a ten-man Burnley team, following the dismissal of Steve Caldwell for pulling down a West Ham player.

Coyle defended his players but if there was a game where supporters began to ask questions about team selections and tactics away from home, this was it:

> Even if it had finished 5–0 it would never have been a true reflection of the game, but we gifted some soft goals and there's no getting away from that. We were the architects of our own downfall and we need to brush up on that because at this level you won't get away with it. At 5–0 we showed tremendous bravery and courage, as we did all day in passing and moving the ball, scored some very good goals and had other chances. It's a learning curve for us all and my disappointment is for my players because they offer me everything day in and day out. But it's not good enough to be that far behind in games and I've said that to them. We'll continue to work hard. As regards the defensive side of things we've got good players and it takes more than a goalkeeper and a back four; everyone's got to do their job collectively.

Nor was he happy with the referee, Chris Foy: 'It was a bizarre game. I don't like to criticise officials but the big decisions went against us. We prefer to be beaten with a bit of quality.' Possibly two of the avoidable West Ham goals stemmed from refereeing decisions, one where he allowed a very quickly taken free kick, and the second a very generous penalty decision.

Coyle still managed to joke at the Press conference afterwards. If he was in a poor mood after the game, he would never dare take it into the house for long when he returned home.

> I usually bring it home with me until my wife gives me a slap. Having a family is very grounding. They put things in perspective. I try to switch off by doing the normal things with my family. My family is the best way to relax. I have more grey hairs now which take the edge off my good looks—but I've been grey for a few years.

But joking apart, there was another reference to finances at Burnley and how the budget would not even be a top-half Championship figure. Such references were now coming on an almost weekly basis.

In away game after away game Coyle had spoken about learning from mistakes. But was he learning from his mistakes, the supporters asked? This was a team set up to attack, not defend. This was a team that basically did not know how to defend collectively. 'We only know one thing and that is to go and attack teams,' said Robbie Blake. The word 'naïve' appeared in more than one Press report. This was the same team home and away, the same tactics home and away, and whilst no-one wanted to see a team that parked the bus in front of goal for 90 minutes, supporters whilst full of admiration for Plan A, were beginning to wonder if it was time for Plan B away from home, or indeed if there actually was a Plan B.

Surely, the first way win would come at lowly Portsmouth, a club in total financial disarray and heading for relegation.

It didn't.

Supporters drove the long journey home after this game wondering how on earth they had not won. The answer was simple. Chances had been missed at one end and soft goals had been let in at the other. Portsmouth's second was particularly galling as just about the smallest man on the pitch rose unmarked to head home. It wasn't even a good header, hitting the ground and bouncing into the net. Avram Grant had just taken over as manager a week earlier and with Portsmouth in their precarious position you might have thought they had won the Cup Final after the game. In truth it wasn't a game in which Burnley fired on all cylinders but one glaring Fletcher miss in the first half was a deciding moment. The worrying thing about this result was that it was against such a poor team and these were the games that demanded to be won. It was a foretaste of things to come. As the season progressed the results against the bottom teams were dreadful.

Coyle bemoaned:

> Normally with performances, results come with it. But we've dominated the game and lost. It's disappointing because we were good enough on the day to win the match and we haven't. We carved them open numerous times through good football, but like anything else, at this level, you have to be clinical because they certainly were. They were two great finishes. I'll take nothing away from the quality but we can certainly do better. The second goal I wouldn't expect to lose in the playground at school. We have to address the fact that it's another game away from home that we've lost.

At this point in early December after 15 games, Burnley were 13th in the table on 17 points. Still to play in December were Wolves, Bolton and Everton all below Burnley. Portsmouth had already been played. Of the 12 points on offer in December against teams, on paper, 'poorer' than themselves, Burnley would take just one single point. Added to this was the point they were lucky to earn in a home draw against Fulham. If Owen Coyle weighed up all the pros and cons when the time came for him to decide whether or not to stay at Burnley, it was results like these that surely helped him to assess the situation and decide that with the budget at his disposal, he could take this team no further. And yet for all that, Burnley's superb display against Arsenal at Turf Moor was worthy of all three points, and an incorrectly disallowed Fletcher goal might well have won the game.

David Conn's article 'Prudence steadies the Burnley ship' provided a telling analysis of Burnley's finances and the chairman's understandable budgetary vigilance.

Owen Coyle's Burnley have won five of their seven home Premier League games but have won only one point away from home. At Burnley Football Club they are still thrilled at their elevation to the Premier League, which rewarded fans for their loyalty, galvanised a town desperately needing a boost and plastered a smile on most of the rest of football. They are not though, losing their heads. The chairman, Barry Kilby, is aware to his bones of the 'catastrophes' which have befallen clubs who have spent too much on trying to stay in Premier League riches. In January Burnley will have 'some money' to spend he says, but will emphatically not 'bet the ranch' on staying up. 'I don't want a disaster on my watch,' he warned.

Burnley's accession to the top flight for the first time since relegation in 1976 was a winningly romantic tale, but came at a cost. The just-published accounts for the year to June are, Kilby shudders, 'a horror story'. They paid £2.3million more in wages than the club even earned, racked up an £11.7million loss, enormous for the Championship, and loans from Kilby and his fellow directors added up to around £9million. Had Burnley, who finished 5th, not beaten Sheffield United 1–0 in the play-off final, Owen Coyle's smart footballing side would have been broken up, and more loans required from the directors as ballast.

Kilby describes the financial gulf between the Football League and the Premier League, which broke away from the other three Divisions in 1992, as 'one of the biggest problems in football, it distorts the game terribly.' He believes nobody ever contemplated the gap growing so large when 'that band (of big clubs) got together and broke away'. The leagues should re-unite, he argues, while conceding that the top clubs would never vote for it. The divide causes problems both ways; Championship clubs mostly overspend to climb up, then clubs are too easily drawn into outsize wage bills which cause them calamities when they are relegated.

Kilby smiles, over fish and chips in the wood-panelled chairman's lounge. 'We're enjoying it, it's fabulous,' he says. 'But we're realistic. The money can now steady the ship, but we cannot take on massive obligations.'

With Coyle's team having won five of their seven home matches, including the marvellous August defeat of Manchester United, but claimed only one point away, Burnley are being drawn into a fight for Premier League survival. In January, they face 'a big decision', about whether to convert the striker David Nugent's loan deal from Portsmouth to a permanent contract, and make 'one or two' strategic signings. 'It is so uncertain,' Kilby warns, 'how hard you dare push it.'

What is certain in January is that Kilby and his fellow directors will, from the Premier League windfalls, be repaid their loans, including £3.7million loaned by Operations Director Brendan Flood from his retail development company, Modus Ventures. Flood, a lifelong Burnley fan like Kilby, has had an awful year. His wife's parents, his own mother and brother's wife all passed away, while his company collapsed into administration. 'It has been the worst 12 months of my life,' Flood says. 'In the middle of it was promotion, which should have been the best day of my life, but I haven't been able to enjoy it.'

He is still being pursued by Allied Irish Bank for £350million they claim he owes in personal guarantees, while Flood is counter claiming for £100million he says the bank had committed to supporting Modus before the credit crunch, when they pulled the plug. Regardless, Modus's loan to Burnley was due to be repaid if the club reached the Premier League, and the other directors, including Kilby, will have their loans back too. 'It's only fair,' Kilby says. 'If the club has the means to pay it, it should.'

Promotion, worth around £40million in television money alone, was further nibbled into by improved wages and bonuses for Coyle and his players. Steven Fletcher, bought from Hibernian for a modest looking £3million, was in fact Burnley's record signing. The club also fulfilled a promise to 7,000 fans who bought season tickets in the Championship, that they would watch for free if the club went up. At around £360 on average for a season ticket; it has cost the club £2.52million.

That still leaves the club significant money but Kilby is reluctant to spend too much of it on players in the first season up. His caution has roots deeper merely than last season's overstretched finances. In two hours of conversation, the Burnley chairman returns repeatedly to one particular match; not the play-off final which he does not mention once; nor the Manchester United victory, which he describes as 'fabulous' but only when asked. The game etched into his supporting soul was on 9 May, 1987, a 2–1 victory over Leyton Orient in the old Fourth Division. That day, other results went in their favour too, and Burnley scraped out of becoming the first club automatically relegated out of the Football League. Lincoln City went down to the Conference instead.

Kilby, born in Accrington, stuck with Burnley in the threadbare crowds throughout that near-total decline. The clawback began there, he believes. 'I think that day the town saw what it might lose.'

He made his own fortune devising bingo and other competitions to be inserted in newspapers or TV formats here and round the world; then sold his company in 1998 for £15million and made his first investment in Burnley. He bought shares steadily up to a majority then reduced his stake to 30% as Flood, later, put £2.6million into the club for 24.5%. In 2006, with Burnley struggling to compete in the Championship and needing money again, Kilby and another director, John Sullivan, bought Turf Moor itself, via a company, Longside Properties, for £3.2million. The club became tenants, paying around £330,000 annually in rent, with an option to buy the ground back. Kilby says he was 'never comfortable being both landlord and tenant' and, given Burnley's stretched state and Flood's inability to put more money in, in March this year he and Sullivan sold Longside, together with Turf

Moor, to another company, Lionbridge. The price paid is not a matter of public record, but Kilby says he and Sullivan about broke even.

'I felt I needed to have cash available, just in case,' he explains. The club still have the option to buy the ground back and there are plans to develop it, worked up by the Chief Executive, the former striker Paul Fletcher, which were postponed when the recession hit.

'If we survive this season,' Kilby says, 'we will look seriously at doing it. But it is a conundrum now; do you spend more money on buying the ground back, or buying a player who could keep you up?' The dilemma has confronted all promoted clubs since the Premier League broke away to stop sharing TV money with the other three Divisions. Parachute payments, a self-serving measure, give relegated clubs money (now £48million over four seasons) to pay players with Premier League salaries still running in the Championship. Several clubs have nevertheless been relegated with unpayable wages and collapsed into insolvency, including Leeds, Leicester, Derby, Barnsley, Wimbledon, Southampton, Ipswich and Queens Park Rangers.

West Bromwich Albion negotiated the divide after promotions in 2002, 2004 and 2008 (and now 2010) by spending carefully, with contracts tailored to adjust financially after their relegations to the Championship. Kilby considers this yo-yo existence a respectable aspiration for Burnley. 'I think West Brom are a model for a club our size. We should not be worried about going down strong.' If that seems a somewhat cautious message from a chairman new to the glittering Premier League, it illustrates how, at Turf Moor, they know intimately how far clubs can fall if they get it wrong. (Courtesy of David Conn)

Chairman Kilby clearly knew that some spending must take place in the January window for any chance of survival to take place. The question was, what level would the spending be? Both Kilby and Coyle knew that it could never be prolific and would be limited. Was this another factor that manager Coyle took into account when weighing up the move to Bolton? It surely must have been.

A *Times* interview with Coyle quickly followed the Conn *Guardian* article. By now much of what Coyle said in interviews was understandably repetitious. It had to be, he was largely asked the same questions over and again, questions concerned with budget, size of squad, and natural limitations. But what he revealed in this interview was that yes, he would be receiving January transfer window money.

There will be incursion into the transfer market next month, although fans should not expect a splurge of money. Even if I had £4million or £5million available to sign a player, I wouldn't be able to match the salary he wanted. And would he and his representative agree to have a relegation clause in his contract like the rest of the squad have? It's something we have to be selective with, getting the right character within our financial structure. I believe in spending money on younger players who can grow with us and evolve at this club. With due respect to the Charlton Athletics and Southamptons, when they went down they did so with annual budgets of £20-£25million. Even now, ours is half of that. From a selfish point of view that might hurt me as a manager, but I have to look at the overall picture.

He was asked did he not fancy Celtic and winning European trophies.

> I've had advances but I've loved every minute of it here and long may that continue. I've shown everybody my feelings for the club. As the manager here I want to build something and have a legacy that will serve them well for years to come. I've got five brothers and three sisters and my mum, who is 78, still comes down to our home games. Because of what we're trying to do at Burnley, it's important we have that family atmosphere, too. I was a part-time player to begin with, so I know what it's like to get up in the morning and do a real job of work, to walk in somewhere and immediately sense whether there's an atmosphere conducive to a working environment. I feel very privileged that football has been my career. If it hadn't, I would still be paying a few quid to go and play five-a-side. It's so important that we have an identity with the local community. I played for a number of provincial clubs in Scotland and I used to find it galling when buses used to leave for Rangers and Celtic every week. Here, all you see is Burnley tops.

The clues as to why Burnley people were so upset when he left the club just four weeks after this interview are clear to see. When a manager talks of wanting to build something, of having loved every minute at the club 'and long may that continue', of identifying with the local community, and having 'shown everybody his feelings for the club'; it comes as a massive shock when just four weeks later, that person leaves. No wonder supporters were shell-shocked at both the departure and mid-season timing.

It is pure conjecture that someone as ebullient and bright as Coyle could ever be dejected or despondent. He could, however, have been forgiven for feeling that way after the Wolves game. Just days before, Wolves manager McCarthy had deliberately fielded a second string 11 against Manchester United at Old Trafford. Of course he didn't say it was a reserve 11; clubs have first-team squads now, and McCarthy could argue that all of them were members of that squad with first-team experience. His argument was that his men had given such a heroic, energy-sapping effort in the previous game, that they would have been unable to give the same effort again at Manchester. Of course it was poppycock most fans said, and the football world surmised that McCarthy was as good as sacrificing three points at a place where he might reasonably assume he would lose anyway, so that his best 11 could be fielded fresh and rested for the forthcoming Burnley game at Molineux.

His fresh 11 beat a sluggish first half Burnley 2–0 thus vindicating his controversial choice. Top clubs regularly field weaker teams for Carling and even FA Cup games, but rarely in a Premier League game. The second half pressure from Burnley was remorseless but to no avail and there might well have been a penalty for a shirt pull on Fletcher. But in seasons when a club is relegated, such decisions are not given. The brickbats that McCarthy had suffered pre-match were forgotten. Burnley made no fuss; made no complaints, such a response not in the Coyle or Kilby style. Wolves incidentally were not relegated at the season's end. McCarthy praised one of his players in particular, Kevin Doyle. 'He was fabulous. He was full of running; amazing what a rest does for you.' This crass remark merely rubbed salt in the wound.

Coyle appeared irritated:

> We came here to win the game and all it does is add fuel to the fire about the away form, and rightly so. I've told the players they are the only ones who can change that. At this level you have to defend well, and I think it was very obvious that we lost two terrible goals. There were probably two or three individual mistakes with the first one. That's the last three games we've found ourselves going behind.

Earlier he had commented on the limitations imposed by the Burnley wage ceiling:

> If the chairman were to come to me and say 'listen here's 3 or 4 million, go and sign a player', you're still between a rock and a hard place. We could spend that money very easily but no representative would recommend their player to come and sign for the salary we're paying. If money's their god, they'll be motivated by money. I understand why people would rather sit where they are and pick up big salaries, but that's not for me, and I wouldn't want that type of player anyway. There will be Championship players earning more than we could pay them and even if you admire them, they might think, 'Why would I want to go for less?' But we can give them an opportunity to play in the Premier League. It's a platform for players to show their quality. Anyone watching Burnley, I would hope, would look and think, 'That's a good team, I love everything about them, the energy, the desire, even the atmosphere, that's the sort of team I want to play for'.

Behind the scenes Coyle was in fact working on two loans—the prodigiously talented teenager, Jack Wilshire from Arsenal, and winger Stuart Holden from the USA. Clearly, buying another player was out of the question.

There were three home games in December. All were drawn 1–1. Against Fulham Burnley were fortunate to get the draw against Roy Hodgson's well-drilled team, having gone 1–0 down. Coyle felt a draw was a fair reflection.

But against Arsenal, Burnley in the second half were in scintillating form, and deserved to take all three points. Again the away side took the lead through Fabregas, the kind of star player that the Turf Moor faithful did not mind paying to see. It was almost a privilege to see him score after he had robbed Bikey. Burnley survived more Arsenal domination but when Fabregas went off injured it was Burnley who had the better of the play, equalising with an Alexander penalty, and then denied a legitimate winner from Fletcher who was wrongly judged offside. Eagles had a superb run and shot that hit the post.

Coyle was much happier but at the end of the day two more points had been dropped:

> Both teams, at different stages, would have thought they could have earned three points. Andre will know he made a big mistake, but the lads dug in and got a grip of the game and Andre's rectified his mistake by being brought down for the penalty. I think both teams had chances then. We tried to stand toe-to-toe and play them, knowing what we were risking with the quality they have. But we were prepared to risk losing the game to try and win it. My lads gave us everything again, against all the odds, and who's to say how valuable that point could turn out to be?

It would in fact turn out to be of no value, but the two points dropped certainly would be, added to the two points dropped in another home draw against Bolton, yet another game where Burnley deserved all three points. In the table, Burnley were still in a 'safe' position, but the points gap between them and the third-bottom club was closing.

Bolton arrived with their fans howling and chanting for manager Megson's dismissal, and then chanting for Owen Coyle as if they could sense something might be in the offing. Megson had never won over the Bolton faithful, by now tired of dull, safety-first, unattractive football. They also happened to be in the bottom three. It was not a happy club. Bolton fans recognised two things; firstly that Coyle had once been a Bolton player, and secondly he had worked miracles at Burnley. There had already been stories of a move by Bolton for Coyle in March earlier in the year. It cannot have gone unnoticed by Coyle that the Bolton fans called out his name and clearly wanted him at the Reebok. Bolton Chairman Phil Gartside must also have noticed. By now it was Boxing Day; Coyle's time was limited at Burnley.

> At half-time I sat with my head in my hands inwardly screaming at the floundering performance from the home side. Only Jordan and Bikey distinguished themselves. Bolton were dreadful, a collection of donkeys and carthorses in a football kit. Against this collection of equine dross, other than a brief passage of pressure we exerted around the 30th minute, Burnley's play was pedantic, inaccurate and toothless. When Bolton took the lead from a generously given free kick, the signs were there that this was going to be another defeat. Bad as we were, their goal came as a complete surprise. The free kick was 90% Davies backing into Bikey and the pair of them collapsed to the ground in a crumpled heap. 99 times out of 100 the decision would have been given the other way. Again and not for the first time we get the referee who is the odd one out.
>
> When the ref missed a damned good shout for a penalty for a nudge in the back on Nugent as he raced into the box; when Fletcher missed an absolute gift of a chance with only the goalkeeper to beat, the first half got more and more depressing. Another one in the second half from just eight yards out was blazed over the bar. At last it was Nugent who got the equaliser from an Elliott cross when he rose high and powerfully headed home. From this point on Burnley swarmed all over Bolton and this would have been a comfortable win if chances had been taken. 14 shots on goal,

and 10 were off target, tells you all you need to know. Bolton were battered as the real Burnley turned up and this was one-way traffic. Near misses, great runs, lovely moves, fast passing, constant forward movement and then McDonald hit the bar. The Bolton goalkeeper began his timewasting routine as early as the 5th minute, blatant and infuriating, and how he escaped a booking is a mystery. But then that was symptomatic of a dreadful Bolton.

This was eight games without a win for Burnley and left us frustrated and disappointed. But Bolton fans must tear their hair out at the dross they watch if this was anything to go by. No wonder they shout for Megson's head. 'You don't know what you're doing,' they screamed at him. Trouble is, if Gartside gives him the boot, will he come calling for Coyle? (Personal Diary December 26th 2009)

Which was exactly what he did just days later (Megson was sacked on the 30th), although Burnley fans could be forgiven for wondering if any behind the scenes, discreet contact took place before January 1st when Phil Gartside telephoned Burnley's Brendan Flood. When asked later about this, Coyle denied that any had taken place.

After the game, Coyle's post-match analysis was as fair as ever:

Bolton are always a threat on set plays, but we had a gilt-edges chance to go in front and never took it and we paid a heavy price, because the free kick was exquisite. Having said that I wasn't convinced it was a foul in the first place. But we roared back in terrific fashion. The two wide players in the second half, Eagles and Elliott, really got at Bolton. We scored a terrific goal and some of Jaaskelainen's saves were out of the top bracket. Bolton are an established Premier League club, they know how to grind out results because they've been doing it season in, season out.

Appointed in October 2007 after a dreadful start by Sammy Lee, with only 5 points from 10 games, Megson guided them to safety and was even Manager of the Month in November 2008. But, in the following year, by the time December came, a period of 50 days saw no wins, a period of five defeats in six games, and huge supporter unrest.

Reporter Alan Nixon maintains that he was set a points target to secure his job, but the key game came at home against Hull City three days after the draw at Burnley. Bolton took a 2–0 lead and all seemed well. Had that game been won, then Megson would presumably have kept his job and there would have been no approach for Coyle by Bolton.

The defining moment came in the 78th minute when Steve Hunt scored his second goal for Hull to level the scores at 2–2. Fans were furious. Megson had taken off striker Klasnic with the score at 2–1 and brought in McCann to stiffen things up and play out the game. It backfired. Boos and abuse rained down. Gartside acted and Megson was sacked. Megson was furious with supporters and with the decision. Bolton, although in the bottom three, had two games in hand. Megson pointed out that the club had been in a mess when he arrived and, 'The problem was that the club was one of the lowest spending'. He was 'leaving it in a better state than when he took over', he added.

Goalkeeper Jaaskelainen commented that the Hull game was the low point.

> He made a couple of changes at 2–1 and we were still cruising, but suddenly everything turned. That was a key point for getting a new manager. It's not easy going into a game when people are not happy with the manager. It does play on your mind. The fans put pressure on the players and it was difficult.

Coyle was immediately the bookmakers' favourite to take over. Gartside regarded him highly, he had seen at first hand on Boxing Day the brand of football that Coyle could produce from his players. He had heard the Bolton fans chanting his name. When Megson had been appointed a poll had shown that few supporters approved. If Gartside could get Coyle, it would be a terrifically popular choice.

Two games remained for Coyle at Burnley and supporters were uneasy at the news of Megson's sacking. They suspected the worst, and the worst was imminent.

13

LAST ONE TO LEAVE
SWITCH OUT THE LIGHTS

It could be argued that once Hunt scored Hull's equaliser against Bolton, then Coyle's last few days at Turf Moor and his final game against MK Dons was an irrelevance. Burnley fans could be forgiven for wondering if there had already been quiet contact between Bolton and Coyle, either directly or via a third party.

The die had been cast. Gartside had heard the fans' anti-Megson chants at Turf Moor and seen the football Burnley could produce. This is the manager I want for Bolton, he must have thought. As visitors to the Boardroom were saying their goodbyes, he called out, 'See you Brendan, we'll be coming for your manager on Monday.'

Flood replied with something along the lines of, 'No chance . . . you'd better not'.

On the other hand if Burnley had won at Everton, and managed to gain another three points, Coyle might just have wondered if it was worth his while to stay. But this game meant it was just one point out of 30 from away games.

So: another defeat although it was the 83rd minute before Everton scored. Full back Jordan's sending off certainly aided them, sent off for a second offence when he pulled back the opponent who was about to race past him. Throughout the game, Burnley fans howled their anger at referee Howard Webb who booked several Burnley players for the most innocuous offences, or indeed imaginary. 'But some constants remain,' said one report. 'Referees will always make mistakes and Burnley will always lose away from home.'

Burnley could certainly count themselves unlucky to have lost, and deserved one point at least. Coyle had just won a Scottish sports award but it was of little consolation. There were certainly no hints or clues in Coyle's post-match words to suggest he was close to leaving: 'I felt we were terrific. But there's a mixture of emotion, certainly disappointment and anger among them, about the fact we're leaving with no points after what we offered.'

Burnley played Bolton on Boxing Day. The Everton game was on December 28th. Bolton would play their fateful game against Hull City on the 29th, Megson's job still safe had they won according to Alan Nixon, but dismissed the day after on the 30th after they threw away the two-goal lead.

Coyle played down speculation on the 31st linking him with the Bolton job saying the things that supporters wanted to hear, and that made them believe in him.

> It's a fantastic job for someone out there but my focus is doing the best I can against MK Dons this weekend. I have had speculation time and time again but, as always, I am concentrating on the job in hand. I love being at this football club and I have shown that. I think the players enjoy working for me, the fans like coming and we are trying to build something at the football club.

On January 1st, the Friday before the Cup game, Gartside phoned Brendan Flood, a friend of his according to journalist Alan Nixon, to let Flood know he would like to speak to Coyle and have 'a chat over the weekend'.

'Flood tells Coyle of the approach and gives Gartside his manager's number,' so they can have their chat, wrote Nixon.

'All parties agree to keep quiet ahead of their Cup-ties.'

This sequence of events prompted a number of questions afterwards. Should Brendan Flood have bluntly refused to give Gartside the number? Secondly, should Gartside's call not have been made to the chairman, Barry Kilby? Then, thirdly, having been given the telephone number; was Gartside able to use this as official permission to offer the post to Coyle? The answer to that emerged later. The fact that things moved so quickly can certainly be attributed to the ease with which Gartside was able to approach Coyle.

None of this is to suggest that had things been done differently, or Flood been uncooperative, Coyle would have stayed at Burnley. 'There were things in his contract that permitted him to speak to other clubs under certain circumstances.' Coyle was soon set on going, but the problems that arose regarding compensation were attributable to Gartside being given the telephone number and using that as permission to speak to Coyle. Under normal circumstances, the correct procedure is that compensation is agreed before any club is given permission to speak to someone else's manager. But then what is 'normal' in football? Premier League rules stipulate that it is illegal to approach a rival manager during the season unless the two clubs reach an amicable agreement. The giving of Coyle's phone number was used by Gartside as the amicable agreement.

Burnley's FA Cup game against MK Dons was on Saturday January 2nd and the day after the game newspaper headlines were asking 'Is Coyle Staying?' or suggesting 'Coyle's Quick Exit Adds To Intrigue'. As this game was being played, miles away at the Reebok, managerless Bolton were beating Lincoln 4–0 with Bolton fans calling Coyle's name.

Coyle remained the last person on the pitch after the Cup game, ironically an away win, 2–1 for Burnley. At the final whistle his waves and thumbs-up had the air, to everybody, of a man saying goodbye. 'The classic symptoms of regime change,' reported Mike Walters in the *Mirror*. Coyle ducked the post-match Press conference, the official explanation being he had a plane to catch to Scotland to see family members. In fact he was with Brendan Flood discussing the new situation.

After the game, assistant manager Sandy Stewart took the conference and fielded questions. Of course he was asked about Coyle and Bolton.

Stewart responded:

> There is nothing to read into this. Owen has not seen his family over Christmas and has to get a flight to Scotland from Luton. If he did all the Press, he would miss that flight, so there's nothing to read into him not being here. The speculation is just the same as the stuff that linked him with the Celtic job in the summer. As of now it remains speculation and until something happens, that's exactly what it is. I do know Owen is very happy at Burnley. We have worked very hard and we think we have done a reasonable job here, so we are quite happy. Owen and I have a great partnership and we have worked together at St Johnstone and Burnley. Hopefully that partnership will continue and right at this moment in time that's at Burnley Football Club. We love it here and we think we are taking the club forward and that's all we are interested in.

When asked about Coyle's wave to the crowd, Stewart replied:

> Anybody who has been to Burnley knows that Owen does exactly the same to the fans after every game. He appreciated the support, especially when they travelled a long distance, so that was a thank you. If you asked every player in the dressing room they don't think it's Owen's last game. We just went out to win a Cup-tie for the fans who travelled today, and that's what we have done.

It is reasonable to assume that Stewart knew what the real situation was while he took the conference. Words like 'we love it here and we think we are taking the club forward and that's all we are interested in,' would be seen later as hollow rhetoric. 'There is nothing to read into this,' was a statement much derided when the pair of them left.

'Owen Coyle To Quit Burnley' wrote Alan Nixon just two days after the MK Dons game. Brendan Flood recalls seeing that and reacting with shock at the speed with which Nixon was breaking the story, wondering too just where he was getting the information from, particularly the revelation that the backroom staff would follow:

> Owen Coyle is ready to walk out on Burnley and become Bolton boss—in time to take on Arsenal in a debut of fire on Wednesday night. Coyle had talks with Wanderers supremo Phil Gartside yesterday after the chairman headed to Glasgow to see him after a family reunion. Gartside was given the nod to speak to Coyle about the vacancy by Burnley Operations Director Brendan Flood and immediately set up the meeting where he persuaded

the highly rated Glaswegian to take the job. Coyle wants to work with serious cash after finding Burnley's shoestring budget was giving him an uphill battle to compete in the top flight—with even Bolton's payroll three times as big. The move has stunned Burnley who thought Coyle was settled after turning down previous approaches. However, the former Bolton striker is hugely ambitious and sees the Reebok as an ideal step. Coyle is breaking the bad news to Burnley and is also in a position to leave, with Bolton prepared to pick up the tab for his compensation, which is around £1million. The negotiations are unusual as Flood and Gartside are friends and the Bolton supremo recommended Coyle to Burnley in the first place, a call that was worth around £60million when they won promotion. Gartside wants Coyle in charge quickly as his club is in the bottom three and running into a tough run of games that includes two meetings with the Gunners, the first at the Emirates on Wednesday, and an emotion-charged match with Burnley. There will be talks over Coyle's backroom staff which could drag on over a few days, but Coyle is now going in one direction and his backroom staff will follow. Burnley are fuming that their 'God' is going but they will instantly look at the market for a replacement. Coach Steve Davis may step in while Flood seeks a new man. (Courtesy of Alan Nixon)

When Nixon wrote, 'Gartside was given the nod to speak to Coyle about the vacancy,' he summed up in a nutshell how the giving of Coyle's phone number was used as permission to offer the job, something that was never Flood's intention or something he envisaged happening.

Nixon's reference to wanting to work 'with serious cash' was ironic. According to the departed Megson, there had been no serious cash available at Bolton for some time. Later in the week Nixon outlined his version of the timetable:

Saturday Afternoon . . . Coyle's team beat MK Dons and he tells the players that he is going to speak to Bolton about a possible move. Boss Coyle decided to head off for a flight to Scotland rather than face awkward questions.

Sunday afternoon . . . Gartside catches a train to Glasgow to meet Coyle and they talk about football for a couple of hours. Coyle is happy with what he hears and contacts Flood that night to tell him he wants to go.

Monday . . . Coyle cancels a day with family at a carnival in Glasgow and heads back for a circus of a different kind at Burnley. He wants to see Flood and Kilby face to face. The meeting goes ahead. Coyle tells them he wants out and the row about compensation flares up. The official line is that they are all waiting 24 hours to think things over, but Burnley know their man wants to go and the cash row with Bolton roars on.

Tuesday . . . The weather stops Coyle taking his players for training at Burnley while the clubs squabble over his move. Coyle sees Flood and Kilby to tell them that his mind is made up. He clears his desk, taking away precious mementos of his stint at Turf Moor. He makes sure he sees every member of staff available, to wish them a tearful farewell. (Courtesy of Alan Nixon)

The story filled the newspapers and dominated Sky Sports News. Was Coyle right to make the move? Yes said some; no said others. Ian Ladyman in the *Daily Mail* suggested, 'This saga leaves a bad taste'.

Sam Wallace in the *Independent* took a different line.

> There will be many who accuse Coyle of disloyalty for leaving Burnley, one of the Premier League's most likeable new teams of recent years, and joining Bolton Wanderers who are a bigger club than Burnley, but not by much. Coyle however is just taking the manager's pragmatic attitude towards survival. When your stock is high, you have to move on. Coyle is a very affable, bright man, who talks ten to the dozen about football. No doubt he will wince at some of the things he said about the importance of loyalty when it came to rejecting Celtic but he should not be embarrassed. Football is a ruthless business and history tells us that if Coyle had not left Burnley, sooner or later they would have got rid of him. Coyle has moved to a club that he feels gives him a better chance of staying in the Premier League. No shame in that, it will be galling for Burnley supporters and some will never forgive him, but if results were to turn against Coyle at Turf Moor, it would be him who paid the price. He presumably feels that Bolton have better resources than Burnley to finish outside the bottom three.

Tom English in *The Scotsman* analysed Coyle's new situation and the pressure now on him, pressure that was never placed on him at Burnley. Bolton have to stay in the Premier League, he wrote, and then went on to describe the monstrous burden of the financial imperative. Their accounts to November 2009 showed a salary bill of over £40million and a net debt of £64million. In Chairman Gartside's eyes you don't see pupils you see pound signs and a whole pile of fear, he wrote, and if Bolton went down it would be a cataclysmic blow.

Local journalist Chris Boden reminded readers of the *Burnley Express* of some of the things Coyle had said in his time at Burnley, the same things that Sam Wallace wondered would make Coyle wince. Boden took *Burnley Express* readers back to March 2009 when there was speculation about Coyle replacing Megson at The Reebok.

> Chairman Barry Kilby and Brendan Flood still carried a stunned look about them on Wednesday; days after it emerged Owen Coyle wanted to jump ship. Here they thought was a man of integrity and loyalty, who, should he further himself away from Turf Moor would go on to bigger and better things.
>
> Regardless of whether Coyle had joined Bolton or Barcelona, the timing of Coyle's departure is all wrong and goes against everything a man of principle had supposedly stood for. If I take you back to March last year, after speculation, incorrect as it turned out, that Coyle would replace Gary Megson at The Reebok Stadium—shortly after Megson agreed a new rolling contract.
>
> 'I've no intention of going anywhere. I love it at this football club.'
>
> 'Our focus is on staying together. I didn't bring players into this club to be up and leaving at the first opportunity.'

'I'm not upping and leaving at the drop of a hat.'

'I want to be here. I don't want anybody to be distracted, there's a job to be done here and I want to do it.'

While promotion two months later was a major achievement, 'the job', as Coyle said, is yet to be done, with Burnley moving closer to a precarious position in the Premier League. The Bolton offer is the first concrete offer he has received, and while Coyle told Kilby and Flood that Celtic and Bolton are the only clubs he would leave Burnley for, again it goes against what he has previously said. What must his players be thinking? Especially those tempted to come because of the enthusiasm and vision of Coyle? They were convinced Turf Moor was the place to be, despite the club offering the lowest salaries in the Premier League, and, as Coyle was oft to note, lower than many clubs in the Championship could offer. Coyle had no interest in players who moved for the money anyway. But if we believe what is reported elsewhere, he will join Bolton on a higher wage, £4.5million over three years, and he has gone because Wanderers have a bigger budget and more money to spend in the transfer market.

As he said only last month: 'If money's their god, they'll be motivated by money. I personally was always motivated by football.' (Courtesy of Chris Boden)

Brendan Flood spoke to Coyle before he flew to Scotland after the Cup win. He wanted to clarify things, see if Coyle really was interested or merely flattered. Boden asked Flood later about the meetings he'd had with him.

> I think you're initially flattered because another club wants you, but to actually move, logically, why should you move? But he's explained his reasons. It's probably better getting them direct from him. But it's still disappointing he's going. I think we tried everything. There was a factual analysis of the two clubs. They've got a bank debt of £44million, we've got none. They don't have a history of spending a lot of money over the last few years, and their owners are probably towards the end of their era of ownership. I think they can say lots of tempting things to attract Owen, but whether they'll deliver on those, I think history will tell. He's certainly been tempted by the ideas that have come forward from Bolton. We would certainly have liked him to stay. We did our best. He does have the ability within his contract to go if certain things happen, so it was his decision ultimately. Perhaps for reasons we can't understand, it's down to your affinity with clubs you've played with. It was always going to be a heartstrings moment for him, and I think that was partly to do with it.

Chris Boden reported that Barry Kilby and Brendan Flood had tried to find more funds for him in January to persuade him to stay. But Kilby said:

> To be honest it wasn't a big thing, other than he wanted to work with a bigger budget. I think he knew the situation of the club and we gave him everything we can, in a way. It wasn't a major, major thing. He was saying the difference between the two, and he wanted to work with a bigger budget, and he obviously felt they had a better chance of staying up in the Premier League than Burnley. Let-down's too strong a word. Football is

185

football. You have to be thick-skinned on these things and I really do think, move on. Sometimes these things happen for a purpose and let's see who we get in now.'

Did Gartside paint an over-rosy picture of the Reebok budgets available? Was that how he snared Coyle? Bolton Wanderers are almost the classic Premier football club, hugely in debt, and with the accompanying philosophy that as long as the debt can be 'serviced' then life goes on. Such clubs then exist, not so much to win trophies, but simply to survive financially. The debt is what drives the club on and it becomes simply a monster that consumes everything. Such clubs have little to look forward to. Survival is the most used word. Certainly what Coyle quickly discovered in the January transfer window as he arrived at Horwich, was that there was no large pot of Bolton cash to enable him to go a shopping spree. All he could do was arrange loans. And, in August 2010, he admitted on Sky that he had to sell, to buy. Nor in the summer of 2010, was there any great spending spree to strengthen the team. As Flood pointed out, Bolton had no great history of being a big spender. Did Megson not say on his dismissal that he had had little money available and one of his briefs was to reduce the wage bill?

Kilby added more about the untimely approach from Bolton:

> I don't think we are the best of pals at the moment. It was at a bad time and an unwelcome approach. I fully expected when Owen did move from here, he was an ambitious manager and we accepted that might happen, that he would go upwards from Burnley, not sideways to a club we are fighting in a relegation scrap. It was a surprise and obviously it has been traumatic for the football club. None of us wanted Owen to go. We had talks and managed to get Owen to delay his decision by 24 hours. We put our case strongly and were hopeful that he would stay with us but he decided to carry on and go to Bolton. He had a fabulous two years here and it was with regret that he went. He said to me there was only Celtic or Bolton he would leave Burnley for, so I don't think he took the decision lightly.

If he was distraught or deeply hurt, Kilby did not show it. Histrionics or public anger have never been his style. And in his philosophical comment that: 'Sometimes these things happen for a reason,' lay an almost Thomas Hardy view of the universe.

In the meantime Burnley were preparing to put reserve team coach Steve Davis in charge of the team for the forthcoming Stoke City game. This was a scenario that had happened once before when Steve Cotterill left and Davis had presided over a 1–0 win at Leicester City as temporary manager.

It would not happen again however. Coyle in an act possibly never before seen at Premier League level in mid-season took more or less the whole of the backroom staff with him, including Davis. The club was stripped of just about everyone who had worked with the first-team squad. The physio joined him in the summer. It was an unparalleled act. Even the Media Director was asked would he like to join him. He said no. Flood put on a brave face saying, 'No players have left the club.'

Kilby drew on his dry humour calling the search for the next manager as 'the beauty parade'. But supporters and local media were utterly outraged. They were outraged by three things, the mid-season timing, the taking of all the backroom staff and all the things that Coyle had said about being at Burnley during his tenure.

An article on the Twohundredpercent website 'Owen Coyle Hasn't Only Let Burnley Football Club Down' (author unknown) made some telling comments. It began with the opinion that here was a man whose words counted for little.

Talk of loyalty is cheap and Coyle has offered enough of that to Burnley supporters over the last few weeks or months. It's worth little to them now.

It is well worth asking the question how this has come about. Some are pointing the finger at *Daily Mirror* writer Alan Nixon, who, in the recently published paperback *Big Club, Small Town and Me*, was said to have recommended Coyle for the Burnley job and has the uncanny knack of providing his employers with Burnley exclusives this season. The biggest exclusive of the lot came when the back page of his newspaper screamed that Coyle had already accepted the job well before any public statement had been made.

Why, though, could he not even wait for the summer? Why could he not sign a pre-nup with Bolton to go to the Reebok Stadium in the summer? Why is it Burnley that have to start their next match, in the middle of the season, with an untried caretaker manager rather than Bolton? The correct answer to this may be 'because life's not fair' but being correct and being right aren't always the same thing. One aspect of this story that has been striking though, and it has been striking to the point of being startling; has been the degree of magnanimity displayed by so many people at Burnley Football Club over the move. There seems to have been an air of resignation about the whole sorry incident, especially considering the fact that Bolton count amongst their local rivals. The silver lining for them is that they are likely to receive a significant compensation package as a result of his desertion, but even the specifics of this are unlikely to be made public in the near future, and figures thrown round in the Press will be conjecture, to say the least. They won't know the true cost of his defection until the last match of the season.

The sadness of the story of this managerial poaching, however, is in the death of another small chink in the romance of the game. The accession of Burnley into the Premier League was one for the football romantics. The small-town club that arguably punched above its weight and became one of the great names in English football had been in the doldrums for years. Their promotion was unexpected as it was refreshing. We all know that players, managers, and everybody associated with the game is involved in it for altogether more prosaic reasons than romance. We like, some may even say need, to maintain the illusion that there is more to it than this, though, and when one aspect of the fairy tale falls apart, yet another small piece of our love affair with the game dies a little.

The bigger question now is whether Burnley can complete their mission and stay in the Premier League at the end of this season. It's less likely than it was a week ago, but Burnley at least still can stay up this season, and those of us that love a happy ending will be hoping that our disbelief can continue to be suspended for a few months yet.

With compensation issues still to be decided and Coyle still not yet in situ at Bolton, Burnley player Graham Alexander revealed his opinions, insisting the players were still fully focused on the games ahead.

I was gutted to be honest and I think most of the players were disappointed Owen has gone. The two years we had here we had a fantastic time. We thought he would be our manager for the rest of the season at least. Deep down I didn't think he would go to Bolton but everyone has their choices to make in life. But, the players have got to put it to bed now. He was the manager for a great two-year period but there are still a lot of players and people behind the scenes who had a lot to do with that as well and they are still here. The end of the story isn't this week. Hopefully we can carry it on and stay in the Premier League and take it on from there. We've got to think about ourselves. We have played under him but we haven't played for him. We have played for Burnley Football Club and that's what we've got to take on. The thing we've got to do is play for ourselves, each other, the fans and the people that pay us. That's all we've got on our minds. There is an incredibly strong group of players in the dressing room who have been through a lot in the past couple of years. As much as a great job Owen Coyle did here, it wasn't down to one man.

If Graham Alexander was 'gutted' when Coyle left, he might have felt even worse and even more shocked had he known that Coyle would also take the 'people behind the scenes', the complete backroom staff.

Just a week after the MK Dons game the thing was settled. It was Alan Nixon who broke the news in the *Mirror*. 'Owen is going in £1m Deal'.

Owen Coyle is the new Bolton boss after his bitter compensation row was sorted with Burnley and a £1million fee agreed. Coyle then went through a final day of haggling and legal wrangles before being cleared to leave his roll-on deal at Turf Moor and sign a contract at the Reebok until the summer of 2013. Wanderers will unveil Coyle at the start of the week but are relieved to end the bickering over the way they took the highly-rated manager from their relegation rivals.

Coyle said: 'I'm absolutely delighted to be back at Bolton. I look forward to the opportunity of bringing back the good times for everyone.' Chairman Phil Gartside stuck to his guns over the fixed fee, based on a year of Coyle's salary, despite Burnley looking for around £3million for the manager who took them to the bigtime. It is a personal triumph for Gartside, who talked Coyle into the move and will get the fans off his back after the appointments of Sammy Lee and Gary Megson. Gartside beamed: 'Owen was our number one target and we are naturally delighted that he has returned to the club as manager. He was an inspirational player who leads by example and is a great motivator and, on behalf of everyone at Bolton I would like to say welcome home.' Coyle plans to take his assistant Sandy Stewart and coach John Henry. (Courtesy of Alan Nixon)

Not only did he take Stewart and Henry plus the goalkeeping coach, Phil Hughes, but eventually also Steve Davis who at the very least would have been Burnley's interim manager. The football world was open-mouthed. This was the total destruction of a club's staff. The question was asked several times, 'Would this not do untold damage to any club's attempts to avoid relegation?'

The irony of the whole situation was not lost on Andy Dunn of the *News of the World*; that if there was a choice for the neutral as to which club they would like to see relegated, it would not be Burnley; that for all his agonising, Coyle had in fact 'abandoned' Burnley; and that the League Managers' Association was strangely silent on the matter. When a club sacked a manager in mid-season they were up in arms, but when a manager walked out, there was no comment. And, most tellingly of all, here was a manager who had worked 'bloody hard' for the success of Burnley while still caring for the financial well-being of the club, yet here he was now going to a club that existed with a potentially disastrous debt level, paying the inflated wages that Burnley so carefully avoided. 'That they will not break the bank marks Burnley as a beacon of hope in a game threatened by an avalanche of debt.'

Undoubtedly, the most savage comments came when Piers Morgan had his say in the *Mail* on Sunday column. His fierce criticisms of Coyle were in direct contrast with his tribute to another Burnley man, Graham Alexander, voted the 'Morgan on Sport British Football Personality of the Year', in the same article.

Sometimes even I am amazed by the loyalty of football fans. I know you're all slightly mad, especially when it comes to your own teams, but the results of my 'Morgan on Sport British Football Personality of the Year Award' votes are simply staggering. More than 200,000 votes were cast of which 168,933 went to one man, Burnley legend Graham Alexander, who has made more club appearances than any player in the Premier League. He beat Craig Bellamy into second place, with 28,915 votes, and Ryan Giggs into third, with 9,915. The common denominator with all three is that, whatever you think of them, nobody could question that they give 100% to every game they ever play. They are what you call 'commitment' players, the kind of guys who never stop running, tackling or trying. I'm thrilled that Alexander won because he personifies the genuine, decent, professional footballer. And let's face it; if ever Burnley fans needed something to cheer them up, then surely it is this week.

For the behaviour of their 'saviour', Alexander's boss, Owen Coyle, has been utterly disgraceful. This is the man who knew he carried the hopes and dreams of a whole town with him when he took Burnley into the top flight. He talked all the talk about how much he loved the club, the fans, the town. But when it came to it, he jumped ship at the first sight of a slightly bigger chequebook. It's laughable that he sees Bolton as a 'bigger' club.

They're not. They will be struggling just as much as Burnley for survival this season. The only thing that is 'bigger' is Coyle's new pay packet. For a few pieces of mercenary silver, he has betrayed everyone with whom he worked and everybody who admired him. Even my old mucker, Alastair Campbell, Burnley's most famous fan, is at a loss to find a good thing to say about this appalling piece of treachery. AND I don't blame him. What can you say about a manager who seemed to epitomise all that is solid, reliable, and loyal about the game . . . but who turned out to be a Judas Iscariot in a claret and blue scarf.

In two weeks time, in a delicious piece of good fortune for everyone like me who loves seeing traitors meet their victims while the carcasses are still hanging from the crosses, Burnley play Bolton at the Reebok. I hope the extraordinary passion that Burnley fans brought to their voting in my awards for Alexander is matched, if not eclipsed, by their passion in howling their fury at Coyle that day. And I sincerely hope that come the end of the season, Burnley stay up and Bolton go down. (Courtesy of Piers Morgan)

Coyle would always argue that personal wealth and salary offers had never been the main motivation in his career:

I dropped salary four or five times as a player just to keep playing. Is that somebody who is motivated by money? People say it is about money, but money has nothing to do with it—not personal money anyway. If it was about money I would have gone to Celtic in the summer when I could have trebled or quadrupled my salary, or whatever.

Whilst the reference to the pay packet might have been a tad stretched, nevertheless the tone and passion of Morgan's piece matched that of Burnley fans. But, at the end of the season Morgan did not get his wish, Bolton did not go down, and Burnley did not stay up. However, fans certainly took their passionate fury and spleen to The Reebok when the match took place.

Quite the opposite view came from Mick Dennis in the *Daily Express* just two days after Morgan's piece, opening with the premise; show me someone who says he would not have behaved like Owen Coyle, and I'll show you a liar. He suggested, without using the word, that Burnley fans were being merely hypocritical about loyalty. Where were they in Burnley's lean years, he asked. Did they themselves show loyalty then? And, were they not happy enough for Coyle to leave St Johnstone during the season, the week before their Cup Final? Did they complain then? Dennis went on to suggest that Coyle would have been 'moved on' had Burnley been relegated. 'The statistics prove it,' he added.

However, Dennis did not know that had Coyle gone down with Burnley, he would not have been 'moved on' and become one of the statistics. No-one would have blamed him one jot, he would have remained a hero and the chairman with his history of patient support for managers would have remained loyal. Barry Kilby would not have sacked him.

But Dennis's analysis of why Coyle might have felt the move a good one was fair enough. Coyle would move to a new modern ground, completely re-vamped training facilities, a substantially bigger fan-base, and a club that had already been in the Premier League for ten years, therefore well established with a modern state of the art infrastructure. Thus Coyle calculated that Bolton were higher up the food chain and had a better chance of staying in the Division. But most Burnley fans were unimpressed. They had bought into the 'dream' that here was man who was too honourable, they thought, to leave them in mid-season. No matter what the attractions were, to leave in mid-season was unforgiveable.

But even then part of Mick Dennis hoped that Coyle was wrong in the calculation that Bolton were the better bet, pointing out that it was Chairman Phil Gartside who once put forward the 'avaricious proposal' that there should be no relegations from the Premier League, this of course being the way to ensure Bolton's debt-laden survival.

Dennis's summary, however, was succinct enough. 'Now like any of us he (Coyle) has taken what he thinks is a better job. That is life. That is football.' That much was certainly true and was a view expressed by a number of supporters who argued that they too would move to a 'better' job at any time if the chance arose, that this was normal human behaviour. Seizing the moment, be it in business, football, or just daily life, being a basic human characteristic.

As the billboard that stands outside Turf Moor was daubed with the word 'Judas' and the personal attacks and criticisms rained down on him in the pubs, local Press and websites, Coyle answered back.

> Ultimately I can understand that people are hurt and disappointed, of course. It is such an emotional game and there was nobody more emotional than me about leaving the football club. I don't mind saying I was crying as I left. The chairman was. It really pulled at your heartstrings. Everybody at the football club knows my mind—I just want to be the best I can be, same as I did as a player. People have used certain words and that has been in poor taste. But I am big enough and thick-skinned enough to deal with that. The local newspaper had a headline that said BETRAYED. If that's how people want to portray it, that's up to them. But I can look in the mirror and know that I haven't told the fans a lie throughout the whole thing. Fans are fickle but the people that know me know what I put into that football club and how hard I worked to take that club on.

And then, speaking about if Burnley were relegated and would he feel guilty: 'I don't know about guilt, maybe regret. I think the world of that football club and I always will. But if Burnley do end up going down, it could have happened with me at the helm.'

That of course was perfectly possible. In fact, there had been a run of nine games without a win before he left. But fans felt there was now more chance of Burnley going down, without him.

With his customary quiet dignity Chairman Barry Kilby attempted to draw a line under the matter with a brief message on the club website.

It's been a turbulent few days in the history of Burnley Football Club. But sometimes these things happen for a purpose, so let's all pull together and work as one for the betterment of this. When I think back to November 2007 and the appointment of Owen, I remember feeling good about the future. I have that same feeling now as we concentrate on replacing him. We have a clean sheet of paper and a reputation within the game that has been enhanced by our promotion. We intend to try to get somebody who will be right for us and keep us in the Premier League. Ultimately, we did all we could to keep Owen here as our manager and that was not enough. But I am not going to throw away all we have achieved by offering up funds we simply cannot afford. You can only work within the budgets you set out with at the start of the season and there is absolutely no way I want to end up like some other illustrious clubs who have, dare I say it, bet the ranch. I don't want that, not on my watch. As 2010 dawns, we are set to embark on another adventure. I am excited by what's ahead and the journey starts here—together. (Courtesy of Burnley Football Club)

Of course it did not draw a line under the saga. How could it? Feelings still ran too deep, and with the game at Bolton still to come, the temperature was sure to rise further still.

We approached the next game against Stoke City with mixed feelings, butterflies in our stomachs of course with points being urgently needed, but at the same time feeling both anger and disappointment. The burning thought was that if there was justice and fairness in the football world (but we all know there isn't) we would win the Stoke game and then the fixture at Bolton as well. What a travesty it would be, we thought, if Burnley went down and Bolton stayed up. The scenario was ripe for either a remarkable Burnley escape if the new manager was the right one or a descent like a plummeting stone if the appointment was the wrong one. Fortunately Darren Ferguson was snapped up by Preston North End. Names began to appear in the hat. Our own solemn-faced Steve Davis, Paulo Sousa from Swansea, the eccentric stand-up comedian from Blackpool, Ian Holloway, the available Curbishley, the available Coppell, the always evergreeen, likeable, scallywag scouser Reid, Gareth Southgate, the young and hungry Hughes from Hibernian, oh, and even Souness got a mention. But poor Barry Kilby, we thought, with genuine empathy, just when we thought it was safe to say Happy New Year, Coyle lands him in it and gives him anything but. Sky news has camped out at Turf Moor to grab as many fans as possible that appear happy to use the word Judas and stick the boot in. It makes gripping TV . . .

. . . Unfortunately, the Stoke game was called off because of the weather. It is possible that it might have been won on a cocktail of adrenalin and pumped up emotion. As it was, when the game did take place, it yielded only one point.

Reading through some of Coyles expressions of loyalty to Burnley I came across one from way back: 'I knew I had to stay on and carry on this incredible adventure,' I began to agree with the guy on the radio one night who labelled him 'a silver-tongued charmer'.

The newspapers were filled with the story. Pundits' articles poured out by the dozen. But one made me smile when it described Owen Coyle as belonging to the Kevin Keegan School of Management. 'Never mind, if you score four then we'll score three.' (Personal Diary January 2010)

And still the Press churned out their copy. Supporters lapped up James Corrigan's piece in the *Independent*—'Let's Hope Coyle Falls Flat on His Two Faces'. He called it a 'desperately grotty story'. Once upon a time when club directors got together to give a manager a vote of confidence, the world knew that the manager was about to receive his marching orders. Now the boot was on the other foot and when a manager said he was happy at a club, then he was probably about to leave for another. Corrigan expressed sympathy for the Burnley fans who 'like the gullible fools they are' had believed Coyle's messages. In the summer he had told them that exciting challenges lay ahead of them at the club he 'loved' and he wanted them to continue. Come January it was quite the opposite. 'It can't be long until a manager's 'I'm here for the long term' speech is regarded as ominously as the Board's 'vote of confidence'. At Turf Moor it already is,' Corrigan concluded.

But Coyle answered back, via Alan Nixon, in the *Sunday People*. The headline was 'THE TRUTH' in bold red with the sub title: 'I'm unhappy being painted as the bad guy . . . I gave my heart and soul to Burnley'.

Emotional Owen Coyle admitted he shed a tear on his way out of the door at Burnley to join Bolton Wanderers. Coyle has broken his silence on the shock exit that stunned the Clarets and revealed his dramatic final days at Turf Moor. And Coyle, in his first interview since moving, has hit back at claims he lied, or was a Judas, as the bad feelings boil over at the club he took into the Premier League. Coyle will be unveiled as Bolton's new boss tomorrow but is determined to put the record straight. In this frank *People Sport* exclusive, Coyle detailed the timeline of his dramatic switch.

He said: 'I had been asked about the Bolton job after Gary Megson left and said I was focused on the FA Cup tie and that is the truth. I didn't know about the Bolton Wanderers approach until Friday night when Burnley told me they were interested in speaking to me. I had the game on my mind but I said I would like to hear what they had to say. I knew the club would tell me if something happened like that because people there, Barry Kilby and Brendan Flood, have got real integrity. They were friends and I hope they will remain that way. I hold them in the highest respect. It was the same when Celtic came in for me in the summer. I wanted to hear what they had to say before I made up my mind and I stayed. So we agreed that I would see Phil Gartside. But, I just wanted to win that MK Dons game and we did. I knew it could mean a lot to Burnley and the draw proved it, if they got Liverpool it could be worth a lot of money to them, which is always a factor. After the game I told my players there would be an approach, I always keep them informed. We have been through so much together and get on so well. Some of them were shocked and a bit upset. I didn't want to tell a lie and never will. I went to see the Burnley people after the game and didn't do the Press conference. I didn't want to mislead people.

'I caught the flight back home to see my mum, who I hadn't visited for a good few weeks. Then I met Phil in a Glasgow hotel on Sunday to speak about the Bolton Wanderers job. I had not seen Phil for years, not since I left Bolton in 1995. I know he put my name in with the strongest recommendation to Burnley but we had not met in that time. Phil was very passionate about his club when we spoke. He didn't have to sell Bolton to me. I have been there already and had two and a half great years. What he told me was about the set-up, the squad, the infrastructure. They have become an established Premier League club and spent their money well. It is something I had wanted for Burnley but I knew it would take five to ten years to achieve. I was immediately impressed with what I heard about Bolton and how far they have come. I have seen those facilities since, the ground, the training centre, the academy, and Phil was telling the truth about what they have built up.

'I told Brendan and Barry how it had gone and that I needed to see them. I wanted it to be a face to face meeting to discuss my decision. I was due to go to the circus with my kids but instead we headed down south. I met Brendan and Barry on Monday night and they put their views. I know how they feel about Burnley, they love the club. You know that any time you listen to them. I said I would go away and think about it, which I did, but I was still of the same opinion. I had come to my conclusion but it was with a heavy heart. The next day training was called off so I could not see the players to explain it all to them. Instead I rang every one of them personally to tell them I was leaving. I emptied my office and said goodbye to people who had become my friends. You can ask Brendan, or my PR man Darren Bentley, how emotional I was in those final moments. Everyone who knows me knows that I put my heart and soul into that club and community. I wasn't happy to see myself being portrayed as the bad guy.

I have kept a dignified silence about it. You will never hear me say a bad word about Burnley. I never did and I never will. (Courtesy of Alan Nixon)

The line about not wanting to mislead people, in Nixon's article was an interesting one. That task fell to Sandy Stewart.

As a postscript to the article, Nixon added another in which he wrote that coach Steve Davis would also be leaving Burnley and that too would upset supporters. It certainly did and for them was the last straw. Of course fans knew Coyle had put his heart and soul into the club but now they saw him stripping it bare of the backroom staff. Steve Davis, it was revealed later, would have been kept on in some senior capacity at the club, 'part of the furniture,' said Brendan Flood, his departure simply adding another distasteful paragraph to the sorry story.

In the *Daily Record* Coyle continued to steadfastly deny that he was guilty of any wrongdoing and argued that he had behaved in an impeccable manner throughout. Betrayal wasn't in his nature; he was only being true to himself. What he did possess, he said, was a sense of realism that came from an upbringing in the Gorbals.

I know what has been written about me on the websites and in the local papers and it's hurt my family and friends more than it has hurt me. I know criticism grows because football is a game that feeds off people's emotions. I understand why people in Glasgow and Burnley have been disappointed but a lot of what's been said about me is untrue. I don't feel I need to justify myself to others. I've always tried to live my life in the proper manner and I know I'm not a money-grabber. I've never been motivated by money. If finance was all that important to me I would have taken the job with Celtic in the summer. A Celtic fan doesn't take that decision lightly but I did it because the Premier League in England is the best in the world. Celtic were the team I supported as a boy and I always will. They offered me the job and I turned it down to stay with Burnley. That puts the argument about being obsessed with money to bed as far as I am concerned. It's a knee-jerk reaction from people who are not in possession of all the facts. I put Burnley in what was previously uncharted territory for them. They'll make a profit for the year totalling millions of pounds, more than they've ever had before. I know I can look at myself in the mirror every morning and when Bolton meet Burnley in 10 days time I'll deal with that situation head on. I've also been flattered by what people in the game say about me. I had Andrew Cole at Burnley on loan last season and he used his newspaper column last week to offer me his support. He said I was the kind of boss who made players feel 10ft tall and had a 100% work ethic. Now, I have a massive challenge at Bolton and I have to meet that head on as well.

It was on the morning of Monday, January 11th, that he was unveiled as the new Bolton manager at the Reebok Press conference. Prior to that, whilst compensation was thrashed out, he had been allegedly placed on 'gardening leave'. But, the League Managers' Association lawyers had advised Burnley that, in fact, Coyle could simply have walked out anyway, the contract having been breached, ironically, by Burnley they said. The figure agreed was £1million and it was Coyle who insisted that this be paid by Bolton, said Nixon. Until it was, Coyle told Bolton he would remain on 'gardening leave', if that is what it was. Because Burnley had allegedly breached the contract, there were suggestions that, remarkably, Bolton had no obligation to pay anything. The clichés can be churned out. Football works in mysterious ways behind the scenes. Football is football. That's life. Since when has football been fair? The ordinary fan shakes his head.

It was a greater opportunity to invest in players at Bolton that was the main reason he moved, Coyle told the assembled hacks and cameras.

One thing I want to get straight is the suggestion that I came here for money. I've never been motivated by personal money in my life. I came into the club at Burnley on one of the bottom three salaries in the Championship and worked my socks off as I said I would. If it was financial I would have taken the Celtic job in the summer which would have been double the salary and everything else. I would have jumped through hoops because that was the team I supported as a boy. But I wanted to be involved at the highest level and the highest level in the world is the Premier League.

This is an unbelievable challenge, but it was a big wrench to leave Turf

Moor. Of course I am excited but the emotional attachment I feel for Burnley has made it a difficult decision. With finance so tight, we all pulled together and achieved promotion. But there was a choice to be made about whether we carried on as we were doing, or maybe invested another £30million to establish the club. That wasn't possible. The level of finances Burnley were at, was always going to be difficult and you risk sliding down the Leagues. I think Burnley will stay up but I was trying to move things quicker than finances would dictate. The job is done in a sense that the football club had been nowhere near the Premier League for 33 years.

Speaking about Bolton he said:

I would say that at Bolton I have an infrastructure that is 5 to 10 years ahead of what I am leaving behind. There's an unbelievable stadium here, and the infrastructure is all in place—the academy and the training centre. Everything is geared for top flight football and it is my job to ensure it. I want to take this football club forward and take them on.

Bolton's style will change, he added, but the priority was to avoid relegation before looking to make improvements. 'I believe there are creative players at the club and we will be looking to get the best out of them.' Referring to the imminent game with Burnley Coyle explained:

At this moment I'd expect Burnley fans to come and vent their frustration, but I hope that's not the case. Whatever the game brings up, I will just have to deal with it as I always do. Whoever used the word Judas, be it websites or newspapers I can't do anything about it.

Asked if he would back Coyle in the transfer window, Gartside said he had always backed his managers in the past. The legacy of the last ten years was an honour to hand on to Coyle. It took five minutes for them to make up their minds when they met on the Saturday (presumably he meant Sunday) and that there was no-one else on the shortlist. He was sure that the fans would embrace Coyle for his bubbly and infectious enthusiasm. 'You can't not like this guy. He's sat there because he'll keep us up.'

'It has been a trauma for our club,' said Kilby. 'It was a shock when all this broke. I fully expected when he did move it would be upwards, not sideways to a club we are fighting in a relegation scrap with. We were all very surprised.'

The legacy of Owen Coyle headlined Jack Keogh in his 'Through the Keogh' column, on Friday January 15th in the local newspaper, the *Burnley Express*. These extracts sum up perfectly the feelings of everyone hurt and embittered by his decision to leave.

The dust has started to settle after last week's devastating news regarding the completely unexpected departure of our inspirational manager Owen Coyle to Bolton Wanderers in what can at best only be described as a sideways move.

Although it came as a complete shock to the system, particularly with the timing of the decision, it had always been in the back of my mind that if

Bolton came knocking there would always be a danger that this could happen; taking into account his association with the club as a player even though that was 15 years ago.

One of the saddest parts of this entire debacle is the lack of loyalty shown by a man who not only breathed fresh air into Burnley Football Club, but who had the ability to work miracles with the smallest of financial budgets, as well as charisma, honesty and integrity which he appeared to have in abundance.

All the good work Coyle has done over the past two years earning him a reputation that has taken him from a virtually unknown manager from the Scottish First Division to almost a household name throughout the football world, has now been tarnished and undone. All respect and credibility, particularly in the eyes of supporters of Burnley Football Club, has gone out of the window.

The decision he has taken has left most Burnley fans with a mixture of emotions, which range from frustration at being left high and dry in mid-season and during the transfer window, to a genuine feeling of anger at being badly let down with all our hopes and aspirations of Premier League survival having now been left hanging by a thread.

What disappoints me is that Coyle has not only let down the loyal Claret fans who worshipped the ground he walked on, but also the team he had assembled during his tenure, in particular the youngsters from Scotland and Ireland whom he had persuaded to join Burnley.

It would have been fitting if he could have left with the blessings of his beloved fans and not with a bitter taste in their mouths. Maybe the real face of Owen Coyle has emerged from behind his famous mask.

The majority of Burnley supporters feel betrayed by a man they would have trusted with their lives. Does he realise the hurt and disillusionment he has caused to an entire town with his selfish actions, and to add insult to injury he has decimated the backroom staff, which included Clarets legend Steve Davies. (Courtesy of Jack Keogh)

Keogh ended with the wish that his team would survive, and Bolton would go down. The wish would not be granted.

Supporters could still not quite believe it as Coyle and Flood began the unexpected task of finding a new manager. The man who came had a hard act to follow. Their choice would be surprising.

14

MISSION IMPOSSIBLE

Where do you apportion blame when a manager walks out in mid-season? Do you blame the manager who is tempted to leave, seduced by the temptations laid before him by those who want him? Do you blame the chairman of the club that covets him, and deliberately seeks to take him away when already contracted to another club? Or is the system to blame which allows it to happen and permits the poaching and tapping-up that seems so rampant in football?

Martin Samuels in the *Daily Mail* had the simple answer to manager-poaching in mid-season. He made the assumption that Burnley themselves would now have to get their hands dirty by taking a manager from another club. There is nothing new in this, he wrote, but one simple rule would stop it. If you cup-tied managers in the same way that you cup-tied players the problem would be solved. A manager who was at a club would not be able to leave until the end of the season. Samuels had advocated this six years earlier. If a few minutes in a Champions League game stopped a player from playing for any other club in that competition for the season, then surely the 23 games Coyle had managed Burnley should count for something and should have stopped him moving anywhere else in January. It would also put a stop to underhand tactics from interested parties making quiet phone calls to someone already employed. As it is, the current situation simply passes disruption down the line from one club to another and will always encourage the tapping-up process.

The Times asked another question. Would Coyle's defection to Bolton not give them an unfair advantage over relegation rivals Burnley? Presumably Coyle and Burnley were planning to sign players in January (they were), which meant Coyle had a clear plan of action for Burnley. That plan was instantly ruined. (In fact Coyle took two players to Bolton he had planned to sign on loan for Burnley and one of them in particular played a large part in Bolton's survival). Would he not be privy to a whole range of information about Burnley, from player wages to transfer targets? Would he not know player strengths and weaknesses (especially important with the Bolton game approaching)? Would all these factors and possession of privileged information not give him a clear and unfair competitive advantage? Did all this not affect the integrity of the

League? Simply put; it should not be allowed unless a manager had been sacked and then he was free to move.

Burnley drew up their wish-list of candidates they would consider or approach and certainly did not discount approaching another club's manager. If this was the system, so be it. Names mentioned included Paulo Sousa from Swansea, Blackpool's Ian Holloway and Leeds United's Simon Grayson. Others were added—Sean O'Driscoll and Lee Clarke from Huddersfield. There was speculation about Mike Phelan. West Ham's assistant manager Steve Clarke was another name. Swansea's chairman quickly warned Burnley off Paulo Sousa.

'As much as we're disappointed,' said Flood, 'There are always young, hungry, winning managers who want a challenge and who want to make their name. I think we would like to have the same recipe again and I think there are choices that we can consider. We just have to meet them and make sure they have the right feeling for Burnley. We will, hopefully make a decision in the next two weeks.' The players during this period were in a state of total limbo.

The target was to have someone appointed by the time of the Manchester United game. The first game for any new manager at old Trafford, could there be anything more dramatic? The word was that Burnley would look for someone bright, youthful, up and coming and not entirely dissimilar to Coyle. Coyle had recommended his friend John Hughes his former co-manager at Falkirk, and currently managing Hibernian.

The short term emergency plan, following the departure of Steve Davis, was to appoint Head of Youth Development, Martin Dobson as acting manager, move up various members of the youth team staff into more prominent coaching roles, and also appoint player Graham Alexander as player-coach. Captain Steve Caldwell also helped with coaching sessions. Craig Mawson became goalkeeper coach. The sheer scale of what the club had to do to fill the gaps was astonishing. Coaching staff who had never worked with senior players before now had to work with a group of seasoned pros who were left high and dry by Coyle's departure. Most of them publicly took the usual line: 'That's football . . . c'est la vie . . . these things happen . . .' but privately they were disappointed. His departure rocked the very fabric of the club and eroded the wonderful team spirit and belief that had taken the club to such heights. Coyle's success was very much based on the power of positive thinking. His dynamic enthusiasm was contagious. Suddenly it was gone.

When 'the beauty parade' was over, it was in time for the United game, and it was with some surprise, and even shock, that supporters (and players) received the news that the new man would be Brian Laws. The first reaction from the Press was that this was an appointment on the cheap. But Chairman Kilby and Director Flood insisted that he was the best of what was available, and the best of those actually interested in the job. Some were discounted immediately when they said, 'Talk to my agent'.

Brian Laws was available because he had recently been sacked by Sheffield Wednesday. There would be no compensation to pay, nor would there be the embarrassment of 'poaching' a manager from another club already in employment, bearing in mind the anger at the way Coyle had been poached from Burnley. But, in truth, just about every journalist was agreed; this was a baffling, underwhelming appointment and smacked of a view that relegation was already accepted and that the club was planning for the inevitable. There would be no short term appointment of a big-name manager and pay a big bonus if the club stayed up.

Supporters were less than impressed, the players privately stunned, but in his favour was a survey that placed him as one of the best managers around, in relation to budgets available and points won, despite leaving Wednesday in the bottom three. It was not an argument that convinced supporters. Yet, there were visible reasons behind his appointment. He had already been first choice when Cotterill had left, but Sheffield Wednesday would not cooperate. He had Burnley links in that he had been a young player at Turf Moor. And he was a 'safe' choice. Here was a manager who had spent his nearly 800-game management career working on limited budgets. He was hardly likely to be using a media friend to be announcing in a national daily that he would need £30million to stand a chance of taking Burnley further. He understood the notion that Burnley were a selling club. At interview he was the outstanding candidate, said Kilby and Flood.

Laws, who had once held his wedding reception at Turf Moor, defended his appointment describing himself as 'the perfect match' for the club and insisted he had the experience to lead them to safety. With a two and half year deal he was aware and acknowledged that some supporters were just a little underwhelmed by his arrival. But he insisted that his life in the lower leagues and the number of games he had been a manager, yet was still young and energetic, would give him the foundations needed.

'I know there will be supporters thinking why have we not got an experienced Premier League manager? But if you want an experienced manager—I'm here,' he said. 'I have got more than 700 games. Not many can boast that in the Premier League, other than Sir Alex Ferguson. I'm only 48. I started very early. If you talk about experience I have got it all. I was at my lowest ebb at Hillsborough, but now I'm like a kid with a new toy.'

The grizzled senior pros at the club hearing that remark and seeing how in his track suit he raced round the Turf Moor pitch like a wild thing on his first meeting with them, might just have been a little wide-eyed, wondering exactly what had arrived. It wasn't the best way for a new man to announce himself. Two of the senior players certainly provided him with just a little resistance to change, said Alan Nixon. It was the classic situation where a new man moves into any situation be it football, school or office and finds people set in their ways and happy to continue working as they have done for the previous boss, especially when it has brought success. Confided Alan Nixon:

> Laws was unsure what to do at times, changing the system, changing the way players thought about trying to win games. Obviously some of the old guard were not keen on that and one or two made their views known. Things always look worse when you are losing and Laws did not know how to stop the trend. But it was not entirely his fault.

When Joey Gudjonsson wrote in an Icelandic newspaper that Laws had lost the dressing room, whilst it might have been an exaggeration, and he later denied saying some of what he was purported to have said, there was presumably an element of fact in it. Laws did not have an easy time with some of the players, and at the end of the season with relegation assured, Brendan Flood commented that some players should have been looking at themselves rather than blaming the manager.

But if some of the players felt that Coyle's ways had brought success, nevertheless they had not won any of his last nine games and the defending was not good enough. Even without Premier League experience, Laws clearly knew this and identified that a modicum of change was necessary. He realised that there had to be a balance between being cavalier and cautious.

Laws said before his first game:

> There's a real plus in being cavalier because it shows no fear. I don't want to stop that and suppress it—there are other trigger points which we can defend a little better as a team. That's something we've got to focus more on, particularly away from home.
>
> I still want the same approach. I still want the players to go out there and play good football. I don't want to snuff it out. There's nothing broken here. I've told all the players we're not here to revolutionise everything and change everything. I think that would be the worst thing you could ever do. They are good players and I wouldn't want to suppress their confidence or the way they want to approach games. I might be putting the reins on a little bit but I won't be pulling too hard. It needs only tweaking here and there.

The tweaks didn't work. Although for 70 minutes Burnley played supremely well at old Trafford, it ended in a 3–0 defeat. Burnley performed valiantly in a 0–3 defeat against Manchester United and then lost miserably at Reading in the FA Cup. At Old Trafford, with fans putting aside their surprise at his appointment, Laws was warmly welcomed by the away end. A new manager is always given the chance to impress. The chants rang out not just for him but also for Barry Kilby. The events of the previous two weeks had produced a bond and togetherness between club and supporters that was quite remarkable. What they had been through was hugely traumatic and deeply emotional. Owen Coyle might never really understand the feelings in Burnley he induced at that time. People and club were devastated. The heart was ripped out of the place. The chants and noise and passion at Old Trafford were a symbol of the feelings for Burnley Football Club that remained. Everyone drew deeply from their wells of affection for the club and their sympathy for, and empathy with, Barry Kilby, as much a fan as anyone else and the man who had lead the club through two quite dreadful weeks.

On the field the team played supremely well. Forced into changes at the back, Duff and Edgar, brought in for the game, were outstanding. But for good chances spurned by Eagles and Nugent and an outstanding opportunity missed by Fletcher, there might well have been a huge upset, and in addition Thompson hit a post. But it was not to be. In the final 20 minutes United scored three times to finish the game with a quite undeserved scoreline. Fans and team left the stadium dissatisfied with the result, but not the performance. It boded well.

Alas the next performance in the FA Cup at Reading was dire and the 1–0 win by Reading was a wretched result, made even more depressing because the Reading winner came so late in the game. The display was entirely the opposite of that at Old Trafford. This was a team that looked confused and unsure, a team in tactical transition perhaps, seemingly uncertain of what was now expected of it—or perhaps just thoroughly demoralised.

But next was Bolton at the Reebok. Tuesday January 26th, 2010 and it was the game every supporter wanted to see, Bolton versus Burnley, the game that Piers Morgan wanted to see a Burnley win. The away end was sold out, the place filled with banners and posters, the chants long, loud, derisive, abusive and vitriolic. This was the opportunity for Burnley fans to vent their spleen, make their feelings known, and shower Owen Coyle with their bitterness and anger. The fates had thrown this game up just days after Coyle had taken his seat as Bolton manager.

Clarke Carlisle was philosophical in his attitude to all that had gone on.

It's an upheaval of course, especially in the middle of the season. But in terms of shock these things happen in football. Players leave that you never expected to leave, managers leave that you never expect to. It's happened and we move on. It often happens, people leave like thieves in the night, and that's just the way it happens. When we get there I'm sure there'll be no animosity. There probably won't be any over-friendliness because it's a professional scenario. It will be no different to bumping into former colleagues.

The result, however, took Bolton out of the bottom three and put Burnley in it. For Burnley fans the result was depressing, and Coyle's walk to the away end at the final whistle to applaud the Burnley fans, simply infuriating.

The day began with another Alan Nixon exclusive as he wrote that

Coyle, who one morning had even found the name Judas scrawled onto his snow-covered car, had revealed that it was he who insisted that Bolton pay the £1million compensation. The *Guardian* reported that he felt aggrieved that his former club claimed he had been placed on gardening leave after he repeated his desire to leave, when, he insisted, the truth was that he had refused to leave Turf Moor until Bolton paid up. 'There was no facility in my contract about gardening leave but I kept a dignified silence and waited. I sat for three days to make sure that Burnley got the compensation.' Nixon elaborated on this in the *Mirror*:

Bolton boss insists he took gardening leave to make sure old club Burnley got their £1million compensation. Owen Coyle has lifted the lid on the bitter row between Burnley and Bolton—and how he made sure his old club got their £1million.

Coyle has taken flak and he can expect more from a 5,000-strong Claret chorus tonight, but put the record straight on the compensation row that dragged out his short move from Turf Moor to the Reebok. He is fuming about some of the cheap jibes aimed at him. He was branded a Judas for moving, but says he showed the patience and principles of a saint.

Coyle was also accused of being a money-grabber when he made the switch, but the real cash dispute was between the two clubs. He was legally advised he could walk out but he chose to stay until Bolton paid the money to Burnley to 'do it right'. It was his final gesture to a club that he had taken to the Premier League and all its riches. He took the flak and even put the move at risk, as the clubs bickered over a figure.

'I conducted myself right every step of the way,' said the Bolton boss. 'I sat at home for three days to make sure Burnley got their compensation. Things happened, but I kept a dignified silence. I wanted to be sure they got the figure in my contract.'

Coyle has kept decent relations with his old Chairman Barry Kilby and Operations Director Brendan Flood. But the fans are not in a forgiving mood. Coyle said: 'It's easy to say things in a crowd but when I meet Burnley fans face to face they are disappointed but realise the job we did.'

It will be tough for Coyle to take on his former team tonight, aware of the emotional ties that still exist with the side. He said: 'Apart from being good footballers they are all top people. I think they would be personal friends if I had not been their manager.'

The bottom line about Coyle's transfer was the size of the budget. He added: 'A week or two after I joined, the club posted a £3.5million loss from the previous year. I sold my top scorer and didn't spend the fee. I brought in Chris Eagles for £600,000 plus add-ons, and I signed Martin Paterson and Kevin McDonald. We were promoted with minus £2million in the kitty in transfer dealings. There is a tremendous foundation at Burnley to kick on with. In time people will realise it was a key moment in Burnley's history.' (Courtesy of Alan Nixon)

The game that same night went Bolton's way, the goal coming from a shot that hit the bar and bounced down a foot over the line. In another season where there was just a little more good fortune, it would have bounced off the crossbar and back into play. Supporters will always lament their team's bad luck and the Bolton goal was typical of the way things were going for Burnley and would continue to do so.

By half-time I was bemoaning the lack of any luck, or any run of the ball coming our way; and the scrappy goal Bolton scored following what might have been an offside decision anyway, according to the Bolton commentary that someone was listening to behind us. I ranted and raved at what a joke scoreline it was cursing the lack of justice in the game. Bolton had hardly been in the game. They could have played till midnight without scoring but somehow they did. God they were abysmal, and we hadn't played that badly, despite seeing both McCann and Alexander go off injured very early—goodbye gameplan. Whilst the gods kicked us in the teeth, they smiled on Bolton, the ball hitting the crossbar and bouncing over the line. We were stunned. The half hadn't been that bad by Burnley, we'd been threatening, sliced them open several times and made them look quite the worst side we'd seen all season. What football there was certainly came from Burnley. Megson, Coyle or whoever; this was pure Allardyce stuff from Bolton, much of their play reminiscent of the 1950s days of Tommy Banks and Roy Hartle. NASA doesn't need rockets to put satellites in space, they can just ask a Bolton player to do it.

Disappointed at half-time, nothing could have prepared for the ghastly, abject, wretched, dismal, demoralising, poverty-stricken second half. It was in this half that I saw football as I know it, die. It was football that two Conference sides would have been ashamed of.

For some reason, manager Laws took Eagles off, for all his faults and blind alleys, still Burnley's one threatening player. On came new boy Nimani, the giraffe lookalike, recently borrowed from France. This meant goodbye to any wide play and any wingman. Now we had three centre forwards all bundling down the middle of the pitch. Paterson who had played with some purpose and clear position in the first half, now just joined in the general chasing and kickabout. Whenever Jensen (or anyone else for that matter) hoofed the ball down the middle, the forwards just raced after it before it disappeared somewhere down the other end of the ground. If they didn't chase it, it was left to Nimani, a fish out of water, at 6"4', to try and jump for it as it bounced high over his head. All football vanished to be replaced by kick and chase, or kick and hope. Not since I was last at Scarborough and saw a bunch of dads and lads trying to catch up with a beachball as it blew down the sand, had I seen anything quite like it.

And it wasn't even as if the two teams were evenly matched. Bolton were even worse. 'I felt some of the play was pleasing on the eye,' said Coyle about Bolton. He must have been at a different game than the rest of us.

Dire as it was, this was not a half that induced sleep or boredom. Far from it; the sheer awfulness of it was riveting. It was hypnotic in its dreadfulness. The football depth it plumbed was spellbinding; toe-curling, buttock-clenching, jaw-dropping dross that under the Trades Description Act should have got all of us a refund.

The score stayed at 1–0. The banners aiming abuse at Coyle were waved throughout. The howls of invective never stopped. Steve Davis disrespectfully punched the air when Bolton scored. So much for loyalty and gratitude there then, football is a selfish business. A last volley of abuse was hurled at Owen Coyle—but no—it wasn't. Through our weary eyes we saw him walk to the Burnley end to applaud his former worshippers. 'The bloody cheek,' said the saintly Mrs Thomas who never ever swears. The last time I heard her swear was when she came back from the hairdresser and I asked, if it was only half finished. The crescendo of boos and jeers increased in volume as he neared the Burnley supporters. Had we won we might have felt magnanimous, closure even, but no, the banner that said 'Never Forgotten but Never Forgiven', summed things up. To add salt to the wound, the result took Bolton out of the bottom three and put Burnley in it.

Coyle draped his arm round some of the players. Some of them looked distinctly uncomfortable. We drifted away cursing football and this sorry result, a defeat totally undeserved, and wondering where do we go from here?

After the game Owen Coyle compared himself to Moses. Something along the lines of: 'They've called me God, they've called me Judas. If we're talking biblical should they not call me Moses for leading them out of the wilderness?' Clearly he hadn't paid much attention in Sunday School. He must have forgotten that Moses was loyal and stuck with his tribe through thick and thin, through plagues and pestilence, and didn't bugger off halfway through the march. (Personal Diary January 26th 2010)

'It's a testament to the job I did there that they are so disappointed that I left,' Coyle told Sky Sports. 'They are a terrific set of fans there and they back their team and they did that tonight. Nothing will change my feelings for Burnley Football Club until the day I die. I asked for that passion in the fans when I was there and I can't complain when it's turned on me now.'

Expressions of feelings for the club 'till the day he died' fell on seething ears.

Laws summoned defensive reinforcements in the shape of Carl Cort and Danny Fox, the signing of Cort effectively ending Bikey's season. Jack Cork came on loan from Chelsea. Nugent's loan deal was extended. It was all to no avail. Chelsea came and undeservedly won 2–1, the fourth consecutive defeat. The first win came against West Ham. It was a fine game with both sides intent on attacking. Football is so predictable sometimes. When the luck goes your way, you win. West Ham were the unlucky ones. Hopes rose but faith in Laws was still low. There was a comprehensive defeat away at Fulham but in fairness to Burnley Fulham were gifted the first two goals by a poor linesman allowing offsides to go unchecked. The third goal came from a generous free kick. But overall Burnley were poor.

Later in the season Steve Caldwell gave an insight into how things had gone pear-shaped behind the scenes. He explained that when Coyle left he and other players were in shock. Burnley should have done more to keep him he added. Coyle was the driving force and everybody was 'gutted'. The players respected him, he respected them. The players had a couple of meetings but it was an unstable time. Some players forgot the team ethic and thought more about themselves than the club. It wasn't impossible to work with Brian Laws, he said. However, within a statement like that, there is usually the unspoken caveat—but it wasn't easy.

Brian Jensen gave an insight into what the players were now missing:

> There wasn't a day when he didn't come into work with a smile on his face. That was his philosophy, crack jokes, have good banter, work hard, but at the same time enjoy yourself. He gave us so much self-confidence and belief and that's 90% of football.

Clarke Carlisle explained the changes, that they'd been re-learning defensive duties, finding a happy medium between attacking and defending. He hinted that during the Reading game they'd fallen between two stools.

> The new manager is trying to implement a new plan, a new focus within the side. I think we saw (at Reading) a big swing from one focus to another. It's marrying the two and that's what makes a successful team and that's what we're trying to do.

It was certainly a ragged performance. And in the background Brendan Flood hinted that some players were resistant to change, and that the camp faced a sudden loss of positivity that drained confidence.

At Fulham Laws claimed that he could see players' heads dropping early in the game. Their mindset was now accepting bad luck and defeats. The legendary team spirit was splintered. They flew off to Portugal for some warm weather, and another defeat in a friendly against Dynamo Kiev. On their return they were promptly hammered by Aston Villa, 5–2. Laws by now was under close scrutiny and whilst some games were seen as definite defeats, there were games on the horizon that supporters felt were winnable and could ensure safety and another Premier season. Portsmouth, Wolves and Blackburn at home were winnable. Stoke City was a maybe. Wigan away prompted optimism. The season was far from dead.

Bottom club Portsmouth arrived at Turf Moor in financial turmoil. No-one expected defeat. How could such a chaotic club rooted at the bottom of the table provide any kind of shock? But, football kicks you in the teeth. The result was utterly demoralising as Portsmouth left with all three points, and with every defeat players lost a little more heart and spirit. This was a result that no-one anticipated.

Portsmouth were compact and organised, ,and counter-attacked with speed and intent. Cork and Eagles the two Burnley flair players were omitted. Bikey was back but not in defence where he was always more effective than in midfield. Portsmouth took the lead in the 25th minute, the goal being the first mistake in a calamitous afternoon for Carlisle, when Piquionne was allowed to pick up a ball that should have been cut out. Burnley rallied and Paterson lobbed James beautifully for the equaliser. The game was set for the Clarets to take control. Alas they did not and the second half was a total anti-climax. Carlisle gifted Portsmouth a penalty with a clumsy challenge. Jensen saved the spot-kick. Stung into life Burnley came back and a cross from Paterson should have been buried by Fletcher but the Scot fluffed the chance. Supporters can blame bad luck, the manager can blame the defenders, but when a centre forward misses gilt edged chances as often as Fletcher did during the season, then the team pays the price. And then Portsmouth scored the winner in the 76th minute. Jensen and Carlisle dallied when Fox took the throw-in and casually threw it into the 18-yard box. Neither could decide what to do it seemed. Carlisle seemed to have the ball but Utaka nipped in and stole possession. Carlisle brought him down and this time the penalty was scored. The ground went silent and then the groans and murmurings of discontent began, along with the sighs of resignation.

After a gallant defeat at Arsenal it was first Stoke and then Wolves at home in the space of four days. The Stoke game yielded just one point. Surely the Wolves game would bring three more and games like this were now assuming a 'must-win' status. Both teams were level on 24 points with Burnley in the bottom three on goal difference. This was the frustration; at no time were Burnley out of touch, they were still in with such a good chance of salvation. It began as such a promising day. Wolves could be dumped in the bottom three and Burnley could climb out. Players were playing for new contracts and Premier wages. What more of an incentive did they want?

At Sunderland in midweek Bolton had been trounced 4–0 and a photograph flashed round the websites. Directly behind Coyle and his dugout two lads in Burnley tops had unfurled a long 'Judas' banner. Sympathetic Sunderland fans joined in the abuse.

Incentives or not, March 13th might well have been the day we said goodbye to the Premiership. On a bitterly cold and windy day Burnley lost 1–2. The fortress that is Turf Moor is no more and Burnley looked like what they were; a Championship side that had somehow stumbled into the wrong room, even though it could be argued they were unlucky to lose.

It was a game when loud boos rang round the ground aimed at Brian Laws when Eagles was taken off and Burnley were losing 2–0. Laws in fact could have taken any one of half a dozen players off. Bikey was misplaced in midfield again. Blake seemed to be yesterday's man.

The goals Wolves scored were of the pantomime variety, there seems to be no other sort at Turf Moor these days. The first came when Mears' underpowered a header back to Jensen and the nearest Wolves forward raced onto it, scored with ease, and said thank you very much at this totally unexpected gift. The second was cruel when a tame shot deflected off Carlisle's leg, changed course by about ten feet and trickled in. Without that deflection it was heading for the corner flag. Without even trying, Wolves found themselves two goals up. We just shook our heads. Blake, generally out of favour and rumoured to be one of the dressing room grumblers, was brought on.

Nugent hit the bar for Burnley. Blake hit the post. There was a shout for a clear penalty in the second half. Any luck had truly vanished. 21 Burnley shots produced no points. The grumbles and criticisms of Laws rained down. General opinion was that relegation was assured and Laws out of his depth with just one win in ten games so far.

'Their luck was cruel,' wrote James Mossop in the *Mail on Sunday*. But, as loud boos rang in Laws' ears, no-one could argue with that. (Personal Diary March 15th 2010)

'LAWS IS NEXT FOR THE CHOP' was the header in the *Sun*. It was not a Nixon article. If it had been supporters might have taken notice. Nevertheless stories were emerging that within the Boardroom there was discontent with the manager and that there were some who wanted to replace him. True or not, the loud boos that rang round the ground during the Wolves game must have shocked Barry Kilby. Reasonable people might have felt sympathy for Laws 'given a hospital pass' said Kilby. But since when has football been noted for sympathy or patience.

Discussions centred round who was available to replace him. If the story was true just who could come at short notice—Curbishley, Coppell, Stan Ternent, Peter Reid, Ian Dowie, Phil Brown—the usual suspects were listed. What was certainly agreed was that the feel-good factor was well and truly gone. Anticipation and optimism were at rock bottom and there was huge disappointment that the season was ending in such a ragged way. And yet 3,500 tickets were sold for the away game at Wigan.

But still the fat lady had yet to sing. There were still plenty of points to play for and room to catch up. Next was Wigan away, a side now struggling near the bottom and out of sorts. It looked set for a goalless draw and no more than Burnley deserved as the final whistle approached. Burnley had raced out of the traps to look for an early goal, caused as many problems for Wigan as Wigan had for Burnley. Paterson might well have scored late on but his looping volley cleared Kirkland but then hit the crossbar. If the Wolves result was cruel, how cruel was the Wigan result? Into the final minute of injury time Moses out on the right skimmed Jordan, crossed and Rodallega headed home. There can be nothing worse in football than losing a game so late on. With supreme irony, had Burnley won this game with Paterson's strike, it would have been Wigan demoted at the end of the season and not Burnley. That's how close it was, that's how near Burnley came to safety at the end of a season when all the pundits, and some supporters, way back in August had predicted an embarrassing and humiliating season.

Laws said the obvious: 'We're still in the fight.' He was justified for he had seen grit, determination and spirit. It boded well for the next game, home to Blackburn Rovers. But in the meantime the rumours of Laws' dismissal had been scotched. Some directors had indeed wanted to replace him, but Kilby had remained loyal and felt he deserved his chance with a fresh start and clean slate the next season if they went down.

Relegation is the culmination of a long hard season. It is never the result of just one game. Every result contributes to the final outcome. But, if Burnley fans wanted to analyse the season and point to significant results, then it was the recent ones against Portsmouth, Wolves, Wigan and the forthcoming one against Blackburn Rovers that would be mentioned time and again. These were the winnable games they felt, and the games that had to be won.

But yet again, against Blackburn, nothing went right, and the game saw one of the worst dives, one of the worst con tricks, and one of the worst refereeing decisions when the referee was totally taken in by the sequence of events. It was a horrible day, in more ways than one.

It was a 12 o' clock kick-off for the Blackburn game with compulsory coach transport for all away supporters and surrounding roads closed off. If the game began in hope, then by two o' clock all hope and even interest had vanished. The words and anguish poured out of the loyal Burnley fans in the pubs, the local Press, and on the websites.

'Gutless, spineless, inept, shameful, weak, timid, outclassed, outplayed, out-thought, tepid, toothless, lacklustre, uninspired, boring, lightweight, abject, clueless, second-rate, woeful, embarrassing, depressing;' it was quite a list that poured from the keyboard warriors and their computers. With some, it was hard to disagree.

But, another one was 'cheated', for no matter how poorly Burnley had played, it was a shameful dive and embarrassing referee decision that lost the points. It was a howler of a decision as the Rovers player went over Jensen without any contact at all. Three sides of the ground were wide-eyed in disbelief. It was cheating of the highest order. But just a few seconds earlier Paterson, unmarked, had hared down the wing into acres of space. He demanded the ball. The quick throw was so obvious. But no, Jensen wellied the ball with one of his trademark stratospheric kicks into the opposition half. The ball came straight back, bingo; penalty.

Fans drove home thinking what a depressing, wasted afternoon it was. Where was the enjoyment or the entertainment? It was now a dismal experience watching this disjointed, mediocre Burnley side lose yet again. The regression was dreadful. Fewer and fewer people believed in the manager, and yet luck, or lack of it, plays such a huge part in the great schemes of things. Where does blame lie, with Coyle for walking out and ripping the heart out of the club and the players; or the players who showed precious little spirit in this game; or the directors who appointed Brian Laws? The debate about his appointment would not go away. Eleven defeats out of 13 was a pretty damning statistic. But if Laws was the wrong man, just who was the right one?

'Can things get any worse?' moaned someone coming down the stairs.

'Yep we could be in Division One and lost 0–1 to Milton Keynes,' said his mate.

Such a wonderful symmetry though, Mike Dean helped us at Wembley with his generous decisions. Today he cost us the game and probably sent us back down again; kind of funny really—or maybe not? (Personal Diary March 28th 2010)

Six games remained, and still only three points behind the next club above; but next it was Manchester City which meant that four out of five games had been at Turf Moor. Just one point came from those home games, and the City game was to be a total, absolute nightmare.

Pre-match, and whilst Brian Laws had spent the week having a go at referee Mike Dean for the 'penalty'; the fans spent the week having a go at the police for the bestial treatment of Burnley supporters leaving the away end as baton blows rained down on their backs. One PC in particular was caught on camera repeatedly beating someone who was on his way out. Of course this particular PC was exonerated by the subsequent report.

Predictions that Burnley would spend a season of crushing defeats had so far been inaccurate. True, they had lost predictably at the big clubs, but on no occasion had they suffered anything like the humiliation Wigan endured at Tottenham. But humiliation arrived in the shape of Manchester City and their galaxy of stars.

> Before the game I had jokingly mentioned that this might be almost an exhibition game seeing as how we were as good as doomed anyway. My jest turned out to be true as for 45 minutes City ran Burnley ragged, producing move after move against a nonexistent Burnley. In the teeming rain, three goals went past Jensen in the first six minutes. Spectators walked out. Laws looked crestfallen, bereft of ideas. By half-time City had rattled in five goals.
>
> Reports vary as to what happened in the Burnley dressing room at half-time but one thing was definite. McDonald subbed at half-time decided to take himself off to a nearby bar to meet his family down from Scotland. This was unheard of at Burnley. Heated views were exchanged between players and Laws. Blake was rumoured to have thumped Laws. It was neither confirmed nor denied. Gudjonnson has written in an Icelandic journal that Laws lost the respect of the players and lost the dressing room long ago and all the players had lost faith in him.
>
> After half-time it really did seem at one stage that the game might be abandoned, but the rain eventually relented but not until the pitch was a quagmire leaving players slipping and sliding and leaving the ball a yard behind them when it stuck in the water. City scored number six and then took a breather for the rest of the game. Fletcher pulled one back, scoring a meaningless goal. If only he had taken easier chances in previous games.
>
> It was a game when most Burnley directors were missing. Perhaps it was that, that saved Laws' job. The crowd with good humour recognised that this was simply a night when Burnley were temporarily in an unfair world and the opposition was not from Manchester, it was from a distant planet. It was a chastening experience.
>
> What was crystal clear, though, was this was a far different dressing room than had been present just a few months earlier. Were the players as baffled by the appointment as the fans? Where was the spirit, the never-say-die attitude that for long spells had played Arsenal off the park in December? Why was Blake taken off at half-time, arguably Burnley's best player despite the debacle? No wonder he was livid at half-time. Were

things so chaotic that a first-team player could leg it down to the nearest pub at half-time? Bikey meanwhile was sat on the bench. (Personal Diary April 4th 2010)

Next it was the *Daily Mail* reporting that Laws faced the sack with the club hierarchy believing that the appointment had not worked, and there was dressing room unrest.

'Lose To Hull And Laws Faces Sack' wrote Jeremy Butler in next day's *Mirror*. But Laws denied internal problems and dressing room rows although he did describe McDonald, who later apologised for his behaviour, as an 'idiot' and 'not the brightest lad'. Butler revealed that Barry Kilby had been in America and would discuss the situation with 'power-broker' Brendan Flood on his return.

'This is ludicrous, irresponsible, damaging and inaccurate,' said Kilby re the stories of a sacking, as news also emerged that the parachute payments for the next four seasons could total a staggering £48million with the proposed new scale of payments. It was tempting to say—relegation—so what, we'll bounce back straightaway. But with Brian Laws, asked the cynical? Get off the bloke's back, urged the others. Kilby, meanwhile, continued his support for the manager. The move to have Laws dismissed was quelled. His job was assured.

Next up was Graham Alexander calling on his team-mates to recover their spirit and to bare their teeth against the Tigers, Hull City. There had been just one win in the last 22 games going back to the previous year. The game against Hull was do-or-die. Win and there was still hope. The prospect of survival was still there. Alexander admitted to staying up till 5 in the morning to watch the City game over and again. They all watched it on Tuesday and Laws brought in a Sports Psychologist to heal the broken minds and rebuild their spirit.

'I want a reaction,' said Laws. 'We've let everybody down. There's got to be a response.'

'This is so big it's scary,' said Hull manager Ian Dowie before the game. And astonishingly, quite amazingly, staggeringly, unexpectedly, Burnley won and not just a 1–0 scrappy lucky win, this was a 4–1 demolition. So still the agony continued, it was still possible to stay up. With the Hull game there were five games remaining. Nine points could possibly do it. If the City game was the nadir, then it could only galvanise the team for a last effort. It began at Hull. For once everything went right. You could see the pleasure in the players' faces and reactions as they celebrated each goal one by one. They had even gone a goal behind but this was a day when good fortune returned, and with that came the win. Alexander scored two from the penalty spot, Elliott finished off in style with a delicious curler from the corner of the box.

But then it was back to normal. At Sunderland in the next game Sunderland were two up by half-time after another lacklustre Burnley show. Blake when he came on livened things up. Burnley pulled one back but time ran out and heads drooped. It was a real disappointment. The show was as good as over and when Liverpool came in the next game it really was all over as they thumped Burnley at Turf Moor 4–0. In truth it was a flattering scoreline. Burnley played so well but Gerrard scored twice. It was goodbye Premiership.

At Birmingham in the penultimate game the two goals Birmingham scored were typical of Burnley's season. For a start Burnley were poor and it was hard to remember that earlier in the season Burnley had beaten Birmingham so easily. Now it was reversed. But goal one was of the pantomime variety as the shot went in off Jensen. Goal two came from a generous free kick following a perfectly fair tackle, and then nonexistent marking allowed the header home, final score 2–1. But the lack of luck played its part. A good penalty for Burnley was denied. Ex-referee Jeff Winter in his Press column said it should have been given.

Tottenham arrived for the final game of the season. A packed crowd, a celebratory, carnival atmosphere, a goodbye to the land of make-believe, and amazingly a make-believe scoreline as Burnley won 4–2. Falling two goals behind, Burnley then outplayed Spurs and looked like they had been a Premiership team for the last ten years. This was the 'old' Burnley, pass and move, quick-thinking, sharp, great movement, and crisp goals. If only they had played like this against Portsmouth, Wolves, and Blackburn, or away at Sunderland and Birmingham.

The second half was quite simply one of the best Burnley performances of the past two years. This was the third game for Brian Laws where we had no bad luck, no defensive blunders, no poor officials and we had what one might call normal, routine, fair share, run-of-the-ball. The others were West Ham and Hull. We won those as well.

At last there was passion, determination, a real will to win and great team spirit. Belief grew with the equaliser and when the third goal went in there was utter delirium as the ground erupted. This was a release of all the frustrations felt since January. Burnley were not a laughing stock after all. Sure they would go down but with dignity and a superb last day win to add to the away win at Hull. They ended five points behind the soap opera that is West Ham.

There is sentiment in football after all. Blake was brought on for the final minutes even though it looks like he will leave. His name was chanted over and again. At his best there were moments of skill on the ball to remind us of how great Jimmy McIlroy was. Some of the goals he has scored have been stunning. Fittingly in his cameo performance there were moments of pure class.

By the end there was a carnival atmosphere. The vast majority of the crowd stayed to wave their farewells and give thanks to the players, who, for all their faults in some games, had largely been the players who got us to the Prem in the first place. Faith was restored along with the suggestion that next season might not be so bad after all. The lump in my throat grew at the thought that I might have seen the last of the little magician, Robbie. And it was there for quite a while as I kept thinking if only we had played like this in other games. If lady luck had been just a little more kindly disposed . . . if only . . . if only . . . (Personal Diary Sunday May 9th)

On the Monday after the game, the Burnley Board met. It was described as a routine meeting but rumours were strong that Laws' tenure was still uncertain. But within days, both local newspapers reported that he was to retain his post, though one suggested that he had ten games in the new season to prove himself. Chris Boden reported that, yes, there was a split vote on his future, but the split was in his favour and it was denied that he had been given a fixed number of games to prove his worth. Laws could only repeat what Stan Ternent had once said after a torrid time: 'Judge me when it's my team.'

Meanwhile, at The Reebok, Bolton were safe, guided there by Coyle. He revealed, at the end of the season, that he was very much motivated by the stick he had received from Burney supporters. 'It was fair to say the stick I got was not particularly nice. I understand where it was coming from. I can't say I enjoyed it, definitely not. But the traumatic things that happened in January gave me the extra steel that was probably needed to deal with stuff that comes my way. I am still a young manager. I don't have all the answers but I am getting better year in, year out. I am better than this time last year and some of that is down to the experiences I have had. It was a family atmosphere at Burnley and it was a real wrench to leave people we have such fondness for. But myself and the staff left for football reasons. The plan put in place at Burnley was the right plan for that football club. So the plan Burnley had was the right plan for Burnley but not the right plan for us, in terms of my development and how hard we'd worked to get to the Premier League. I had wanted as much funding as possible to maintain that Premier status. We worked as hard as we could as a staff to get to the Premier League but accepted the club could go no further in terms of finance. We were like players, though. You want to be at this level for all your days. We wanted to stay there and progress. It was an emotional decision. People will think I don't mean what I said about how hard it was to leave—but it is true.' In addition he argued that Burnley were safe when he walked:

Burnley were safe when I walked. Owen Coyle revealed his pain at watching Burnley go down, but refuses to be the scapegoat for his old team's failure. Coyle who quit to become Bolton boss in January and kept them in the top flight, is annoyed by suggestions that he left Turf Moor successor Brain Laws 'a bad hand'.

Coyle said: 'I think about those boys and everyone at the club every day. I still believe they were good enough to stay in the Premier League. It saddens me they didn't. I left them in 14th place and on 20 points. They are a terrific group of players and an unbelievable set of fans, a unique club. We'd have given it a really good go if I'd stayed; you never know what would have happened.'

Coyle admitted it was not ideal to have moved in mid-season: 'I accept I left at a bad time. But I don't think I left them with a bad hand. I heard what the chairman Barry Kilby, a man I respect, said about that. But I just take it as a compliment because of the job we had done before that. Every second I was there I put my heart and soul into it.' (Courtesy of Alan Nixon)

With their fate settled, Chairman Barry Kilby summed things up:

> It took us 33 years to get back into the top flight, and to go back after just one season is disappointing, but we will go down strong and we will do everything to get back again. Brian didn't have a great hand given to him halfway through the season. We will be sitting down and having a chat about what our plans are for the future. January was a massive thing for us. It wasn't just Owen going, it was the clearing out of the backroom staff that really did for us. We had a manager and a coaching set-up in place and in seven days it disappeared. Owen went on a Tuesday and by the following Monday I had to get Terry Pashley and Martin Dobson to coach the team, and we were playing Manchester United at Old Trafford the following Saturday. I certainly didn't see it coming. I wouldn't have thought he'd go to Bolton, and what he had with the fans and everything. If Aston Villa or someone like that had come in I would have understood.

Quite definitely, following his departure, some players were deeply affected, having lost heart in several games, simply going through the motions. The 'nice' football continued in a number of games, but passion, the will to win, and determination had gone in several others. There was the feeling amongst supporters that they were 'not playing for Laws'. A good bunch of pros was drifting and leaderless. 'Some of the old guard were not keen on the way Laws was trying to change systems and the way they thought about trying to win games.' One or two made their views known. They became a soft touch and there was no rush from other players to distance themselves from Gudjonnson's claims that there was deep dressing room unrest.

The Championship beckoned. The top flight stay had been short-lived. Coyle was gone but far from history. The wounds still festered at the end of the season and the feeling remained that Owen Coyle's walkout was the root cause of relegation.

Astonishingly, not many months later, the Carling Cup draw would bring him back to Turf Moor. It would result in another of those special Turf Moor nights beneath the floodlights.

15

CLOSURE

In October 2010 I visited Owen Coyle at the Bolton training ground. From September 2010 until December, I talked to some of the people at Burnley Football Club closest to him—Brendan Flood, Barry Kilby, Clarke Carlisle and Paul Fletcher.

The Chief Executive, Paul Fletcher, was pragmatic in his judgement.

Owen was one of the biggest heroes there's ever been at Burnley Football Club. Sadly within a few weeks he was being cast as a villain when he not only left but he took some of our senior coaching staff with him. What he did was right for Owen Coyle but wrong for Burnley Football Club. The episode showed how football has changed off the field since I was playing. When I played the fighting was on the field. Now it's behind the scenes in the Boardrooms. Many years ago it was a dirty game on the field but in the Boardroom the game was run by gentlemen. Today's game is cleaner on the field but the activities in the Boardroom are much dirtier due to the massive revenues involved. It's a tough game out there and sometimes clubs hurt other clubs. You've got to look after yourself. That's the dogfight you find yourself in, especially when the stakes are so high as they are in the Premier League. And maybe the experience we went through losing Owen toughened us up and taught us a few lessons.

Personally I always got on well with Owen. He became a good friend and still is a good friend but I've been in football long enough to realise that all is fair in love, war and football. These things happen in this strange game and it's been my view and the Board's view that life goes on so let's get on with it. I know the fans don't always see it like that and will look for every opportunity to express their disappointment. If Owen had left Burnley to join a top Premier League club like maybe an Aston Villa, or Everton or even Liverpool I think the Burnley fans would have said 'thank you very much, you've done a great job for us, all the best and we'll watch your career for evermore'. But the fact that he joined a rival at a time when we were battling relegation, as Bolton were, and they survived and we didn't, was the extra disappointment for our fans. We were close to staying up last season and if we hadn't had the major disruption in the middle of the season we may have got the extra five points necessary. January, 2010 was a tough time for everyone at Burnley.

When Fletcher talked of 'learning a few lessons' it is reasonable to suppose that he was referring to the ease with which Phil Gartside was allowed to talk to Owen Coyle, and the speed with which an offer was made to him.

Time might have mellowed the initial feelings of anger and let-down felt by Brendan Flood and the disbelief that Coyle wanted to leave, but the memories and the details were still fresh and clear in his mind. How could they not be? For over two years they had spoken regularly, sometimes as often as three times a day. Brendan Flood looked back and spoke of how he felt anger at Gartside. He felt he had taken advantage of him and their friendship 'and there had been a breach of trust having known him for several years in a business capacity'.

Flood talked of immediately feeling uneasy about giving Coyle's number when Phil Gartside phoned him, but reasoned that contact would be made anyway, so he gave the number 'for the sole purpose of allowing Gartside to chat to Coyle off the record. He told him he would be wasting his time and told him, 'He won't come'.

Flood recalled Gartside saying, 'I've got the number in the office . . . do you mind if I have an informal chat with him'. Flood says that Gartside then asked him to do him a favour and text the number.

Brendan Flood immediately phoned Coyle to tell him of Gartside's call. 'Are you interested?' he asked.

'I might be,' Coyle answered, 'but at this stage who knows?'

Flood then emphasised to Coyle that he would be very unhappy to lose him. By giving the phone number and immediately speaking to Coyle, Flood felt that at least he was 'managing' the situation and exercising some measure of control over the events inasmuch as he had at least some idea of what was going on.

After the MK Dons game Coyle did not appear for the Press conference because he was in the physio's room talking with Flood. 'I knew straightaway he wanted to go,' he recalled. 'I asked him why on earth he would be interested in a Bolton offer. I just can't see why you would want to go. Did you hear the crowd singing your name in the second half? As much as they love you they will hate you if you leave now. But Owen replied that he would like to speak to Bolton and if he were to leave it would be purely for footballing reasons.' At that point Flood knew he was intent on leaving.

It was when Burnley went to Bolton for the League game that Coyle did indeed discover that Flood was right. And then later in the year in September at the Carling Cup game when Coyle discovered the bearpit that was Turf Moor, he was reminded again of how right Brendan Flood had been. Burnley fans turned up in their thousands to vent their spleen and make their feelings known. There was an attendance of 17,600 for a game that under ordinary circumstances might have attracted something around 6,000. The hostile atmosphere was unparalleled with stewards ever present to 'protect' Coyle, although their presence was not a request from Coyle himself.

Flood outlined how it was on the Monday morning at breakfast that he received the call from Gartside who informed him that Bolton now wanted to talk officially. Flood immediately explained that this could not happen until he had informed the Board and the chairman (who had been away) to obtain their consent. But you've given me your consent already, Gartside responded explained Flood, and Flood knew in that instant that he had been taken advantage of, never expecting Gartside to have already offered Coyle the job either in their 'off the record chat', or on the Sunday in Glasgow when the Bolton chairman met him. Nor did he anticipate that Coyle would be in the slightest bit interested in accepting.

That same Monday was the snow-filled night that Coyle, after he had driven back down from Scotland, visited Flood and Chairman Barry Kilby in the latter's home. Flood says he had already given Phil Gartside a tirade on the phone and called him several unpleasant names. He no longer speaks to him. Now in Barry Kilby's conservatory while the chairman made coffees in the kitchen, a shocked Flood gave Coyle what he described as a broadside. He felt they had been 'buddies' at Burnley, had worked so closely together and that he had been seduced by Bolton.

Flood, in his own mind convinced that the whole thing had been 'stage-managed', so that it appeared that Burnley had given their consent, related: 'I told him if he felt comfortable working for Phil Gartside knowing how the move had been engineered, then he was welcome.' At this point Flood felt that Coyle was unsure about leaving.

Meanwhile in the best traditions of media coverage, Sky Sports News had gone to the wrong house. Camera teams turned up at Brendan Flood's house not the chairman's to record the outcome. It was Brendan Flood's daughter Sinead they filmed driving away.

'Is your dad inside meeting Owen Coyle?' the crew yelled at her.

'Hah,' she responded mischievously as she sped away. Later that evening she sat watching Sky Sports News. Flood knowing that she had no interest in football asked why. Because Sky came to their house, and she was watching to see if there would be anything on, she told him.

Flood was by now also experiencing the machinations of Boardroom politics. In his early days as a director able to support the club financially, he had had a controlling voting position. Not all directors however were quite in tune with him, especially the more cautious. And, with a Board of ten members there were bound to be sub-groups. Once his Modus business had gone into administration, he 'the wounded animal' as he described himself, spoke of his position in the Boardroom being diminished.

Even in the early part of Coyle's first full season, the promotion season in fact, but a season that had started badly, Flood suggested there had been muttered mumblings of discontent at the appointment and mumblings about exactly where the club was heading with Coyle at the helm, as results tailed off in mid-season with five consecutive League defeats.

Now, with Coyle seen as 'Flood's man', by association Flood received blame for Coyle's departure and that he had been unable to persuade him to stay. Both in business and at the football club Flood had been prepared to take risks in order to progress. The unknown Coyle was seen as one of those risks and now he had gone. Thus Brendan Flood took a good deal of the flak for the way it had happened.

In the contract was the compensation figure of £3million if Coyle left for a top-six club. The actual figure received was £1.2million.

After Coyle had gone a small group of senior players were consulted as to what type of replacement was needed. Individual names were not asked for or discussed but simply the attributes needed.

Brendan Flood said:

> We probably spoke to a dozen people. We wanted to speak to Alan Curbishley but he wasn't interested. Those dozen were narrowed down to a small preferred list of four; Brian Laws, Lambert from Norwich, Grayson of Leeds and Sean O'Driscoll from Doncaster Rovers. On the final day we spoke to Sean O'Driscoll and Brian Laws. We chose Brian. Both of us felt we could work with him.

Barry Kilby was in Switzerland when the approach was made. He came back a day early on Friday 1st January, not because of the impending crisis about which he still knew nothing, but because his wife Sonya had injured her ankle. It necessitated a trip to a hospital in Preston on Saturday the 2nd, and the first he heard of the approach from Bolton was a phone call with Brendan Flood while he stood outside the hospital on the day of the MK Dons game.

'There might be a bit of trouble,' Flood told him.

Before the game, Kilby and Coyle spoke on the phone about the team. Nothing else was mentioned. At this stage and during the day it was still seen as just a bit of trouble, but one that would perhaps go away.

The day after, on Sunday, Kilby went to the Rangers v Celtic game, a game he had always wanted to see with tickets provided by Coyle. It was with some irony, unbeknownst to Kilby; that at the same time Gartside was on his way to see Coyle in Glasgow. Kilby remembers it was a beautiful sunny day. But the next day, Monday, came the snow that caused havoc in Burnley and in the narrow country lanes near Kilby's home.

All this time Barry Kilby was still confident that Coyle would not leave. 'Why on earth would he want to,' he asked himself mindful of the plusses of working at Burnley where Coyle was hero-worshipped, and that Bolton was a club deeply in debt. Still on the Monday, Gartside phoned Kilby and Kilby told him you have not got permission to speak to him. But we have, was the gist of Gartside's reply, it came from a senior director; referring of course to the Friday night call when Brendan Flood had given Gartside Coyle's phone number. In less than an hour a solicitor's communication was received from the Bolton solicitors informing Burnley what they didn't want to hear, that Coyle was to be offered the Bolton job.

Kilby was flabbergasted at the speed with which this happened. His eyebrows were raised even more when the League Managers' Association contacted the club to suggest there were issues to do with 'constructive dismissal', in connection with the club saying they now needed a new manager before Coyle had actually left. 'What else were Burnley supposed to say with the prospect that the manager was about to leave?' wondered Barry Kilby.

On Monday afternoon after more discussions between Coyle and Kilby it was arranged that they would all meet at the chairman's house in the evening and go through things again. Kilby was still confident that they could turn things round and was convinced that when the 'manager' left the house it was still 50:50 and that he had still not definitely decided to leave.

Alas when Coyle visited the club offices on Tuesday morning Kilby knew the game was up and he was going. Today they text each other but Kilby suggested that they are not best pals, which, having been a chairman for so many years, is as close as Barry Kilby ever gets to public criticism of anyone.

At the Carling Cup game at Turf Moor, months later, he was contemplative, and looking around, wondered if the fabulous atmosphere would be a reminder to Owen Coyle of exactly what he had given up; the dark night, the packed streets and approaches, the passion of the crowd, the 'proper football club', debt free, the respect of all other football clubs, the vibrancy of the unique stadium, the sense of excitement, games to truly look forward to. He wondered exactly how he had been persuaded to join a club with such huge financial commitments, a soulless stadium; a ground that was simply part of a shopping precinct rather than part of a town and a community. 'I don't think he really expected or understood the depth of feeling waiting for him.'

'What have clubs like this got to look forward to, other than survival? In all our talks I can only recall one thing that he gave as a reason for leaving and that was being able to pay much higher wages. But if Bolton go down, with the commitments they have, they are in huge trouble.'

Coyle's reported comment about Bolton that 'everything I want in a football club is here', which could only refer to the superb facilities at the Reebok and the training ground, produced an instant response from the Burnley chairman. 'No, it's people that make football clubs; people and the community.'

It's now 12 months on and the question is still asked: Coyle—good manager or lucky manager? The successes he had at St Johnstone and Burnley suggest both. But what was his secret. Just how did he do it? Many Burnley fans remain astonished at the run of good fortune, the clean sheets, the wonder goals; the generosity of referee Mike Dean at

Wembley, all the things that Burnley enjoyed in the final six games of the promotion season. But as the saying goes, you make your own luck and no manager can be successful without it. And, good fortune is also very often a by-product of playing the Coyle way, taking risks, with confidence and without fear.

Speaking of luck, Barry Kilby recalled the game at Blackpool in the atrocious conditions. He still sees this as the game that kickstarted the promotion run-in during 2009. When the referee went over to ask the managers did they want to continue, Kilby recalled that it was Coyle that said no, stop. Blackpool manager Tony Parkes said carry on. Kalvanez went on to win the game for Burnley. Or, looking back, was it not an injury time goal against Charlton, when six minutes were added, in 2008–09 that turned the season. Managers have no control over things like this.

'Coyle stirs loyalty because he looks after people,' wrote Henry Winter and that was something also related by Alan Nixon. Winter wrote of his 'compassion' so that even after he strode across the Wembley pitch, victorious, he had time to remember that Brendan Flood's mother-in-law had passed away the day before and thoughtfully consoled him. 'Such kindness binds people together. So the directors worship him.'

Do they still—no they do not. Brendan Flood described the Carling win over Bolton as 'collective, mass therapy'.

But several staff at Burnley FC still speak of him fondly; he was a man who made impressions because he had the human touch. 'He came down to collect the post himself many a time,' said one receptionist. 'When he did that the first time I thought, he'll do for me.'

When groups are given tours of the ground and anyone groans or points to any picture of Coyle with abuse, they are quickly told, 'Don't forget this is the man who brought Premiership football to the club and town.'

'Grounded and accommodating,' wrote Moira Gordon about him in *The Scotsman*, 'with a warm and obliging smile.' Regarding the move to Bolton, it was nothing personal, simply a move dictated by ambition, for football reasons. If the decision had been based solely on emotion, he would still be at Burnley. 'That's why I don't mind when people say it was selfish . . . I have ambition and worked hard to get opportunities and in an ideal world Burnley and I would have gone on where I want to go together but . . .'

What is abundantly clear is that Coyle is a man driven by the need to keep moving up, and the need to improve. Only by moving when your stock is high can you continue upward movement. As both St Johnstone and Burnley FC discovered, that can mean leaving a club in mid-season when an opportunity presents itself. The desire to be the best he can be is an oft heard quote. Along with that came the desire to make players better at Burnley. He talks of the glass ceiling that British managers must break through to get the top jobs in the Premiership. Taken to their logical conclusion, his comments point to an ambition to become a manager of one of the big four.

It was certainly possible to find references to Coyle's management and style, his character and personality by trawling through media interviews and Burnley player features. Twelve months on it is easily possible to distil all the words spoken about him by colleagues such as Davis, and players such as Blake, Jensen and Caldwell into a summary of his 'secret'.

At Burnley he still played and an understanding of what it felt like to play made him empathetic with other players, particularly strikers. He was forever positive, cheerful, smiling and infectious, with limitless enthusiasm. There were references to how he could make the place relaxed; players played without fear, he encouraged flair, honest mistakes were accepted. He showed respect to those who gave one hundred percent. His philosophy was based on what appeals to all players, keeping things simple and being entertaining. His focus was on winning, his substitutions were invariably forwards not defenders. He was never one to stick 10 men behind the ball and hope for a 0–0. Players referred to his motivational skills. He was able to listen to others and give individual encouragement. Mental strength enabled him to make tough decisions. On the touchline he was like the proverbial jack-in-a-box, cajoling, barking instructions, gesticulating, shouting, clapping, and when necessary haranguing referees over their decisions. And, he was supremely fit, toned, trim, weighing not much more than he did as a player. He provided a physical model of how to look after yourself.

Andy Cole commented on his ability 'to make players ten times better. He made players feel ten feet tall and that included me. He was enthusiastic, preached good football and was dead honest. On the touchline he was always shouting, energetic and on his toes. He made the Burnley players ten times better than they were.'

Key player Clarke Carlisle was both fulsome in his praise for Coyle and like ex-player Paul Fletcher, realistic in his opinions, echoing Coyle's own theme of taking opportunities when they arose. Carlisle played for all three managers, Cotterill, Coyle and then Brian Laws. Although Carlisle arrived at the club after the long run of 19 winless games, nevertheless he was able to point to different qualities each manager had and help explain how Owen Coyle was able to transform the same players who had reached the end of the road with Steve Cotterill.

> Adrenalin, ideas and energy became worn out and training and tactics stayed the same with Steve Cotterill. He had got as far as he could with that bunch of players. Nor did he have any money to replace players he might have wanted to change to get different results, and at the same time the lads on the periphery became fed up and disillusioned because they could see the results but still couldn't get in the team. So things stagnated even more.

Then Owen Coyle came in with fresh energy and for everyone there was a clean slate so everyone was out to play well and impress. No-one knew a thing about him when he came, all we knew was he was from some small club in Scotland, and we'd heard he loved endless running, and that's the thing that players dislike and we thought 'oh no'.

But, that wasn't so at all, in fact he hated running so he tried to make everything fun and enjoyable. And, he was able to train with us; he was young enough to play and liked nothing better than shooting practice. He joined in the skills sessions and 5-a-sides; everything was competitive; players are naturally competitive so the losers had to bring pop and cakes in. And if players are competitive, they also hate putting their hands in their pockets when they lose. But it made it fun. From that grew camaraderie.

But just what was his management secret, how did he transform those players? 'He constantly encouraged. He was always positive. He made you believe you could be the best. Even if you had a rubbish game or in training, he'd say stuff that we knew was tosh but we believed him because he drummed it into us over and again.'

Carlisle smiled at one point when I mentioned that supporters still wondered how Burnley had actually managed to win promotion. He admitted:

The players do too. Stevie Caldwell was here the other night for the Barnsley game and he said the Wigan players, where he is now, just didn't believe him when he told them some of the stuff Owen used to say to us. It was simply the power of positive thinking. It's a confidence thing. You fake it to make it. You give people confidence, from that you play better, from that comes more confidence and then you do become a better player. He could make an average player good, and a good player excellent. If he had a secret, this was it.

But in training there were no set piece practices with Owen Coyle.

Oddly there was no positional play practice, set-plays, corners, free kick routines. I can maybe remember two or three, that's all. In fact there was one time it happened and we all looked at each other amazed. He encouraged spontaneity, thinking on your feet, ad-libbing when the opportunity arose; just make the most of whatever comes on offer.

But Steve Cotterill was a set-play man. With him it was do this, do that; he told you exactly what he wanted you to do. Under Cotts I had a job to do, there were no grey areas. If you didn't do what you were told you were subjected to, verbal violence, shall we say? He was in total control but he only had a one-method-fits-all when it came to man-management and man-management is all about treating people how they need to be treated, some it's an arm round the shoulder, and others it's a kick up the backside.

Clarke Carlisle said he understood the supporters' anger and bitterness. Supporters are with a club forever, but players are not, he explained:

For the fans Burnley is their club, so of course they feel let down. But players are different. We move, sometimes like ships passing in the night. If someone moves I'm just grateful for what they did and for what I've learned from them. So yes, it was a turn up for the books when he left, we were surprised at the timing, but in no way did we feel angry or bitter even though it was mid-season and in no way did we feel it was catastrophic. Career moves are a normal part of human life. For fans, Burnley is their club, it is part of them, but it is not their job.

And, we played for us not Owen Coyle. For a footballer it is a job. I play for me first, my family second, there is a mortgage and bills to pay; for my personal success and I play 100% for Burnley while I am there. I want to return the faith placed in me. But astuteness comes into it when decisions are based on career moves.

When they first heard from Owen Coyle in the dressing room at MK Dons that he was listening to what Bolton had to say Carlisle explained that they were like employees in any other works situation when the news comes that the boss might be leaving.

Conversation centred around did we think he would actually go, or would he stay and of course who might be the replacement; those were the big questions. And eventually, yes, some players were surprised when it became clear who the final two would be.

So Brian Laws came in and said he wasn't going to change much but he had noticed that we hadn't scored a goal from any corner or free kick play so he set out to remedy that. There was a period of transition, everyone on tenterhooks about would he want me or not; our futures were on the line and a manager can't be everyone's best friend. So you have to knuckle down and get back to trying to impress the new manager.

Three games came up in the conversation. One was the Carling Cup Tottenham game.

We felt not just hurt, desolate and in despair but we also felt how totally unfair it was that we had beaten them at the end of 90 minutes and then why should they have a second chance to win the game? That was totally unfair. But what it also did was make us think that we were able to beat Spurs 3–0 and we played like that in the Championship we could deal with anyone. And that belief stayed with us—especially after the game away at Blackpool. The conditions were atrocious, but it was a game we never thought we'd lose. It was a horrible, horrible night, you'd no idea where the ball would blow or swerve or move around in the wind. Your one thought is don't succumb to the conditions, don't be the one who makes a mistake because of them. If in doubt get rid and just do the simple things.

And then there was the Manchester City game—was it 5–0 at half-time? Of course the dressing room was understandably volcanic as inquests took place. What the 'bleep' is going on you're asking. Anger in those circumstances is the norm. We saw a sports scientist after that game. But that's only effective if every player buys into the message. If you have 20 players and four are sceptical and make fun the whole thing is wasted. At Watford with Aide Boothroyd it worked though. All of us believed in what the messages said and then it becomes very powerful. We went out feeling like warriors and it worked for us and brought success.

But with Owen Coyle we believed the message that he constantly told us and his message was that we were quality.

Brendan Flood pointed to how Coyle wore his heart on his sleeve, was utterly committed, he looked after players individually, had a philosophy of 'if it ain't broke don't fix it'. His biggest skill was man-management and keeping people happy. At the same time, if some players didn't measure up to his demands, they could be frozen out and players whose faces didn't fit, or rocked the boat, were certainly moved on.

'He was the perfect manager from a club point of view,' one senior employee confided. 'Knew us all, took a genuine interest in what we were doing; was obliging where he could be, right until the moment he left us and then came back and tried to rip the heart out of the club. It felt like being dumped by your first girlfriend—love and hate in equal amounts.'

There were a few texts between Owen Coyle and myself and then I arranged to meet him in October at the Bolton training ground. Owen Coyle insists that he did not leave Burnley solely for a bigger wage packet. He is ambitious and wants to work at the highest possible level. It is as simple as that. He refuted any suggestion that he was 'tapped-up' prior to the meetings with Phil Gartside, in fact he was quick to point out that he had conversations with Burnley before anything was officially sanctioned with the wry inference that if any tapping up took place, Burnley too were guilty and they had no qualms about taking him from St Johnstone just days before a Cup Final. He was adamant that there was no contact with Bolton until the MK Dons weekend of January 2nd.

Yes, he did talk to Celtic in May 2009; and but not until two days after Wembley. Would he have joined Celtic if Burnley had lost at Wembley? The question was neatly answered. 'I never had any doubts they would win.'

He knew nothing of any Gary Megson points target, and dismissed the idea of being placed on 'gardening leave' by Burnley when he left. 'It was just not in my contract.'

The facilities at Bolton are amongst the best in the Premiership, the player-wages budget larger than Burnley's. What remained unspoken though was that there is no big player-purchase budget, or that if this was a 'promise' it has not materialised. But, the huge debt is not a problem, and if anything happens to benefactor Eddie Davies, 'then things are in place'.

The infrastructure is based on many years in the Premiership: 'Ten years as opposed to Burnley's 15 games.' The site encloses five full size pitches all to the standard of the Reebok surface. Buildings contain an enormous, luxuriously-equipped keep fit centre, boot room, physiotherapy suites and doctor's room with medical facilities. There are enormous changing rooms, and the 'cryopod' (a chilling chamber for boosting athletes' recovery processes). There is a huge café/dining area, carpeted hallways, reception area, and conference room. There are two chefs and staff, a pool, 'tranquil room' and a Pilates studio. The manager doesn't just have an office; he also has his own private lounge with picture windows overlooking the pitches.

By comparison what is currently on offer at Burnley's training area at Gawthorpe is primitive and the idea of Burnley players driving back to Turf Moor covered in mud in their cars is positively archaic. (The players, the bread and butter of the club, privately grumbled when following promotion, large sums were spent in the directors' areas at the club, but minimal amounts on player facilities.) However, moves are currently afoot to build brand new facilities at the training area and planning permission has been granted.

Words pour from Owen Coyle like a torrent. Sometimes they run away with him. He answered the suggestion that he had said things at Burnley, perhaps said too much, that came back to haunt him, for example 'I'm here for as long as the club want me': 'I am what I am, my heart's on my sleeve, whatever I say I mean it at the time.'

Bolton FC on the field are however nowhere near where he wants them to be. But with no immediate cash windfalls coming his way, if they are to improve it has to be because of his motivation, his cajoling; his inability to accept that mid-table means success, the latter regardless of the financial constraints. He has to convey to players, convince them, that they can be better than mid-table. One player who has hugely benefited from his arrival has been Johan Elmander, the enigmatic striker. Supporters have seen an improved style of play and better relations off the pitch. The place is more positive than it was 12 months ago. But if he went to the Reebok thinking, or believing, that there was big money to spend, he was sadly mistaken. In truth, in some ways the spending situation is not unlike that at Burnley, except one division higher, and the constraints are in more luxurious working conditions.

It was in September, 2010, that Burnley hosted Bolton Wanderers in the Carling Cup. When the draw was heard, there was a collective gasp. Was this not the tie that fans had said they wanted? Would this not give them the chance to express their continued bitter resentment at Coyle's timing, and the wholesale harvesting of the backroom staff? Would a victory bring closure to the saga?

'Ouch,' texted Brian Laws to Owen Coyle.

'I'd better put my tin hat on,' texted Owen Coyle to Brendan Flood. His jocular, tongue in cheek, little quip perhaps showed how he underestimated the depth of feeling waiting for him at Turf Moor that night.

Burnley were simply magnificent for long spells. This was no fluke victory and the first 45 minutes was as good a display by the Clarets as anything seen over the previous seasons. Elliott's goal was no less than they deserved, Chris Eagles was outstanding.

Before the game Coyle vowed that he would not hide.

> I expect there will be a fair bit of criticism, or whatever they call it. But ultimately, as you'll know as kids growing up, they can only call you a name once. Once you've been called it, you've been called it. If the fans want to come along in that vein and voice their disapproval then that's up to them. I'm under no illusions about how difficult the game and the night will be.

Eight months might have passed since Coyle had left, but Clarets fans had not forgotten. As he walked from players' tunnel to the dugout, his face was set, undaunted and defiant. He was booed and whistled every step of the way. From the first minute to the last he was subjected to a barrage of abuse and scorn. If the players had been earlier knocked for six by his departure, those who remained showed him how well they could play. Match programme pleas to remember his deeds fell on deaf ears. The barracking was merciless. Fans were even there to jeer him as the Bolton bus arrived. He was booed even louder at half-time when he confronted the referee Mark Clattenburg to challenge the Burnley goal.

Tim Rich in the *Guardian*, described how former hero Robbie Blake was also howled down as he went to take a corner. When Luis Figo returned to Barcelona with Real Madrid, a pig's head was hurled at his feet. The jeers rained down on Blake but there was no pig's head. Pig's head and trotters is a Lancashire delicacy, too valuable to be thrown at a footballer at Turf Moor—even one such as Robbie Blake.

Mark Ogden was there.

> Burnley manager Brian Laws called on the club's supporters to draw a line under their ferocious condemnation of Owen Coyle after Wade Elliott's first half goal sealed Carling Cup victory against Coyle's Bolton. Coyle who resigned as Burnley manager to move to the Reebok in January was subjected to a chorus of 'Judas' chants and jeered mercilessly by the Turf Moor crowd on his first return to the stadium. With hostility levels alarmingly high, the Scot was accompanied to the visitor's dugout by eight security personnel who remained in close proximity throughout this third round tie.
>
> The off-field atmosphere only served to overshadow a stirring performance by the home side who deservedly claimed the scalp of their Premier League neighbours, and Laws insisted that the result should serve as the final word on the Coyle saga.
>
> Laws said: 'From my point of view, it's nice to put it to bed now because, if we hadn't won this game, the whole thing would have been hanging round the club for a very long time. We needed this in order for the supporters to get it off their chest, but they have done that, so maybe we can look forward to a new era now. I'm sure that Owen wants to move on too, but let's hope our paths cross again in the Premier League next year. The atmosphere was breathtaking and it drove us on. This place is

notoriously difficult for visiting teams and the fans helped make it happen tonight.

While admitting that he had anticipated the malevolent atmosphere, Coyle insisted he had no qualms at being subjected to the fury of the Burnley supporters. He said: 'Where I grew up in Glasgow, if people called you a name once, then they couldn't call it you again. You had to fight tooth and nail for everything you got and not let names bother you. Football is about entertainment and heroes and villains. For two years I was a hero here, but some people now see me as a villain. That's fine. But I would have been happy to walk on my own to the dugout. The security wasn't a request from me.'

It was events on the pitch that proved more of a distraction for Coyle, with Burnley impressing from the first minute as Chris Eagles twice went close to opening the scoring. The game was settled by Elliott's goal on 44 minutes though, when the midfielder volleyed in from six yards. Confusion initially reigned, with referee Mark Clattenburg appearing to award Burnley a penalty before changing his mind after consulting his linesman.

Coyle insisted that the goal should have been ruled out due to handball in the build-up. He said: It was a great volley by Wade and there is doubt that the ball crossed the line, but Chris Iwelumo clearly punched the ball in the air. It was like a volleyball punch and it was as clear as day, but Burnley have benefited from good fortune. Mark Clattenburg mustn't have seen it, that's the only explanation I have for it. (Courtesy of Mark Ogden)

Legitimate goal or not, Burnley's win over Bolton Wanderers and Owen Coyle in the Carling Cup brought an end to the affair. There was the general feeling that after the win, everybody could move on. At Turf Moor, Barry Kilby certainly wanted everyone to move on. Honour was satisfied, bragging rights assured. Whilst his huge achievements could be remembered, the bitter taste of his exit could be left to fade.

The final score was Burnley 1 Bolton Wanderers 0.

Rarely can a Carling Cup game have meant so much. When Owen Coyle left, the 'feel-good' factor went with him. With the win it was very much restored. As far as supporters were concerned this wasn't Burnley 1 Bolton Wanderers 0, it was Burnley 1 Owen Coyle 0.

Life could go on.

It was closure.

16

ANNUS HORRIBILIS

The hundreds of games Brian Laws had amassed as a football manager certainly stood him in good stead. They had given him a bloody-minded determination to weather any storm. In 2009–10 he had been through a torrid time at Sheffield Wednesday, leaving them in the bottom three when he was dismissed (or left by mutual consent as seems to be the norm these days), and experienced an even more torrid time at Burnley when he was unable to stop the slide towards relegation. If the word 'surprise' was the one most used when he was appointed to the Burnley job, the same word was used more than once when he kept his job at the end of the season, although he came perilously close to losing it.

Brendan Flood recalled: 'I proposed that we change the manager in preparation for the '10–11 season. All of the Board was supportive except for the chairman, Clive Holt and Martin Hobbs. In terms of shareholdings the weight of commitment was to change.'

Chairman Barry Kilby however, was determined that season 2010–11, was Laws' chance to build his own team, consolidate, and push for an automatic return to the Premiership. Brendan Flood agreed to support the chairman subject to the team being in the top three after 10 games. Laws survived.

Born in October 1961, in Wallsend, Tyne and Wear he began playing football at the Wallsend Boys Club, a club that produced several great footballers. Aged just 17 he signed his first professional contract at Burnley and was a firm fans' favourite especially in the promotion season of 1981–82. He was an outstanding full back with pace, great tackling, able to get forward and he scored some excellent goals. For some reason his face did not fit with John Bond when he arrived and he was shipped out for a derisory sum to Huddersfield Town. Shell-shocked by this he would come back to watch Burnley games from the terraces with his pals.

From Huddersfield he moved to Middlesbrough and then the move came that made his name—to Nottingham Forest and Brian Clough for six years. With Clough he won two League Cup winners medals, and runners up medals in the League Cup and FA Cup.

He described Clough as:

Frightening, absolutely frightening. He ruled that football club with fear. If he liked you, you survived. If he didn't like you, he'd ruin you. I didn't believe the phone call in the first place. I thought it was Peter Beagrie winding me up. He said it was Brian Clough and I told him to do one. There were a few more words I used and then I put the phone down on the guy. It rang again and it was that voice . . . I realised it was him and he told me: 'Now young man if you ever put that phone down on me again it will be the last thing you ever do. Do you want to play for Nottingham Forest or do you want to stay where you are?'

I said I'd love to play for him and all he said was: 'Good, I'll see you tomorrow at 11pm sharp'. And then he put the phone down on me.

So he sat me down and asked me, 'Are you a good player or a bad player? I'm asking you a question son . . . I haven't seen you play. That's why I've asked you the question. So if you are a good player and you become a good player you tell everybody that I signed you and I've seen you son. If you're crap, he signed you, and don't you forget it.'

Laws had six great years at Forest, the pinnacle being an FA Cup Final. It was an occasion when everyone wanted a Forest win for Brian Clough. He was almost ready to retire and the players wanted to win it for him. It was the Final remembered however for Gascoigne's wild challenge on Gary Charles. It was a poor game, Stuart Pearce gave them the lead but Forest lost. The after-effects spread into the next season; Forest were relegated and Clough retired.

Laws was there at the Hillsborough semi-final against Liverpool when the disaster claimed so many lives.

I'll never forget it; as long as I live I'll never forget that day. It really knocked everybody back. It's still fresh in my mind. I can picture people's faces; that's how clear it is. I know a lot of players had counselling, we just couldn't comprehend it. We said afterwards we can never win this game and it was true, we lost it.

To leave Nottingham Forest (for Grimsby) was a big decision. That obviously started my career in management. I was the first manager to sign a footballer from Serie A, Ivano Bonetti. I was the first manager to bring one in and I was the first manager to knock one out. It was my second season. If there's ever a time you want players to work hard it's in the League, because it's really vital. I can't stand players that do not give their all. The supporters didn't like it, I didn't like it. Unfortunately I was player-manager at the time . . . we lost 2—1, and seriously I could have hung all Bonetti's clothes up and there wasn't a bit of sweat on. It was embarrassing. All hell broke loose and I ended up with a player with a broken cheekbone. That was a big regret. Your emotions are just tangled up, there's no common sense in your thoughts. I do regret it but it was a learning curve . . . but everyone thought that was me finished. But I had a lot of good support from experienced managers and the Board stuck with me. It's something that could have finished a lot of people. I got through it and it made me a better person.

At Scunthorpe, Laws, on a shoestring budget, achieved promotion twice in 1999 and 2005, credentials that impressed Barry Kilby and Brendan Flood. From there it was to Sheffield with little money but big expectations simply because this was a so-called 'big' club.

Known as 'the colonel' at Grimsby, and welcomed to Sheffield Wednesday by a chairman who said he welcomed a bit of 'Brian Clough' style management; Laws has some firm views. Comparing the game now to his own days when apprentices swept the terraces and painted the fittings at the ground, he commented:

> What we earned in those days was just a couple of hundred quid. The way football has become now, an entertainment business, they're treated like film stars. It's getting ridiculous, average players are multi-millionaires, it's like winning the lottery. If they had the grounding that we had as a youngster they'd appreciate everything they've got. Football is a commodity now. It's making a hell of a lot of money.

Only one person was allowed to assume 'film-star' or big-head status at Forest and that was Clough himself. Wednesday Chairman Dave Allen was a Clough admirer. 'I like Laws, he comes from the Clough camp, and I'm a great admirer of the Clough camp.'

He took over at Wednesday in November 2006. There was a promising start but it did not last. The highlight was the double over rivals Sheffield United in 2008–09 but by December of 2009 fans were dissatisfied with poor results and four straight defeats saw the club sink to 20th. He left in the same month. Wednesday were relegated at the end of the season hugely in debt, and with very little money available for managers.

Of 154 games at Sheffield Wednesday, there were 52 wins giving a win percentage of just 33.7%. Only at Scunthorpe United between April 2004 and November 2006 was there anything like a respectable win percentage of almost 42%. At Burnley the statistic that impressed the most was the Deloitte and Touche survey that placed him at the head of managers who could cope on a shoestring. The more cynical supporters referred to it as Deloitte and Tosh.

Ten games on in the Championship season at Turf Moor, Laws had weathered the wave of supporter apathy his appointment produced. Handily placed in the top six, with new players Iwelumo, Marney, Wallace, Cork and Grant, only Blake and Caldwell of the top names gone, they would have been even higher and even closer to a top spot if in preceding games six shots that had hit the post had gone in and Graham Alexander had converted a missed penalty. Supporters by now were quietly satisfied, if not over-excited; although in fact there had been one truly memorable game against Preston North End and of course the Bolton game. In the Preston game they had not played well and at 3–1 down with Preston coasting it looked like a home defeat was on the cards. But, three Burnley goals in the last seven minutes gave the Clarets an improbable and inspirational victory. Overall it was a solid start, helped by a first win at home in the opening game.

At the 11 game stage full back Mears had got his act together again and was back to his rip-roaring best, Chris Eagles was on fire and Cork was a diamond in midfield. But at this stage, more or less a quarter the way through the season, a 3—3 draw at Sheffield United, saw Burnley slip out of the top six, and the statistic that Burnley had won just four of the 11 games. Now it was just 7 points from the last 18. At Bramall Lane a two-goal lead had been squandered, the lead regained in the 90th minute but then another equaliser in the 94th. Manager Laws afterwards, deeply disappointed, said: 'I don't want to win plaudits for attractive football; I want to win football matches.' It was a not unreasonable sentiment, but not something you would have imagined coming from his predecessor.

With Eagles earning rave reviews, Everton's David Moyes was at Turf Moor to see the next scintillating performance against Barnsley from a winger at the top of his game. Mears was again outstanding going forward. 'A sublime' second half, said Laws as Eagles scored twice and Moyes and his assistant gave each other knowing looks when Eagles' first, a 25 yard screamer, went in. With Cardiff and QPR well ahead in the top two spots the second half demolition of Barnsley was well timed. Yet still there were groups that remained unconvinced by Brian Laws, referring to defensive weaknesses that were still unsolved, and the inability to win away—and the next away games were at Aston Villa, QPR and Norwich of all places. The final score of 3–0 against Barnsley could have been double that and for the seventh and eighth time in the season, the woodwork intervened yet again. It was a peach of a performance in the second half.

Sometimes a game ends and supporters wonder just what went wrong; how did that happen? The home game against Reading was just such a game with a final score of 4–0 to Reading. It was easy to see how it happened on this occasion. A poor display by the Clarets allied to an appalling display from referee Miller, with the result hugely influenced by a penalty awarded to Reading that another referee might have decided was just outside the area; and then Burnley denied an absolute certain penalty when Iwelumo was brought down, created the final score. It would have levelled the score and changed the course of the game had it been converted. Cardiff and QPR went 9 points ahead at the top with fans becoming unhappy at seeing them pull away.

The Carling game at Villa Park saw the end of further involvement for Burnley. Conversely this was a game when supporters came away wondering just how did Burnley not win. When the opposition goalkeeper, Brad Friedel, is man of the match you know that football does not always deal out fair results. It was the same in the home League game against Bristol City when only a superb performance by David James denied Burnley the win. But at Villa Park Brian Laws shook his head at the final whistle knowing full well how close Burnley had been to the win following a superb performance in a rip-roaring Cup-tie. Villa manager Houllier breathed a sigh of relief.

By the end of October another point at QPR made it five wins, six draws and three defeats. The goal Burnley scored at Loftus Road was the first to be scored there by the opposition. Travelling fans reported that this was another game Burnley could have won. The number of times this had been heard so far was increasing, but sadly, 'coulds and shoulds' have never won games or points.

The draws continued: 2–2 away at Norwich with Norwich getting the equaliser in injury time when the referee failed to spot the handball when the scorer clearly controlled the ball on his arm. It was a sickener. That plus the dreary second half performance in the next game, a 1–1 draw at home to Doncaster, and the debate began once again. 'Was Brian Laws ever the right man for the job?' His critics churned out the statistics. So far during the season, just five wins from 16 games and an overall Burnley record of 8 wins in 34 games. The less kind had by now dubbed him Average Brian; the downright cruel, Inspector Clouseau.

At the same time, the club announced pre-tax profits of over £14million. The more mathematically inclined supporters added to this the £16million parachute payment. Barry Kilby had once announced some years previously, during Stan Ternent's term, that the jar on the mantelpiece was well and truly empty. In November 2010, with various commitments, the jar was not quite overflowing but at least there was a little loose change available after the £13million wage bill. But at Bolton Wanderers a totally different scenario had emerged. This was now a club, according to Sky, with an overall debt of £94million. The loss for the year had been £34million. Chairman Gartside at the same time cryptically explained that they were a trading club not a selling club, but that the overall wage bill needed to be reduced and in January they might need to sell two key players Cahill and Elmander. Just re-structuring the management team had cost them £4.2million. The player wage bill alone was over £46million. If the latter had been the factor that prised him away from Burnley, there were now demands, already made on Megson, to reduce it.

What was going through Coyle's mind at this point? He could be forgiven for thinking that this job as described wasn't doing what it said on the tin. Sitting in sixth place in the Premiership after only two defeats, and following a stunning 4–2 win over Tottenham, it might well have looked that he had made the right choice in moving to Bolton Wanderers. But, against a background of threatened cost cutting and player sales, nor was it rocket science to suppose that he might already be dissatisfied and would look to move on to, as he once put it: 'A club with a better chance of staying in the Premiership.' The irony was lost on no-one. Burnley with money to spare but now it was Bolton with the empty jar on the mantelpiece. Nevertheless he had made Bolton into an attractive attacking team and the plaudits were beginning to arrive.

Alan Nixon explained Coyle's situation:

Bolton boss Owen Coyle is counting on secretive super-fan Eddie Davies keeping his club as a Premier League force. Coyle has faith in the multimillionaire who made his fortune mass-producing elements for kettles, and will carry on backing him with cash. Coyle has got to know Davies well enough in his 10 months in charge to believe he is committed to keeping the club in the top flight. 'We speak all the time, he's a terrific man,' said Coyle. 'Bolton Wanderers are very fortunate to have someone of that ilk behind them. He loves his football and this club. He is desperate for good times here at Bolton; to do that you have to work very hard together and he's been very supportive.' Davies shuns publicity, refuses interviews and lets Chairman Phil Gartside run the club—but very much under his watchful eye. (Courtesy of Alan Nixon)

Meanwhile, on the same day that Nixon wrote his piece, Burnley's Barry Kilby wrote his Watford programme notes celebrating the fact that his club was in the black with a healthy return on the short Premier League stay. As far as supporters were concerned, notwithstanding the healthy bank balance, it might well have been the game, they wondered, that saved any Boardroom discussions about Brian Laws' future. For 66 minutes Burnley laboured and fumbled to produce any decent passage of football. But, losing 1–2 with the crowd increasingly restless, Laws then made two substitutions that changed the game and resulted in a 3–2 win. The crowd went home happy at the result but certainly worried yet again by the lack of inspiration and zest, along with the first half formation and tactics. Nobody could say that this was a team firing on all cylinders and this was the first win since mid-October. Had this game resulted in just another draw, or even a defeat, as far as many fans were concerned, the manager's position would have been judged fragile at best. However, the win took Burnley back into sixth place—just. Stephen Cummings in the *Lancashire Telegraph* neatly summarised supporters' opinions so far:

> Should Brian Laws be looking for an alternative career any time soon, he may wish to consider the position of poster boy for Marmite. Like Marmite, Laws is polarising opinion.
>
> To his supporters he is a man who inherited a poisoned chalice from the previous manager and is making steady, if unspectacular, progress in keeping Burnley in and around the top six. His detractors would argue that sixth spot is the minimum requirement this season given the squad and the resources he has at his disposal. To be fair to both camps there is merit in both arguments.
>
> Taking over the reins from the club's most successful manager was never going to be easy. Owen Coyle had led the Clarets to the land of milk and honey. And although the club were not comfortable in the top flight, when Coyle departed for his former club, there was still a realistic chance that Burnley would scrape together sufficient points to survive.
>
> Instead, Laws put the brakes on the attractive football, brought in a raft of uninspiring signings and never looked remotely like keeping the club in the Premier League. But if relegation was grudgingly accepted, it was with the caveat that a strong promotion challenge would follow, this term. Sadly the campaign has been stuttering rather than strong.
>
> With the exception of the 4–0 home defeat to Reading, the Clarets have

coped reasonably well with the demands of the Championship but it has been very much a case of coping rather than commanding. Burnley have never suggested that they will take the Division by the scruff of the neck in the way that QPR and Cardiff occasionally have.

Winless away from Turf Moor, rarely convincing even in victory and with question marks over the manager's selections and strategy; the Burnley public is not united behind Brian Laws. (Courtesy of Stephen Cummings)

'You can only influence what is in front of you,' said Owen Coyle in November 2009. In January 2010 what he could see in front of him was a struggle to keep Burnley in the Premiership. He had got the players as far as he could. Without investment and ambition to match his own he deduced that he would get them no further. In crude, blunt terms he made the correct decision and after the Burnley defeat at Coventry a shift in supporters' opinions emerged; that they now understood why he had moved and were prepared to say so. If they did not approve of the manner of it, nevertheless as they saw Bolton Wanderers briefly in fourth position in the Premiership after another stunning win, this time 5–1 over Newcastle United; many of them could see exactly what his motivation was in leaving. Bolton it was clear would incur debt to stay in the Premiership, Burnley would not. Bolton had to stay in the Premiership. For Burnley, whilst it might have been an ambition talked about at Boardroom level, it was not a burning priority. The understandable priority for the chairman was to stay in the black, establish financial stability, keep the club on an even keel 'and not bet the ranch'. He had already spent ten years keeping the club just about afloat.

Nobody more than he, according to journalist David Conn, knew the pressures of the financial mess in season 2008–09 with a published loss of over £11million and in addition directors' loans totalling £9million. His caution was therefore laudable enough and earned him huge respect in the football world; but meanwhile supporters saw Burnley slide into 10th place in the Championship after another poor display and few, if any, now believed that an immediate return to the Premiership was likely. This was a team that had still to win two consecutive games but only a few miles away Coyle was delivering the goods yet again with very much the same players that he took over.

'His personal ambition outstripped that of the club. Every day that goes by I understand his decision more and more.' Perhaps this one comment about Coyle, on one of the main Burnley messageboards, summed up most of the dozens that appeared on the subject as people began to look back at the good times that Coyle had brought. The derision expressed when he left, was now tempered by realism and disappointment at the mediocrity at Turf Moor.

Ironically a 'Megson' scenario was developing at Burnley with many fans dissatisfied with Brian Laws. At Coventry they made their feelings known. The decision to appoint him had always been a sore point. But, when he did arrive the 'fairness' of the football supporter had kicked into action with a willingness to support and get behind the new man and give him every chance. It manifested itself passionately and unanimously in his first game at old Trafford. That willingness had by now almost evaporated.

After the Coventry game Brendan Flood again proposed that Laws be replaced. He had the support of two other Board members. The Board now comprised just five members, streamlined from the previous ten. Nevertheless the chairman wanted to give Laws until early January and then review again.

Surely, supporters argued, but not knowing any of this, if there was a poor result in the next home game against Derby County, the Board would act. All that, plus emerging stories that although the players as a group might have a good team spirit amongst themselves, as a group they were less than enamoured with the manager. All in all, at the end of November, whilst the situation was far from crumbling; Turf Moor was certainly not a positive, vibrant place.

'Is 10th good enough? No it isn't,' announced Brian Laws prior to the Derby game. 'But we also know we are just one point away from the play-offs and we believe we are good enough to be consistently in the top six. It's pure frustration at the moment because the only thing we can criticise is that we are not finishing teams off.'

But whilst he was looking for answers and fending off supporters' frustration, the accolades were pouring down on his predecessor. Coyle was Premier Manager of the Month for November 2010 and a flurry of media articles spotlighted his achievements so far in the season. There was even a story that he was earmarked to replace Arsene Wenger at Arsenal at the end of the season. Of course one of the stories was by Alan Nixon:

> Bolton boss Owen Coyle has revealed that his happy Wanderers are racing up the table, on the back of a funny but painful dressing room prank. Skipper Kevin Davies gave the game away when he celebrated one of his goals last week by gesturing that he was using a pair of scissors. And one of the secrets of the Bolton success story is the latest game that has the squad howling in more ways than one behind the scenes.
>
> Coyle said: 'Footballers are just big kids at heart. I know these lads are working hard—but they are also doing it with a smile on their face. The lads do a scissors, paper, stone thing, and there is a punishment for the loser. So they are getting good at playing it. The loser gets his ears flicked and it is painful. I stay out of it with the size of ears I've got. But it is great to see them having a bit of fun together. There is a great spirit in this group. It's always great to have talented players at your club, but if you get the right characters to build and foster team spirit it helps you in difficult times. There is a sense of togetherness and camaraderie between these lads. I always enjoyed that as a player. I was in some terrific dressing rooms, full of good players and good people. I want that among this group and it is clear

that they enjoy each other's company. I like us to get together when we can and not just go home after training. There are a lot of big characters. Robbie Blake has been a breath of fresh air and right among things since he came. It is important that players get on well together. It's easy when things are going well and you are winning, but there will always be times when we are up against it and that is when the spirit comes through.'

Coyle's only worry at the moment is that his players will let all of the good publicity they have generated so far go to their heads, but he is sure they will keep their minds on the job of pushing on in the top five.

He said: 'It's good when people say nice things but I have been in the game long enough to know how quickly that can change. Our focus is to drive ourselves on and be at our best. The only target I am setting the players is to go from game to game. We are not a big club that can plan ahead; we do just go from game to game.'

Coyle also believes that one of the main reasons for this season's heady campaign is the players who are outside the first-team pick. He explained: 'My biggest difficulty is picking the team and leaving some of them out. There are so many who deserve to start. People know that if there is any loss of form there are others ready to step in and they all want to play.' (Courtesy of Alan Nixon)

Meanwhile there was a full page spread about the Coyle magic in the *Sunday Times*, whilst in the *Guardian*, no less, Bolton were being described as 'a beautiful thing these days'. The *Daily Telegraph* was less kind to Brian Laws when he was rated as number ten in the top ten most underwhelming managerial appointments:

> When Owen Coyle made his acrimonious move to rivals Bolton, Burnley fans were calling out for an inspirational figure to help them retain their Premier League place. Instead they got Laws, who led the club to 15 defeats in the remaining 18 games and relegation back to the Championship.

Whilst it might have been inaccurate in that it was 'only' 14 defeats, the message it contained was almost brutal in its terse brevity, and was more than accurate in its summary of fans' feelings at the time. Those same fans were furious at the end of the home game against Leeds United. A 2–0 half-time lead was squandered and Leeds United went away with a 3–2 win after a superb second half performance when they attacked at will and cut Burnley to pieces. Yet again Laws publicly criticised the players saying they were unprofessional and complacent. After an unacceptable defeat Coyle would have his say in no uncertain terms but this was almost always in connection with players going away and feeling sorry for themselves after a defeat. He had no time for such players. Laws' criticisms however had a far different tone, giving an appearance of blame-shifting, the sort that might leave players feeling resentful. In this he was ignoring one of the fundamentals of good management in any job, that when there is criticism, it stays behind closed doors.

The matter surfaced at the December AGM. Not for years had there been any fireworks at a Turf Moor AGM but at this one Brian Laws expressed his anger at the *Lancashire Telegraph* reporting of his post-match comments and the sub-editor's headline 'Don't Blame Me, Blame The Team'.

'We are united,' he said and then expressed his annoyance. 'I have had to have a meeting with my players because of that rubbish . . . but whatever agenda they have it hasn't driven a wedge between me and my players, it has actually galvanised us. We had a very positive meeting today and we are angry.'

The *Lancashire Telegraph* and reporter Suzanne Geldard remained undeterred. Unbowed by this rebuke they ploughed on with the next piece. 'It's D-Day for Laws as Burnley Board Meets'.

In it, Geldard wrote that her understanding was that the Board of Directors were due to meet to debate Law's future after the under-fire boss had come under criticism again when his team for the third time had lost a 2–0 lead and were now four points behind the top six. At the AGM Chairman Kilby had explained that a position outside the top six at the end of the season would be seen as failure. 'Our aim is the play-offs. That was our sensible expectation this season. If we don't land in the play-offs; it will be deemed failure in our eyes this year'.

The *Daily Mail* joined in: 'Brian Laws on the brink at Burnley as Clarets lose the faith. Burnley boss Brian Laws faces increasing threat to cling onto his job at Turf Moor. Concerns have been growing over Laws' ability to steer the club back into the top flight'.

No meeting took place however according to the *Telegraph*, in a follow-up piece, an authoritative source revealing that the Board were due to meet after the AGM but that it had been cancelled at the eleventh hour. However accurate or inaccurate these reports might have been, they did spotlight the increasing disquiet and unsettled situation. Not even Steve Cotterill during his 19-game winless run had received anything like the level of disparagement and vilification now aimed at Brian Laws on messageboards and Facebook.

Following the disappointing run of results, columnist Stephen Cummings in the *Lancashire Telegraph*, was next to add his voice with 'I'm Sorry but Laws must go'. It was a piece that reflected the views of dozens of supporters.

> It is with a heavy heart that one advances the opinion that someone should lose their job. Brian Laws is a Claret. He is also clearly a decent man. And nobody would challenge the view that he wants anything but success for Burnley Football Club. But it's just not working. To invoke the ghost of Stan Ternent: 'It's nothing personal. It's business.'
>
> Taking over the reins from the club's most successful manager for a generation was always going to be a poisoned chalice for whoever took it on. And while one has a degree of sympathy for Laws in that respect, he never really rose to the challenge. The brakes were applied to the fluent and attractive pass and move game introduced under Owen Coyle,

unimpressive and costly additions were made in the January transfer window and while it may be wrong to claim relegation was accepted, Burnley disappeared with a whimper rather than a bang.

Backed in the summer, Laws had an opportunity to bring in his own men and mould his own team. Sadly, both the signings and the campaign have been hit and miss. At no point has one ever felt that we were witnessing a genuine promotion push. Having surrendered a two-goal lead to an ordinary Leeds side, things hit a new low. And not just on the pitch. Laying responsibility for the defeat at the door of the players was not only poor leadership, but also sounded like a manager running out of excuses and hiding places. His startling contention that his charges didn't follow his instructions was sufficient reason alone to set the alarm bells ringing. After all, if they aren't listening to Laws, then what is the point of him carrying on as their gaffer?

Most football chairmen could learn much from Barry Kilby about loyalty. It's to his immense credit that he has stood by all his appointments. And, as with Stan Ternent, Steve Cotterill and Owen Coyle; Kilby has leaned over backwards to support Laws. Yet surely even he must concede now that with the current manager, a return to the Premier League is but a pipe dream. The time to act is now. The Clarets are still well placed for a play-off push; funds are available and there is enough talent already at the club. With all due respect to Brian, it is time to write a new chapter at Turf Moor. (Courtesy of Stephen Cummings)

Kevin Clarke in his Sky Sports blog was even more outspoken, saying that he was stunned in the first place when Laws was given the job. He pointed to the average track record, even using the word mediocrity. Most fans, he argued, had by now had enough. 'We've been abject for a while but on Saturday threw away a two-goal lead for the third time in eight weeks and that was the final straw for even the most positive of fans.' Clarke wasn't suggesting that Burnley should be romping away with the League but this was a club that was not skint and should be pushing QPR and Cardiff City. 'The atmosphere at the ground is awful,' he continued. 'The club is in limbo and this is our absolute best chance of establishing ourselves as a decent club by following the West Brom format.'

A 'normal' Board meeting, in fact, did take place at which, amongst other things, discussions included the manager. He had already been perilously close to dismissal by the Board after the final Premier League, Tottenham game, and then after the 0–1 defeat at Coventry. Reports brought it into the open that three of the five-man Board wanted to replace him, but the chairman held on to the view that he should be allowed until January which gave him just two more games, both of them away. The first of them was postponed.

If 2009 had been magical, then 2010 had undoubtedly been an annus horribilis. The Coyle debacle, the Laws appointment, the Board's failed hope that he could grind out a survival campaign, the ensuing relegation; and then the first half of the new season one of total underachievement (said pundit Chris Kamara) the result of not one away win, not one instance of two consecutive wins, the throwing away of two-goal leads and a mid-table points total closer to the bottom club than the top. The majority of supporters were disenchanted and sorely disappointed. To see Bolton doing well with Coyle and Steve Cotterill reviving Portsmouth added fuel to the fire.

Behind the scenes it was Chairman Barry Kilby and Director Clive Holt who favoured giving Laws yet another chance. Brendan Flood, Mike Garlick and John B wanted change and wondered should they 'force the issue' with their controlling number of shares. Had the Cardiff game been played and been yet another defeat, it is likely they would have done so. Thanks to the weather, Laws received yet another reprieve.

December 2010 and two more games to go, barring postponements, before the end of what had been a horrible year. Early in the month, Burnley 'keeper Brian Jensen brought out the English version of his book *Beast* in time for Christmas. There were some startling revelations about Steve Cotterill, various insights into Owen Coyle; but with Jensen beholden to him for the goalkeeper's jersey, understandably little comment about Brian Laws. Jensen was savage in his portrayal of Steve Cotterill. It had been a number of years since he had played for him, but the anger was still fresh. The glimpses he provided of Coyle were a reminder to supporters of what might have been had he remained at Burnley and gave a picture of the charisma of the man and the type of leadership he provided. For a start, how could players not respond to a manager who still turned out for the reserves and scored?

Jensen began:

> I had it to hell with Steve Cotterill, He turned on me whenever he had the chance . . . intense and self centred . . . more and more burdened by the pressure . . . handling adversity poorly and it rubs off on the players . . . a manager who never saw eye to eye with several players . . . who never achieved the level of support from them he craved . . . the roar of the manager's Aston Martin every morning outside the dressing room at the training ground. It was, some felt, purely to impress everyone . . . he slagged people off for no reason. He was moody . . . in my view he was an arrogant beggar who had his head so far up his own ass that it was quite painful . . . I could get fed up with Gary Megson's methods, but still joke with him and get on with him. But with Cotterill there was absolutely nothing . . . Phil Hughes who ironically was brought to the club by Cotterill, told him that in his opinion, during that time the manager ruined the confidence of not one keeper but two.

But Brian's saviour arrived in the shape of Owen Coyle:

> Coyle praises and talks constantly . . . in the five a side games, he plays as an attacking midfielder so he can coach his forwards better . . . however they never practice set pieces . . . Coyle's logic is that it never comes off in a match, so you may as well spend time on something else . . . Coyle's

commitment is contagious; you simply burn to train with him . . . eloquent, gracious and friendly, his playful eyes signal humour and ambition. A man in the prime of life, in balance with himself, life and the job he loves . . . a player's man when outside threats loom . . . the manager is like a shepherd with his flock and no-one should point a finger at them without checking their facts . . . I am very protective when it comes to my players. I make sure they are treated fairly . . . if they criticise one of my players I take it up . . .

Jensen was astonished to learn from the authors the details of the conversation Coyle had with Bascombe from the *News of the World* who was out of order in his report on the Dane in the Wigan game when Jensen was injured. You can feel the admiration for his manager.

Coyle makes a key remark to the authors: 'You can be a hero one year and a villain the next.' Jensen refers to him as a man with many faces.

Coyle had a huge impact on the Dane's career . . . and he was not just well thought of by Brian. With insight and patience, Coyle modelled a winning team out of unfinished raw material. This is what he managed better than anyone else Brian has played under . . . overall to this day Brian has a big appreciation . . . but he has also learned that the Scot is a man of many faces and is better than most at hiding behind the mask . . . Brian Jensen's eyes still shine, however, when he later characterises the hyperactive bundle of energy that was Coyle. He had the energy of a small child and was simultaneously boss, friend, and role model . . . A guy who earned immense respect and you could chat and confide in.

But when he left there was the inevitable reaction:

Among the players the feeling of being let down is strong. Coyle made boys into men and got them an invitation to dine at the top table but his exit has sent them back onto the street. When he disappeared the tyre was punctured. Burnley's players will never forget the months of constant progress ended with Coyle scarpering down the motorway to a club with massive debts . . . when Coyle left the magic disappeared. Nevertheless we still believed we could given time get it back. But at some point I could see the task was too much. Some constantly find excuses . . . a lousy attitude affects the squad. We have too many who just spit the dummy out and it got worse . . . they said Burnley's spirit disappeared with Coyle. But there was no Burnley spirit. It was a Coyle spirit and it evaporated when he left . . . at times there was insufficient effort from several players.

Jensen understandably says little about Brian Laws in his book; after all he was dependent to him for the goalkeeper's jersey. But he does mention the outburst from Joey Godjonnson where the Icelander laid into Laws saying he had lost the respect of the players. Is it significant that Jensen does not refute it? From Laws he at last received his contract extension and it irritated him immensely that Coyle left without sorting it. The new one is the best and the highest paid he has ever had in his career: Laws was amazed at how low his old one was.

Those supporters that read Beast's book, including me, found that distant memories were re-awakened and hazy images of Wembley and the good times that Coyle brought, came back into focus. Supporters had long discussed and argued about what the exact effect of his departure had on the players. Jensen's book provided some of the answers and also such a telling line: 'At times there was insufficient effort from several players.'

17

THE AXE MAN COMETH

Arctic temperatures and dreadful conditions decimated much of the December football programme and Burnley had fallen two games behind in the run up to the Boxing Day fixture at Barnsley. Supporters had already groaned when they saw this fixture. When was the last time they won there, they asked? Boxing Day wins were rare enough anyway. Rumours abounded. Laws would be dismissed on Tuesday 21st. Laws must win four of the next six points to survive. Laws must do this or do that. Laws would be replaced in January. He was under pressure and Phil Brown was waiting in the wings. The Burnley football messageboards and Facebook were relentless in their fervent wish for a replacement.

'I can't worry about the sack,' responded Laws defiantly and went on to say all this was part and parcel of the job and he would carry on until he was informed otherwise. 'Clarets can bounce back,' added the manager who by now had demoted Brian Jensen to the bench and replaced him with Lee Grant who had arrived at the club in the summer. The words 'bounce back' were beginning to annoy people.

'In my opinion I have been dropped for no reason . . . I'm not happy about it and it is a hard one to take,' the goalkeeper commented in a Sunday sports paper. Perhaps too there was a small insight into the world of Owen Coyle and how it differed from that of Laws. 'The difference with Owen's side is that we were really together. Now we are missing something,' he added. Jensen's transfer request followed.

Iwelumo's announcement that Burnley could be 'unstoppable' when games resumed after the postponements was greeted with merriment. But at Barnsley of all places there was hope that he might in fact be right. At a place where Burnley had not won since 1932, there was a most improbable 2–1 victory, the first away win of the season. With lowly Scunthorpe next at Turf Moor hopes were high that the next hoodoo could be broken—the absence of back to back wins. With Burnley having played so well in the second half at Barnsley and Scunthorpe having lost their previous five games few people had thought of a defeat at Turf Moor. The scene was set for a return to the top six and a possible Happy New Year especially with Coventry having lost earlier in the day. A good display, a win, a move up the table, another reprieve for the manager—all seemed set—until Scunthorpe arrived with other plans.

In the history of Burnley Football Club there can have been few performances as badly received as that of Tuesday, December 28th, 2010. It certainly wasn't the worst ever, for that you have to turn the clock back to the Fourth Division wilderness years, but nevertheless it was a display and result that left the vast majority of a 15,000+ crowd incensed. It was totally devoid of any verve, self belief, momentum, confidence, energy or spirit. The dejection was palpable.

When Scunthorpe scored their second goal in the 84th minute most of three sides of the ground simply erupted with cries of 'Laws Out'. It was instant, deafening, ugly and prolonged. This, briefly, was not Turf Moor; this was the Coliseum in Ancient Rome. This was a crowd baying for the manager's head, to be despatched quickly by the chairman's sword; and after the game most people were agreed, no manager previously had ever been subjected to this level of intense abuse, not even John Bond or Chris Waddle. Entertainment levels had been despondently low during Steve Cotterill's final season, but he had battled on, people had appreciated that, and had never subjected him to this level of barracking.

The chairman was not at the game. He was in New York. Had he been at Turf Moor he would undoubtedly have been taken aback if not shocked by the mass demonstration of fury. It was reasonable to assume there might have been an immediate Board meeting had he personally witnessed the scenes.

But the players too were certainly guilty of letting down the people who paid their wages. Their tame surrender of the Premiership place was by no means forgotten. Andrew Greaves expressed the feelings of many in the *Lancashire Telegraph*, a newspaper banned from Turf Moor Press conferences as a result of previous articles.

> The boos are becoming as much a fixture at half-time as the R n B hits and the line of kids firing footballs at a giant pie. And after another woeful first half you could not help but feel sympathy for the Clarets faithful. The win at Barnsley on Boxing Day has merely papered over the glaring cracks that exist at the moment. I'm not bothered who the manager is but the simple fact is, with the squad we have, in a weak Championship, this is not good enough.
>
> Brian Laws may be the easy target, but as he rightly said after the Leeds capitulation, some of the lads need to take a good look at themselves. Andre Bikey, frustrating even at the best of times, was nothing short of awful. Not much better was winger Ross Wallace who can count himself very lucky not to have been hooked by Laws at half-time. Instead it was Wade Elliott who made way, prompting the introduction of Chris Eagles.
>
> The second half did start better, the Clarets—albeit temporarily—looking more energetic after a sluggish first 45 minutes. But still we failed to create a clear cut chance and that is a worry. Scunthorpe looked more of a threat than we did and when Chris Dagnall slotted home a second, the mass exodus and the 'Laws Out' chants could not be ignored. A home defeat to Scunthorpe is not something that can be explained away easily, and I mean no offence to the opposition when I say that because they thoroughly deserved this result.

He may think he's been given a rough ride in recent weeks but the evidence is mounting against Laws. He is clearly not the man to lead Burnley and if he's not going to walk away after this latest shambles then Barry Kilby needs to wield the axe fast. This year started with a departure and should end with one again. Twelve months is a long time in football and it's frightening how far back we have gone in that time. (Courtesy of Andrew Greaves)

Barry Kilby needs to wield the axe fast, wrote Greaves. He could not have imagined it would happen so fast, faster than anyone thought possible. Brendan Flood in the *Lancashire Telegraph* the day after the Scunthorpe game announced that the Board would meet in the next few days to discuss Brian Laws. With the chairman in New York where blizzards raged he revealed that yes, it was time to make a decision, to back him or make a change. Aims were not being met and he wanted to communicate his concerns to the fans. But there was no hint at all of an immediate sacking. 'Discussions will be in the next few days. I can't really say any more than that.'

But then even as fans were digesting that, the announcement came on the official club site during the afternoon.

Burnley Football Club can announce that first-team manager Brian Laws has today stepped down with immediate effect. The club would like to place on record their thanks for his hard work and commitment to the club since he took the role in January 2010.

Chairman Mr Barry Kilby said:

I have telephoned Brian today and have asked him to step down as manager of Burnley Football Club. Everyone is naturally disappointed and frustrated that recent results have not gone as we would have hoped. The Board of Directors has therefore decided we need a fresh approach in order to achieve our goal of returning to the Premier League.

And so after less than a year it was all over. More than a few people were desperately sorry for Laws however, pointing out that he had been placed in an intolerable position from the very start; that it had been an ill-fated appointment, leaving players stunned. All of it doomed to failure from the beginning. How could any manager recently sacked from a club in the bottom three of the Championship be given any credibility on his arrival at Turf Moor. He had not one but two Everests to climb—the players, several of whom openly admitted to being shell-shocked at his appointment, and then the supporters who were simply disbelieving. He was the last name any Burnley supporter would have suggested.

Alan Nixon months earlier had posed the question just who was there that could replace Coyle? Yet how and why he was appointed was really quite simple. The first two choices of the final preferred four candidates became unavailable. The third choice O'Driscoll then became the first choice, but for undisclosed reasons was not appointed although the rumour mill suggested that he had been critical of the infrastructure. The job, according to one report was his for the asking, but the training facilities were so utterly important to him, seeming to matter to him more than anything, that his criticisms left each party unimpressed with the other. Thus by accident, as it were, Brian Laws the outside choice, became the only choice and could barely believe his luck to be offered the job.

Ironically over the last six games Brian Laws had achieved a 50% win record. But a win then lose, win then lose again scenario was unacceptable. In terms of sympathy and patience from the fans he was past the point of no return and had been so since the Coventry game. Any good will gained by the Carling win over Bolton Wanderers had long since evaporated.

Brian Laws gave a short and dignified departing statement that he was leaving the question of a settlement to the League Managers' Association. They sprang to his defence and expressed surprise at his dismissal.

> The LMA shares Brian's disappointment at his leaving the football club and we find the timing of his dismissal very strange in all the circumstances. The club is only two points off a play-off place with a game in hand. Burnley have the third best home record in what is a really competitive Championship. They have lost only six games this season and have not suffered back to back losses. In the Carling Cup the club enjoyed a memorable win over Premier League outfit Bolton Wanderers and were only just edged out in extra-time at Villa Park in the next round. Boxing Day's win at Oakwell was the first time Burnley had beaten Barnsley away in 79 years. Further, Burnley are currently the highest placed of the three clubs relegated last season. (LMA website)

It went on to list his qualifications, his vast experience, his two promotions, his UEFA Pro Licence and graduation from Warwick University with a Certificate of Applied Management. It was all very positive. Unfortunately it did not list the negatives or make mention of the awful scenes at Turf Moor during the Scunthorpe game. It did not mention what he had not achieved; two consecutive wins for example, or the belief of the supporters.

Within 24 hours it was announced that Stuart Gray would be caretaker manager for the next three games knocking on the head any idea that Phil Brown would be appointed immediately. The *Guardian* had been first on the scene with that prediction within hours, and that he was ready to be installed the very next day. He wasn't. Alan Nixon in the *Mirror* was next and tipped Sam Allardyce and wrote that he had made his interest known to the Burnley bosses.

> Sam Allardyce wants to be the next Burnley boss after the club yesterday axed Brian Laws. Big Sam has already put in for the job and pals say he is desperate to get stuck in again after being sacked by Blackburn Rover's new Indian owners a fortnight ago. Laws was given the boot over the phone by Chairman Barry Kilby after Tuesday's 2–0 defeat to Scunthorpe left Burnley 9th in the Championship. The club are due to appoint a caretaker boss today and are not expected to name a successor until after Monday's game against Reading.
>
> Kilby said: 'Everyone is naturally very disappointed and frustrated that recent results have not gone as we would have hoped. The Board of directors

have therefore decided that we need a fresh approach in order to achieve our goal of returning to the Premier League.'

Also understood to be in the running are Huddersfield's Lee Clark and Phil Brown who was axed by Hull in March, as well as Doncaster boss Sean O'Driscoll, the Clarets' first choice to succeed Owen Coyle a year ago. (Courtesy of Alan Nixon)

Surprisingly few names were bandied around. Eddie Howe of Bournemouth was one and so was Derek McInnes from St Johnstone. In a poll of 2,000 people on one of the major Burnley websites, Claretsmad, Chris Hughton and Sam Allardyce were the two preferred contenders.

By day two feelings towards Brian Laws had mellowed a little and some sympathy emerged especially in an article by Clarets writer Richard Oldroyd who wrote that callous though it might sound, Laws had been a sort of human punch-bag at Turf Moor. With dignity he had taken all the flak and the brunt of everyone's frustrations, the root cause for which was not of his making. Quite definitely it was agreed that he had been let down by the players. However, although the season had been below expectations so far, it was far from disastrous, the side was stable and he had put in place various means by which young players might be brought on. His commitment and passion for the job was never in doubt.

In some ways therefore the question was asked was Brian Laws simply the fall-guy and the patsy. Psychologists talk about aggression-transfer, the process by which people take out their anger with one person, in this case Owen Coyle, by aiming their frustrations at someone else, quite clearly Laws. Its most common form is when mums, angry with their husbands, take it out on their children. More ruthlessness would have seen him removed in July following relegation and spared him much of the ordeal. But, Barry Kilby had always had a tradition of giving his managers every chance. But not even he could not ignore the verdict of a brutal crowd during the Scunthorpe game.

The next game with Stuart Gray acting as caretaker manager for the next three games crept up almost unnoticed. New Years Day and suddenly there was a game to think about. Gray was in charge for Sheffield United, Reading and the Cup game against Port Vale. The players made the right noises as they always do, when they agreed, yes, they had indeed let Brian Laws down. But, as one red-top journalist commented perhaps a little harshly, 'Players change their opinions as often as they change their socks'.

After a 4–2 Cup win and a happy crowd, the speculation continued. Nixon suggested that Burnley were now turning to Malky Mackay of Watford. Burnley want a deal done quickly he added. But, Big Sam was apparently in Dubai. Nevertheless in a Talksport telephone interview Allardyce said he was flattered to be linked with the post, but used the word speculation. A few days later with a defeat at Reading in between, Nixon hinted next that a possible Allardyce deal had broken down and so had any approach to Malky Mackay. Burnley then issued the first official statement to announce they had made a formal approach to Norwich for permission to speak to Paul Lambert. It was immediately rebuffed by Norwich City who announced they would fight tooth and nail to keep their manager and his team. Under no circumstances, they added, would they wish to give permission. The formality and protocol of it all, contrasted hugely with the way in which Coyle's mobile phone number was surrendered to Phil Gartside and how that ploy was used as permission to offer the Bolton job to him within hours of their weekend meeting. Whilst Burnley on the one hand made it so easy for Coyle to be prised away, Norwich had no intention of following suit. Nor had Paul Lambert and within hours announced his full commitment himself to Norwich City. That plus Big Sam allegedly dithering and hedging his bets; and a Lambert rejection—where next?

Where next was supposedly Malky Mackay but he elected to stay at Watford. Eddie Howe was linked but in a BBC Radio Solent interview announced he was staying at Bournemouth, when he turned down Crystal Palace and Charlton Athletic. Nevertheless it was a story that refused to go away. Stuart Gray was given another game to be in charge, this time QPR. Names were bandied about, McInnes, Megson, even Strachan, Curbishley again. Several players pleaded Gray's case. Meanwhile Burnley had indeed contacted Bournemouth after Howe had turned down Palace and Charlton.

When all the dust and media speculation and rumour had settled, as far as Burnley were concerned it had in fact been between the two lead candidates Paul Lambert and Eddie Howe, the two preferred targets. The part played by Director John Banaszkiewicz had been highly significant. On his first introduction to Brendan Flood prior to the tour of Singapore he had immediately remarked: 'Ah Brendan great to meet you I've read your book twice.' Flood feigning surprise that anyone had even read it once replied: 'You are in a very elite club.'

The tour of Singapore had almost been a test run for John B to show his mettle as it were and convince other Board members that he was a serious Burnley Board contender and to demonstrate his full engagement with the club. His introduction as a shareholder enabled the restructuring of the Board with Flood, John B, and Mike Garlick forming the 'younger' element, whilst Barry Kilby and Clive Holt remained to provide the 'steady' hands within a small group that could make decisions with greater speed and dynamism. It had certainly aided the search for Laws' replacement.

Brendan Flood proposed that the two lead candidates for the new manager post should be Lambert and Howe whilst attempts to meet half a dozen of the other better managers were made. Malky Mackay according to Flood was never really close but his agent made a few attempts to push his candidacy. Derek McInnes' case was presented by his agent Trevor Steven. Sam Allardyce and Chris Hughton were not interested, preferring Premier posts, but Flood did speak to Allardyce's agent, Pete Cowgill, and then directly to Big Sam himself. He was complimentary about Burnley but said he wanted to wait for a Premier job and went on to recommend Phil

Brown and Keith Hill.

Perhaps the most bizarre moment, said Brendan Flood, was when Chris Kamara phoned him. Flood immediately thought this was live on Sky but it turned out it was simply Kamara plugging his mate Gary Megson's case.

Lambert, they thought, was interested in coming but with that notion dispelled the remaining target was Howe. Whilst he was being courted by Palace and Charlton it needed a big sales pitch from Burnley. There were three late nights of phone calls to Howe's agent and then Howe himself who was flattered by the Burnley determination to get him and the clear vision of what was wanted. Compensation was sorted at £300,000 with Bournemouth having initially asked for £1million. Then there was the compensation for Laws and Wilcox. All this was underwritten by John B and Mike Garlick. The more youthful Board had secured its youthful manager.

Meanwhile for Owen Coyle, still 7th in the Premiership, all was not running smoothly at Bolton as the team hit a rough patch without a win in six games. 'Scotch on the rocks,' one article was headlined. Coyle pointed to injuries and 16 major decisions that had gone against Bolton. Certainly Bolton were miles from the drop but the potentially fairy tale season was now stuttering towards mid-table mediocrity. Down at Portsmouth, a rejuvenated Steve Cotterill had brought his side up from the bottom places to a position only two wins away from a sliding Burnley but then a poor run saw them heading downwards again.

At last Sunday, January 16th, 2011 saw the official appointment of 33-year-old Eddie Howe, from Bournemouth, as the new Burnley manager. Preceding chapters in the Burnley history books were closed. Managers come and go, as do players, directors, chairmen; each of whom play their part. Some are remembered longer than others. Some are loved and become legends. Others become infamous. Some fade into obscurity and are seldom mentioned. History treats some of them kindly and others less so. One by one they pass away as did the much revered Ralphie Coates in December of 2010. Meanwhile the Football Club itself as an entity goes on and on, the constant in so many people's lives. The new man, Eddie Howe, moved within its embrace.

And so began the next chapter.